Financial Integration in Latin America

A New Strategy for a New Normal

EDITORS

Charles Enoch

Wouter Bossu

Carlos Caceres

Diva Singh

INTERNATIONAL MONETARY FUND

Cataloging-in-Publication
Joint Bank-Fund Library

Names: Enoch, Charles | Bossu, Wouter | Caceres, Carlos | Singh, Diva | International Monetary Fund.
Title: Financial integration in Latin America: A New Strategy for a New Normal
Description: Washington, DC: International Monetary Fund, 2017. | Includes bibliographical references.
Identifiers: ISBN 9781513520247 (paper)
Subjects: LCSH: Latin America--Economic integration
Classification: LCC HC123.F55 2017

ISBN 978-1-51352-024-7 (Paper)
978-1-47557-713-6 (ePub)
978-1-47557-711-2 (Mobipocket)
978-1-47557-714-3 (PDF)

Please send orders to:
International Monetary Fund, Publication Services
P.O. Box 92780, Washington, DC 20090, U.S.A.
Tel.: (202) 623-7430 Fax: (202) 623-7201
E-mail: publications@imf.org
Internet: www.elibrary.imf.org
www.imfbookstore.org

Table of Contents

Foreword

REGIONALIZATION OF FINANCIAL SERVICES WITHIN A GLOBAL CONTEXT

Latin American financial sectors are once again at an important crossroad. Amid economic transition and important developments in global financial markets and regulatory frameworks, there is a growing case for greater financial integration and cooperation. In this context, this book analyzes the scope for—and benefits from—further "regionalization" of domestic financial services among Latin American countries.

Following the financial crises in the 1980s and early 1990s, Latin American countries opened up their financial markets to foreign participation. This brought in North American and European banks, which were regarded as a source of capital, expertise, and know-how, as well as an opportunity for diversification from domestic shocks. Moreover, this was accompanied by a fairly cautious attitude toward risk and thus the adoption of prudent regulatory approaches. Most regional regulators opted for a model of self-standing subsidiaries, ring-fencing of domestic capital and liquidity, and in some cases limiting domestic residents' holding of foreign currencies and binding constraints on foreign investments by local financial institutions (for instance, pension funds).

Since the global financial crisis, Latin America has been facing a rapidly changing global financial landscape. Whereas global banks were previously seen as a source of strength, policymakers need to internalize that these banks could now represent a source of weakness for domestic financial systems. Global banks are retrenching from non-core business areas and regions. The implementation of worldwide regulatory initiatives has triggered moves toward fragmentation of global financial systems, thereby heightening the risk for further withdrawals of global banks from Latin America.

Moreover, the region is currently experiencing an important economic adjustment. Rebalancing of growth in China and the end of the commodity super-cycle are putting pressure on fiscal and external sectors in several Latin American economies. Consequently, there is a need for renewed sources of long-term growth throughout the region.

This changing environment, as well as the need to alleviate long-lasting supply-side bottlenecks, calls for a sound, efficient, and forward-looking financial sector. In this regard, regional financial integration could provide an important additional boost to financial intermediation and ultimately growth.

TIMELINESS AND RELEVANCE OF THE MAIN THEMES OF THE BOOK

This book includes comprehensive coverage of the financial sector viewed through the lens of further financial integration in the region. Latin America has been characterized by the predominant role of banks within the financial sector. However, there is also significant scope for financial integration in the region through nonbank financial sectors, as evidenced by the growing number of initiatives in those areas.

The banking sector has experienced first-hand the withdrawal—or significant downsizing—of global banks from the region, leading to increased consolidation of domestic banking systems. Other financial sectors, such as pension funds and insurance companies, have expanded rapidly in recent years. At the same time, limited availability of marketable securities at home combined with restrictions on investments elsewhere challenges the efficient allocation of resources in these sectors.

Regionalization could attenuate some of the existing and potential difficulties. Regional banks could fill part of the intermediation void left by departing global banks in domestic markets, and the possibility of investing in mutually recognized, well-regulated regional financial markets would allow for greater efficiency and diversification of pension fund portfolios.

Finally, important regional initiatives provide a platform for further integration. Broad-ranging initiatives, covering a large number of areas beyond financial integration, such as Mercosur and the Pacific Alliance, are important examples. But these can be complemented by more targeted initiatives such as the Latin American Integrated Market (MILA) initiative, which seeks to integrate the stock exchanges of Chile, Colombia, Mexico, and Peru. Political support for regional integration is ample.

BENEFITING FROM FURTHER INTEGRATION WHILE KEEPING RISKS AT BAY

In summary, regional financial integration, although not a panacea, does offer a large number of benefits for Latin America. As highlighted in this book, these benefits include increased diversification of market risks, enhanced competition, economies of scale and cost reduction, transfer of know-how and operational best practices, and convergence of regulatory practices toward higher financial standards, among others.

Undoubtedly, greater integration also brings risks. Analysis suggests that most spillover risks are currently low and there is ample scope for further integration. However, this does not mean that there is room for complacency. Financial integration needs to go hand in hand with strengthening of regulatory frameworks, adoption of best practices, and increased cooperation among supervisory entities.

To conclude, Latin America is in need of a more dynamic financial sector that fosters robust and sustained growth. Regional financial integration could prove to be a key ingredient in this new growth recipe. This book provides some useful insights on how this can be achieved in practice.

Alejandro Werner
Director
Western Hemisphere Department
International Monetary Fund

Preface

The idea of a regional financial market in Latin America is not new. Several initiatives were launched in the past with this objective. However, after the repeated crises in Latin America in the 1980s and 1990s, many countries in the region opened their financial systems to the outside world, particularly Europe and the United States, to attract capital, gain expertise, and cushion themselves against regional shocks. At the same time, they sought to protect themselves against external spillovers: foreign banks had to enter as self-standing subsidiaries, currency controls limited domestic residents' holdings of foreign currencies, and investment regulations severely restricted the external exposure of pension funds and insurance companies.

This strategy worked well for much of the past 15 years and Latin America recovered rapidly, fueled by the commodity super-cycle and growing demand from China, with prudent domestic economic management adding potency to the mix. Indeed, even the global financial crisis did little damage to this previously crisis-prone region.

The end of the commodity super-cycle and economic rebalancing in China have seen growth slow dramatically in most of Latin America, exposing the need to identify new, alternative avenues for growth.

Latin America has also been particularly affected by the fragmentation of the international banking system in the wake of the global financial crisis. European and U.S. banks have dramatically cut their involvement in the region, either withdrawing completely or downsizing. There are various factors behind this trend, including the regulatory pressure of the post-crisis reforms that have had a negative effect on the risk-return payoffs of certain business lines, the enforcement of sanctions against tax violations, and stronger anti-money-laundering regulations. No major European or U.S. bank has entered Latin America to replace banks that have left, leading to increasing consolidation of domestic banking systems in many countries.

In the nonbank financial sector, pension funds and insurance companies have been growing rapidly, and indeed have in some cases outgrown the domestic markets in which they are—to an extent that varies across countries—constrained, potentially undermining competition and reducing the efficient financing of capital across the region. Meanwhile, stock exchanges are facing increasing challenges, with volumes declining in many cases as a result of heightened market and regulatory pressures in the post–global financial crisis environment.

STRUCTURE OF THIS VOLUME

This book is a study of seven Latin American economies (LA-7): Brazil, Chile, Colombia, Mexico, Panama, Peru, and Uruguay. It looks at the financial landscapes of these economies, and sets out the case for them to pursue regional financial integration: growth has slowed across much of the region and a stimulant is needed, at a time when fiscal space for expansionary policies is very limited or nonexistent. In addition, global banks have been withdrawing from the region and, unless they are replaced from outside national boundaries, there is a risk that competition in the national markets could be undermined. Benefits from regional integration include risk diversification, in that national risks across the region would be pooled, there would be increased growth from enhanced efficiency in the placement of assets or activities, and economies of scale could be realized. Higher financial standards, through the assimilation of regulatory and operational best practices from regional leaders, as well as technical know-how, could also accrue. Global integration remains an end goal, but is hard to achieve in the short term, and regional integration now can be a step toward global integration in the long term.

Chapter 2 quantifies the benefits that could be derived from regional financial integration. It shows also that Latin America is less integrated than other regions, so there will likely be scope for increasing this integration.

Latin American financial integration is constrained by a number of barriers. A central theme of the book is that there should be a comprehensive, if gradual, reduction in these barriers, together with actions to mitigate associated risks. Chapters 3 to 6 look at barriers to cross-border regional activity in banks, insurance companies, pension funds, and capital markets, respectively, and provide recommendations to address these barriers.

Chapter 7 looks at regional financial integration from a legal perspective. The chapter looks at domestic laws and regulations that constrain cross-border financial activity.

Two important blocs covering these countries have regional integration at the core of their mandates: Mercosur,[1] and particularly its financial wing ("financial Mercosur"), and the Pacific Alliance.[2] Chapter 8 suggests that these two groupings could make significant contributions toward financial integration, putting together, separately or in coordination, a program covering many of the recommendations here. One umbrella recommendation is that, in order to carry the other recommendations forward in a consistent and comprehensive manner, the Pacific Alliance establish a small secretariat. As regards financial Mercosur, a revitalization of the alliance, and establishment of a comprehensive financial integration agenda among interested members, would also be timely and productive.

---

[1] Comprises Argentina, Brazil, and Uruguay, as well as Paraguay and Venezuela.

[2] Comprises Chile, Colombia, Mexico, and Peru.

Finally, Chapter 9 looks at measures to mitigate the risks in cross-border financial integration. The authors indicate that risks of spillovers to other countries in the region from problems in one of these countries seem limited at present and can be mitigated, particularly through enhancing consolidated supervision across countries as well as across the various entities within cross-country conglomerates. Without achieving high standards in cross-border supervision, regional financial integration could jeopardize financial stability and substantially set back growth.

This book also contains appendices that describe the financial sectors in the seven countries covered.

LEVELING THE PLAYING FIELD ACROSS THE REGION

Ensuring a level playing field among financial institutions from across the region could have a significant impact on enhancing regional integration. The book contains an array of recommendations to establish such a level playing field.

Country authorities should, in countries where this does not yet exist, develop an explicit, open, objective, and nondiscriminatory statutory and regulatory framework for entry of cross-border financial institutions. Regional financial organizations such as the Pacific Alliance and Mercosur could play a role here to ensure that such frameworks would be consistent across their memberships. The authorities could also ensure that within their countries domestic and cross-border banks have equal access to credit bureaus and to deposit insurance,[3] as well as to regulatory authorities for physical branching permits.

Convergence of tax rates and arrangements are among the key factors cited by financial institutions that could encourage more cross-border activity. This could initially be facilitated by the development of stable and transparent tax rules for domestic and cross-border financial activities across the region, buttressed where appropriate by agreements for the avoidance of double taxation. Over time, regional bodies could work toward harmonization of tax regimes and further tax convergence.

Similarly, accounting and prudential regulatory frameworks should be harmonized, through consistent and timely adoption across the region of accounting principles compliant with the International Financial Reporting Standards, as well as of the Basel III prudential framework for banks, including consistent capital, leverage, and liquidity definitions. There should also be consistency across regulatory regimes for other parts of the financial sector, including Solvency II–type regimes for insurance companies and harmonized consumer protection arrangements.

Pension funds and insurance companies in nearly all countries in the region are heavily limited in the extent to which they can invest their assets across borders.

[3] In the long run one might envisage a pooling of information across credit bureaus, or a single regional credit bureau. There would also be benefit in harmonizing deposit insurance across the countries of the region, to avoid risk of arbitrage by financial institutions or their customers.

Abrupt changes in these restrictions could cause disruptions in their respective markets. The countries' authorities should, however, announce that over time they would relax these restrictions, in those cases where the restrictions are in place, so that the maximum cross-border investment ratio for pension funds and insurance companies across the region could be raised to 50 percent or higher. They should also ensure that procurement bids for financing infrastructure projects be open to institutions from around the region, and identify routes whereby limits on sectoral concentration for pension fund and insurance company investments do not prevent cross-border bidding for infrastructure projects.

MITIGATING THE RISKS

Past banking failures, for instance that of the Bank of Credit and Commerce International in Europe, have frequently been caused by a lack of cross-border collaboration among national regulatory authorities. Enhancements to cross-border banking therefore need to be accompanied as a matter of urgency by cross-border consolidated supervision across the region, and with formal agreement, such as through memoranda of understanding, among the respective supervisors to ensure full cooperation in the exchange of information. In some countries, this may require legislative action to ensure that banking secrecy laws contain exemptions to allow the exchange of information with supervisory agencies in other countries. For banks with a significant presence in more than one country it would be useful that supervisory colleges be set up, where these do not already exist, so that the supervisors in all the countries where the bank has a significant presence meet regularly and have a full and up-to-date picture of the soundness of the bank. Importantly, supervisory colleges could also facilitate the adoption of best-practice supervisory standards across the region, encouraging a "race to the top" and preventing the anachronistic practice of "light touch" supervision that some countries (also beyond the region) have sought in order to try to achieve a competitive advantage.

Many major Latin American banks are part of industrial conglomerates, with the banks being subsidiaries of nonbank holding companies. This generates a dangerous supervisory lacuna where supervisory authorities do not have the power to also supervise the nonbank parents of the banks. In countries where this issue exists, legislative changes will be needed to broaden the powers of the supervisor. In general, conglomerate supervision will need to be combined with the cross-border consolidated supervision discussed above. In instances where this is not possible, regulatory limits will need to be set for intergroup exposures within banking groups, and between bank and nonbank parts of conglomerates. Moreover, the supervisory authorities will need to have the power to stop any intragroup transfers if they see that the conglomerates, in whole or in part, are in difficulty.

As the international community moves on from supervisory reform to resolution reform, this too should be a focus for regional banks in the context of financial integration. Legal frameworks for resolution and restructuring should be harmonized across the region. Restructuring colleges should be established so that—unlike during the global financial crisis in North America and Europe—the failure of a cross-border bank can be handled smoothly and efficiently.

Similar arrangements are needed for cross-border activities for nonbank financial institutions. Consolidated supervision is needed for cross-border nonfinancial institutions. For conglomerates, coordination is needed between bank and nonbank supervisors; usually a lead supervisor should be identified, based on the supervisory structure in the country concerned and the relative size of the banking and nonbanking activities of the conglomerate. Colleges of supervisors are also needed, and insolvency regimes for nonbank financial institutions need to be harmonized. Pension funds and insurance companies require oversight of assets purchased across borders. And though it is recommended (see the discussion of the Pacific Alliance countries below) that licensing of market players such as broker-dealers be passported, at least across the Pacific Alliance countries, so that a dealer who is licensed in one member country can operate in all the member countries, it is an important proviso that they nevertheless be subject to supervision in both their home and host countries.

Risk mitigation is a critical concomitant to the proposed liberalization of cross-border financial activities in the region. Indeed, liberalization—such as allowing pension funds to invest a higher share of their assets across borders—should only be permitted where arrangements are fully in place for these to be properly supervised, together with remedial actions in the event of difficulties or failure.

OTHER MEASURES TO FOSTER REGIONAL FINANCIAL INTEGRATION

The home countries of global banks are intensifying anti-money laundering efforts, as well as efforts to combat the financing of terrorism (AML/CFT), both in Latin America and elsewhere. Failure on a national level to comply fully with these efforts, and with the Financial Action Task Force (FATF)[4] standards that underpin them, could increase the process of fragmentation of a country's financial system from that of the global economy as global banks withdraw from correspondent banking and other relations with the country. Full compliance with FATF requirements, and additional measures that may be sought by the home countries of the global banks, would foster a more thriving domestic financial sector and provide impetus for enhancing regional cross-border activity too. Harmonizing AML/CFT efforts across the region could serve to raise the standards overall, provide a stronger signal to global banks' home countries regarding the seriousness of the region's AML/CFT efforts, and avoid the stigma of being found to have given shelter to the sorts of activity that AML/CFT is seeking to eliminate.

Central counterparties (CCPs) are widely seen as potentially carrying systemic risk. Latin American countries should assess the compliance of the regulatory

[4] The FATF is an intergovernmental organization established by the Group of Seven countries during their 1989 Summit in Paris to combat money laundering.

frameworks of their CCPs through peer reviews across the region using the CPSS-IOSCO Principles for Financial Market Infrastructure (PFMI) methodology.[5] Integration will be fostered and financial activity more generally stimulated if, upon demonstration of compliance, countries of the region recognize each other's CCPs and/or regulatory frameworks. Over time, there should be progressive harmonization across key characteristics, in order to embed best practices, with long-term potential for cross-border mergers.

More broadly, countries should review where they still retain exchange controls. Such controls clearly inhibit regional integration, although they likely remain in place to help the country's authorities achieve other macroeconomic goals and financial sector prudential policies. Relaxation should therefore be progressive, eliminating remaining controls in a sequenced manner. These measures could include, for instance, permitting individuals to hold foreign exchange accounts onshore.

Regional financial integration is arguably hampered by the absence of a common currency, and the need to pay "double fees" to exchange one regional currency for another through transactions involving the U.S. dollar in New York. Mexico has already established netting arrangements under which certain Mexican banks can net their dollar assets and liabilities so as to reduce the volume of transactions that need to go through New York. Other member countries may wish to examine the possibility for extending such dollar netting arrangements to their own countries. Beyond that, in conjunction with the IMF,[6] they may also wish to examine the possibility of regional currency settlements in non-dollar currencies, and ultimately cross-currency.

BRAZIL

Brazil has by far the largest financial markets in Latin America, comprising about half of the total activity. Relaxation of some of its restrictions on cross-border financial activity could serve as a signal for greater openness, strengthen Brazil's financial markets further, and reduce the cost of finance across the region. Although many restrictions can already be circumvented using offshore entities, use of such entities has come under increased suspicion, and is likely to come under further scrutiny. It would be useful for Brazil to stay ahead of this curve; where activities are permitted to Brazilians, it would in general be better for them to be undertaken onshore.

At the moment it is not permitted for non-Brazilian bonds to be sold onshore in Brazil. Eliminating this restriction could be a significant step toward integrating

[5] PFMI, established by the Committee on Payment and Settlement Systems (CPSS) and the International Organization of Securities Commissions (IOSCO), are intended to "ensure that the infrastructure supporting global financial markets 'is even more robust and thus even better placed to withstand financial shocks'" (quoted from the website of the International Capital Market Association).

[6] IMF involvement is important for any measures in this area, given the countries' obligations under the Articles of Agreement to not maintain multiple currency practices.

Brazil's financial markets with those of the rest of the region. Brazil could also reduce the fragmentation of its own public bond market by eliminating the current practice of requiring separate legislation for each issuance. And although institutional investors are permitted to invest abroad, this currently must be undertaken through Brazilian asset management vehicles. This restriction is outdated. A limited liberalization in this regard would be to allow cross-border regional investment to be undertaken through regional asset management vehicles. This would also serve to encourage the development of such vehicles, possibly stimulating regional institutional development more generally.

Brazilian institutions have been expanding across the region in recent years. Bank Itaú now sees itself as a regional bank, with the region as its home market. And the Sao Paolo stock exchange has bought 8 percent of the stock exchange of Santiago, thus following a trend that is well-established elsewhere in the world, of increasing cross-border integration of stock markets. These trends are market driven; however, the Brazilian authorities could publicize that they welcome such developments. To offset possible nervousness among partner countries in the region, such clarifications should be accompanied by measures, such as reducing restrictions on cross-border activity, encouraging inward investment into Brazil, or raising financing in Brazil for other countries in the region.

Brazil was a founding member of Mercosur, an alliance that has among its objectives the financial integration of its member countries. Although Mercosur registered impressive achievements in its early years, it has been less active recently. This may be a good time to revive the financial Mercosur. On the Brazilian side, financial Mercosur may be a good vehicle for the initial stages of financial integration, taking integration measures with those fellow members of Mercosur that wish to participate. Among other countries, the new government of Argentina has expressed its support for a revitalization of the body. Active pursuit of an integration agenda by Brazil—together with Argentina and other interested countries—could achieve significant success.

Four countries of the region have together formed the Pacific Alliance, the aim of which is also to foster financial integration among its members. Although Brazil is unlikely to wish to join this alliance in the foreseeable future, the Pacific Alliance could make a good partner for Brazil's own integration efforts elsewhere. Areas for Brazil to explore jointly with the Pacific Alliance would include increasing cross-holdings of ownerships in stock exchanges and harmonization of capital market practices.

PACIFIC ALLIANCE COUNTRIES (CHILE, COLOMBIA, MEXICO, PERU)

The Pacific Alliance should establish a small secretariat in one of its member countries, tasked with preparing and disseminating a comprehensive framework for integration, including timelines and sequencing; maintaining momentum; ensuring consistency; coordinating the political big-picture announcements with the technical specifics for taking the process forward; and gaining the benefits of proceeding through reciprocity. Its work would be both inward- and outward-looking: the inward-looking aspects including ensuring that all members of the Pacific Alliance are moving forward together, and providing assistance if any of the member countries is facing difficulties. Its outward-looking work would include arranging activities to encourage investment into member countries, participating with other regional groupings such as the Association of Southeast Asian Nations (ASEAN), with which the Pacific Alliance already has close links; working to achieve interregional liberalization and integration; and liaising with prospective new members. The establishment of close links with ASEAN is one of the success stories of the Pacific Alliance to date; further progress in this regard is likely to continue bringing economic benefits.

Pacific Alliance countries could foster integration by permitting a higher tranche for investment into other member countries and, beyond that, by allowing cross-border investments within the Pacific Alliance to be counted as domestic, once appropriate supervisory arrangements have been put in place. Also, remaining ratings-based country limitations for pension fund investments across member countries should be replaced by specific foreign currency and corporate limitations. Insofar as a member country (existing or prospective) has not yet signed the IOSCO Multilateral Memoranda of Understanding, it should be required to do so.

The Latin American Integrated Market (MILA) initiative, which covers the Pacific Alliance countries, has received considerable publicity, but very few trades have so far been conducted. The authorities should urgently discuss measures to help kick-start MILA with markets and other private participants in member countries. To enhance its role, MILA should be expanded beyond its present capacity, which includes primary and secondary markets for equities, to also include sovereign and corporate bonds. Operational procedures for member country capital markets should be harmonized, including all aspects of listing requirements and technical arrangements, such as opening hours. Broker-dealers registered in a member country should be passported to operate through the MILA membership area, subject to effective supervision in both home and host countries, as recommended for Pacific Alliance countries. Further cross-ownerships across the exchanges of the member countries should be considered.

Pacific Alliance countries should also examine the possibility of harmonizing their financial sector safety nets, so as to move toward best practices and to reduce the risk of intercountry arbitrage. Bank deposit insurance and capital markets investor protection programs are two areas for initial work on harmonization. In the long term, the countries may wish to consider a common fund and a single investor protection regime. These could serve to increase the visibility and credibility of financial institutions and markets in the Pacific Alliance countries, and serve to increase participation from both within the member area and outside.

Finally, Pacific Alliance countries can enhance contacts among national regulators and supervisors, including through bilateral exchanges of staff and secondments to the proposed secretariat. This would serve to increase awareness of best practices in other parts of the area, and provide a corpus of officials that would take a broader, regional perspective.

PANAMA AND URUGUAY

Panama and Uruguay are considerably smaller than the other countries in the study. They are therefore particularly affected by developments in neighboring countries, and may have a special interest in integration efforts among their neighbors.

In recent years Panama has made great strides in developing as a regional hub in a number of economic sectors, such as transportation. Its role as a regional financial center, historically relied on a model of "light touch supervision" that nowadays is obsolete. Panama can nevertheless reestablish its position as a regional hub by refocusing on the provision of high-quality services, and ensuring that capital, disclosure, and other prudential requirements are at least as strong as those of other countries in the region. As a hub, Panama should be particularly supportive of moves toward regional integration; and the authorities should continue to look closely at the Pacific Alliance, and consider the potential benefits of joining. From the point of view of the Pacific Alliance, the inclusion of Panama would also be useful, providing added linkages inside and outside the current membership, including through Panama's use of the U.S. dollar as the national currency.

Uruguay is a founder member of Mercosur, with the headquarters in its capital. The country would have an interest in supporting the revitalization of financial Mercosur, to take forward the integration agenda on a broad front.

Uruguay still maintains tight restrictions on the extent to which it permits its pension funds and insurance companies to invest outside the country, notwithstanding the relatively small size of the domestic economy. Uruguay should consider raising the foreign asset cap on Uruguayan pension fund investments, and ending the restriction that pension funds' foreign purchases must only include securities from multilateral institutions. Uruguay could also look into the possibility of cross-country integration more broadly, including, for instance, partnerships for the Uruguayan stock exchange that enable the exchange to maintain a critical mass of activity and continue to provide services.

Acknowledgments

This book was prepared under the general guidance of Alejandro Werner, Director of the IMF's Western Hemisphere Department. It derives in large part from visits to Brazil, Chile, Colombia, Mexico, Panama, Peru, and Uruguay from May to July 2015 by most of the authors of the chapters in this book, as well as from analysis at IMF headquarters. We wish to thank our counterparts in each of these countries, both in the private and public sectors, who gave generously of their insights and time. We also thank Marco Piñon for his contributions during these visits. Papers from these visits were reviewed by country authorities, and by colleagues at IMF headquarters, and were presented at a seminar at the 2015 IMF Annual Meetings in Peru and to the IMF Executive Board. We thank all who participated.

We extend our appreciation also to Joanne Creary, Joe Procopio, and their colleagues in the IMF's Communications Department, who coordinated the editing and production of this volume. Excellent assistance was provided by Modupeh Williams.

CHAPTER 1

Introduction

CHARLES ENOCH

Many factors indicate that now may be the time for Latin American economies to work toward greater regional financial integration. This would not be a substitute for wider integration in the world economy; some Latin American economies are among the most active in global initiatives. However, given the recent economic slowdown in much of the region, limited progress in pursuing global agreements, and the widespread withdrawal of global financial institutions from emerging markets (including those in Latin America), regional financial integration could help buttress the economies of Latin America, enhance competition, and—over the medium term—lead the way toward global integration.

Regional financial integration could not only facilitate inward investment and enable Latin American markets to achieve minimum viable size, but it would also add a dimension of diversification, so that these economies would not rely solely on domestic or global developments to progress. In particular, regional financial integration would enable Latin American economies to reap benefits from the economic stability of other countries in the region, facilitate the adoption by Latin American economies of best practices in areas such as supervision and accounting, and serve as a step toward wider integration at a later stage.

Important public initiatives are currently fostering financial integration in Latin America. Since 2011 the presidents of Chile, Colombia, Mexico, and Peru have met regularly to further the agenda of the Pacific Alliance. On July 2, 2015, they issued the Paracas Declaration, reaffirming their commitment to foster market integration among their countries. In June 2016 the rotating leadership passed to Chile, and the presidents met in Puerto Vargas on July 1. Countries in Mercosur (a more long-standing organization comprising Argentina, Brazil, Paraguay, and Uruguay plus, more recently, Bolivia and Venezuela) may also revive the momentum of its financial integration agenda.

Regional private sector endeavors are underway as well. Banks, particularly those of Brazil and Colombia, are establishing themselves as regional institutions. Stock exchanges are establishing a regional presence; for example, the Latin American Integrated Market (MILA) initiative aims to foster equity and bond market integration across the Pacific Alliance countries, and the Brazilian stock exchange has bought 8 percent of the Santiago exchange, perhaps as a step toward greater Brazil/Mercosur/Pacific Alliance links. Nonfinancial firms are also expanding across the region, especially retail institutions from Chile and conglomerates from Brazil and Mexico.

An understanding of the evolution of financial sectors in Latin American economies can help elucidate the relevance of regional financial integration at this juncture. Between 1982 and 2002, all major Latin American economies suffered economic and financial crisis—in many cases, repeated crises—including the Mexican crisis of 1994 that IMF Managing Director Michel Camdessus called the first crisis of the 21st century. In nearly all cases, the countries undertook IMF adjustment programs (see Table 1.1) that over time contributed to fundamental transformations of their economies. The current financial systems of Latin America are to a large extent legacies of the manner in which the various countries responded to crises. Usually this response involved the initial nationalization of a significant part of the banking system, followed in many cases by sales to foreign banks, particularly those in Europe and North America. Mexico was an extreme example, with only one large bank remaining in domestic hands. At the same time, the crises forced many countries to reduce their vulnerability to losses of confidence. For example, Brazil and Mexico placed tight limits on residents' holdings of foreign currencies as well as on banks' exposures to foreign currencies; many of these limits remain in place.

The opening of their economies to global financial institutions reflected a view in many Latin American countries after the crises of the 1980s and 1990s that this strategy could protect them from regional instability, provide much-needed capital, and help them import managerial and technical skills. The strategy worked well and, aided by gains from the commodity boom and improvements in macro management, growth recovered strongly in most countries. No large Latin American country needed financial support during the global financial crisis, despite their exposure to global banks. Indeed, foreign bank subsidiaries in Latin America, buttressed by their reliance on domestic deposits, in some cases were a source of strength for their global balance sheets, including through the provision of liquidity to their overseas parents. From 2002 until recently, the region has experienced sustained growth: GDP in 2014 in the seven Latin American countries covered in this study is estimated to have been 52 percent higher in real terms than in 2002, compared with 25 percent for the United States and 16 percent for the countries of the European Union.

TABLE 1.1

IMF Lending Arrangements with LA-7 Countries since 1982

Country	Number of Programs	Total Borrowing (Billions of SDRs)
Brazil	6	41.3
Chile	3	1.4
Colombia	3	0.0
Mexico	5	17.9
Panama	7	0.4
Peru	9	1.1
Uruguay	10	2.8
All IMF programs	371	314.5

Source: IMF staff compilation.

Nevertheless, although Latin America was less affected by the global financial crisis than other regions, the crisis demonstrated that extreme volatility could originate from outside the region and that the region would not go unscathed. Weakened in the global financial crisis and facing the costs of additional regulatory demands, reduced profitability, and increased funding costs, European and North American banks have been downsizing. In this process, some major global financial institutions have left countries in Latin America and other emerging markets or have markedly reduced their exposures. No new bank from Europe or North America has established a significant presence in Latin America. The withdrawal of global banks has led to increased consolidation among leading local banks (for instance, in Brazil), potentially undermining the competitiveness of the banking systems and liquidity in the local markets. The pressure on global banks to withdraw may increase further as regulators implement a range of reforms, including the systemic banks' capital surcharge requirements, the requirements of the Key Attributes of Effective Resolution Regimes of Financial Institutions, over-the-counter derivatives reforms, and ring-fencing. Recently, Deutsche Bank announced its withdrawal from investment bank activities in 10 Latin American countries, including some in which it has had a presence for over a century.

The nonbank financial sector is also challenged. Volumes and liquidity in a number of exchanges are declining as U.S. regulations for derivatives trading have increased the cost of doing business in emerging markets. For some exchanges, their continued viability on a stand-alone basis is in doubt. For pension funds and insurance companies, regulatory restrictions constraining the bulk of their activities to domestic markets are causing increasing friction and may create bubbles, especially among the region's smaller markets.

Regional initiatives are not substitutes for further integration with the rest of the global economy. Latin American countries are deeply involved in major global initiatives. However, the ongoing retrenchment of global institutions from the region could leave countries underfinanced or with less competitive systems unless they are able to attract new institutions. Global agreements, particularly on financial integration, are not reached quickly; substantial mileage may be achieved by going further and faster on a regional basis. Indeed, to the extent that regional integration involved raising financial standards generally, it could facilitate wider integration in the future. Moreover, regional integration initiatives bring greater visibility, and more investment, to Latin American economies: in September 2015 the presidents of the Pacific Alliance conducted a joint road show around major global financial markets, and the Pacific Alliance was invited as an observer to the Association of Southeast Asian Nations meetings in the Philippines in November 2015.

Currently, Latin America as a region is less integrated across national financial markets than other parts of the world (see Chapter 2). Various factors—including size, history of crises, and regulatory structures—may contribute to this. Integration can help foster depth, and deeper financial markets have been shown to positively affect growth, at least up to a certain point. The usefulness of deep and strong financial markets becomes ever more apparent as prospects for growth in a number of Latin American countries (for instance, Peru) currently hinge on large infrastructure projects financed mainly through public-private partnerships.

Many Latin American economies are under strain, which is partly conjunctural. With the end of the commodity super-cycle boom and the slowdown in China (which had been the key impetus for much of the growth experienced in the region, particularly for countries in South America), countries need to find new drivers for economic growth. Among the possibilities, financial liberalization and regional integration may help new growth sectors emerge. The current strain is also the result of structural factors. For instance, investment restrictions are hampering synergies between the rapidly growing pension and insurance funds in the region and countries' needs for long-term and large-scale financing. Legislative and regulatory reforms in a number of Latin American countries—most significantly Chile—have generated rapid growth in these funds, but domestic capital markets do not provide sufficient investment opportunities. In addition, the infrastructure needs of the region require large investment initiatives, and domestic funds might be unable to invest enough and still avoid overconcentration, thereby jeopardizing the viability of such projects.

Regional financial integration could thus be an important response to Latin America's current economic challenges and circumstances, for the following reasons:

- Growth for most of Latin America has been closely related to the expansion of the Chinese economy, which drove both higher volumes of commodity exports and the resultant higher prices at which they were sold. With the slowdown in China and the end of the commodity super-cycle, growth through commodity exports may no longer provide sufficiently strong support to the region's economies. The prospect of tighter global financial conditions further complicates the economic outlook. New industries will require financing, which in turn will require strong financial markets, in terms of both banking (which still dominates the financial sectors of all Latin American economies) and capital markets (where pension funds in particular are growing rapidly and could potentially supply much of the financing for the emerging needs of the region).
- The global banks that have been major players in many Latin American economies have been withdrawing since the global financial crisis; a number of them were weakened in their home countries and have been forced to retrench, and the global regulatory agenda has increased the cost of prudential compliance in response to the global financial crisis. Insofar as the departing banks are not replaced by cross-border institutions, concentration will increase in domestic banking systems, with a potential loss of competitive forces. For instance, the purchase (announced in July 2015) of HSBC's retail operations in Brazil by Bradesco, Brazil's second-largest private bank, will add

to the consolidation of the Brazilian banking sector. More recently, Deutsche Bank announced its withdrawal from investment banking activity in 10 Latin American countries.

- Although the intent of the international regulatory agenda has been to reduce overall risks, in its initial stages it appears to have inflicted a number of unintended consequences on emerging markets. The increasing cost of cross-border activities (for instance, by requiring haircuts on cross-border collateral and centralizing business on exchanges) and of dealing in markets outside major financial centers has led to shifts in capital market activity toward exchanges in advanced economies. A withdrawal from Latin America by global institutions and markets could affect the region's ability to develop new products, which could in turn increase costs of and reduce access to finance (particularly for second-tier institutions) and transfer intermediation fees outside the region.
- Trade links in the nonfinancial sector are increasing across Latin America, not primarily through trade among Latin American countries but through the cross-border establishment of Latin American firms, including some of the major conglomerates. Companies from Brazil, Chile, and Mexico have been particularly active in this regard.
- Increasingly, size matters in building and maintaining financial infrastructures. For instance, the information technology, legal representation, and compliance costs needed to achieve competitive parity with the major financial centers may be prohibitive on a national scale in all but the largest Latin American countries. Without the integration of regional markets, prospects for maintaining active markets may be limited in some Latin American countries.
- In the nonbank arena, the ongoing rapid growth of pension and insurance funds in a number of Latin American economies threatens to overwhelm domestic capital markets. Given the dearth of domestic investment opportunities for these funds, the limited pool of assets in these markets may be largely held by the funds to maturity, depressing liquidity and limiting investment opportunities for smaller retail investors.
- As a corollary, the next phase of growth in Latin America is likely to involve projects with large financing needs (for instance, infrastructure), and it will be challenging to finance these projects solely through domestic markets. Countries' domestic pension and insurance funds, which are generally subject to concentration limits, may provide an insufficient pool for financing on the required scale. Permitting increased cross-border investments by pension funds and insurance companies, at least within the region, will enable them to diversify their risks and thus facilitate the financing of large projects. Of course, such an increase in cross-border investment would need to be accompanied by appropriate risk management.

- Increased integration would not be risk-free. Cross-border activity without robust risk management can potentially threaten financial stability, but it is possible to mitigate such risks. Enhanced cross-border consolidated and conglomerate supervision should enable supervisors to keep track of banks' and financial conglomerates' complex cross-border activities. Careful monitoring of intragroup transfers and ring-fencing capital should dampen spill-overs from the home countries of parent institutions. Higher quantity and quality of capital and liquidity requirements should make banks safer. Supervisory and resolution colleges, together with memorandums of understandings (MOUs), should provide early warnings of problems and help deal with those that occur. With this expanded toolkit, countries may be more willing to accept the benefits of regional integration, notwithstanding the initial costs of enhancing the regulatory regime to protect financial systems from systemic risks.
- Although ensuring domestic protection from potential cross-border spill-overs by looking outside of the region may have been the most prudent response to the Latin American crises of the 1980s and 1990s, regulatory reforms since then provide a complementary route for protection. In addition to tighter bank capital, liquidity, and disclosure requirements, regulators have increasingly recognized the need for consolidated supervision. Consolidated supervision and conglomerate supervision, together with upgraded MOUs and colleges of supervisors for all banks with significant cross-border activity, are designed to mitigate the risks of cross-border activity. Macroprudential measures too are increasingly being adopted and refined to address systemic risk concerns and to limit spillover risks from global market volatility.
- Finally, differences across the region in the speed of application of the new global regulations, as well as continuing limitations on the range of permissible activities, generate their own costs and lead to anomalies. In an environment of consolidated supervision, each institution has to follow both home and host country regulations, putting banks from countries with more advanced regulations at a competitive disadvantage. And while banks from some countries are able to make cross-border investments, their home countries may not be very accessible for inflows. Brazilian Banco Itaú, for example, takes an explicitly regional perspective for its operations; however, its expansion might be more welcomed in target countries if institutions in those countries found it easier to enter and do business in Brazil.

In sum, regional integration of banking and capital markets could help counter the negative conjunctural and structural factors presently affecting Latin American countries. Integration would create a larger internal market, thus enhancing competition and potentially fostering economies of scale. It would reduce the costs of the withdrawal of global institutions and diversify the risk exposures of Latin American economies, making them less vulnerable to volatility in global markets. Capital market integration would allow pension and insurance funds to diversify their investments and enable large projects to find a wider range of potential investors. Deeper markets would likely be more liquid, reducing costs and increasing access for participants generally. Increasing access for regional banks to operate across borders would enhance competition and enable the spread of best practices. Some form of "passporting" broker-dealers recognized in one country would help the process of establishing a unified capital market, as long as the passported firm is subject to full supervision in both home and host jurisdictions. Retaining financial intermediation within the region would help markets develop new products, facilitate access for second-tier companies (for whom intermediation on global markets may be difficult), and generate income from financial market activity. As a prelude, harmonizing tax, regulatory, and accounting frameworks would help provide a level playing field and would also likely stimulate investment into the region from overseas.

Ongoing initiatives may provide a model for taking regional integration forward. The combination of political and market enthusiasm may make the Pacific Alliance a more successful initiative than earlier regional attempts. For example, the integration through the Pacific Alliance of Mexico (a large manufacturing country) and the three medium-sized commodity exporters (Chile, Colombia, and Peru) could bring particular synergies. Among the Pacific Alliance's various plans for integration, the MILA initiative, which seeks to establish a unified capital market, is worth highlighting. Although MILA activity so far has been minimal and the process has come under criticism for achieving few results, the impediments are interrelated and would benefit from a comprehensive and coordinated approach to making the market work. With strong political support, this would be a good time for Pacific Alliance countries to make a push for enhancing financial integration among themselves and more widely by removing remaining barriers. Meanwhile, the Mercosur alliance has been a vehicle for integration among its members for many years. Although it has been relatively dormant lately, factors such as the recent changes in external economic policies in Argentina suggest that this may be a propitious moment for its revival.

The argument of this book is that financial integration within Latin America, with appropriate management of the risks, could bring needed diversification to Latin American financial sectors and set the stage for further integration into the global economy as conditions permit. The aim of the book is not to propose measures that artificially stimulate financial integration in Latin America if there is no underlying economic case. Rather, the book seeks to identify barriers to integration that are a legacy of measures introduced for other reasons and whose removal could pave the way for regional financial integration and thereby support growth.

The analysis in the book covers seven Latin American economies: Brazil, Chile, Colombia, Mexico, Panama, Peru, and Uruguay (LA-7). All are at a relatively similar stage of economic development and have taken steps to liberalize in recent years. Five are among the biggest Latin American economies; the other two are much smaller but are closely related. One—Brazil—represents almost half of the entire Latin American economy and is somewhat separated from the others, partly because of geography and language but also owing to its regulatory regime. Four of the countries—Chile, Colombia, Mexico, and Peru—are actively engaged in an integration strategy through the Pacific Alliance and its capital markets component MILA; their efforts are now at a critical stage. Finally, the two smaller countries (Panama and Uruguay) have large financial systems relative to their size, are closely related to their regional neighbors, and have economic prospects that will be greatly influenced by regional relationships.

The book first quantifies the possible benefits of regional integration. It then covers prospects for integration in the various sectors of the financial markets in the seven countries: banking, pension funds, insurance, and capital markets. The book identifies regulatory and legal barriers to regional integration and describes possible measures to contain the risks arising from integration. Recommendations are provided for each section and are summarized at the end of the book. Appendices briefly describe the state of the financial systems in the seven countries.

CHAPTER 2

Benefits of More Global and Regional Financial Integration in Latin America

LUC EYRAUD, DIVA SINGH, AND BENNETT SUTTON

After a period of endemic economic and financial crises during the 1980s to 1990s, many Latin American countries opened up their previously closed economies to international financial institutions at the turn of the millennium, aiming to attract capital, gain technical expertise, and cushion themselves against regional instability. In some extreme cases, such as Mexico and Uruguay, the financial system came to be completely dominated by global banks, with few or no domestic banks remaining. In addition, their experience with financial crises prompted most Latin American countries to implement stricter financial regulations. The strategy of importing global institutions and know-how, together with tighter regulations, appeared to have served the region well: with the exception of the Argentine and Uruguayan crises of 2001–02, none of the largest Latin American banking systems have suffered a financial crisis in the new century. Even the global financial crisis of 2008–09 caused relatively little harm, with high commodity prices fortuitously buffering exports and growth in this resource-rich region.

Nevertheless, the global financial crisis marked a turning point; in its aftermath, global banks, particularly from the United States and Europe, began retreating from Latin America and other emerging markets to their home bases and core markets, weakened by slow growth in advanced economies and encumbered by significantly tighter banking regulations. Adding to this, the end of the commodity super-cycle and the slowdown in China saw the main growth driver of the Latin American region evaporate, indicating a new reality and a need to identify alternative, noncommodity avenues for growth. Developing these new avenues would require fresh investment and deep financial markets. The retrenchment of global banks from Latin America began at a time when the countries of the region faced a need to further develop and deepen their financial systems and markets rather than see them shrink. Although this was certainly inopportune, it has perhaps created an opportune moment for Latin American countries to look to each other for potential synergies that could provide the scale and support their financial systems needs. In other words, if current circumstances preclude the possibility of advancing financial integration at the global level, the timing may now be as propitious as ever to investigate the scope for enhanced regional integration in Latin America, and to act on this.

Regional integration would not be a substitute for the goal of expanding ties with the global economy but rather a complementary subset of this broader goal. Given the current trend among global banks to continue withdrawing from Latin America and other emerging market economies, increased regional integration, to the degree economically feasible, can serve as a useful step toward further global integration in the future. If for example, as a result of regional integration, Latin American countries were to assimilate technical know-how and regulatory and operational best practices from regional leaders, this would raise financial standards across the region, leaving the countries well prepared for eventual deeper linkages with advanced economies and others.

Important initiatives are underway to promote financial integration within Latin America, and they seem to have garnered a considerable degree of political support. For example, in 2011 the Pacific Alliance countries (Chile, Colombia, Mexico, and Peru) put forward the Latin American Integrated Market (MILA) initiative, which seeks to establish a unified capital market among these countries. Progress has been limited and activity on the platform has been minimal, but this appears to be due to a lack of coordination among the Pacific Alliance countries on technical, logistical, and regulatory elements rather than to a lack of political support, which has been ample. In addition, the relatively dormant Mercosur alliance (comprising Argentina, Brazil, Paraguay, Uruguay, and Venezuela), established in 1991 with the ultimate objective of establishing a common market among its members through harmonized regulations and taxes, may have a chance at revival given the recent change of regime in Argentina.

Taking all this into account, the timing seems ripe to pursue greater regional financial integration in Latin America; failure to capitalize on this situation would represent a significant missed opportunity. This chapter examines the scope for further financial integration in Latin America, based on economic fundamentals and comparisons with other emerging market regions, and quantifies the potential macroeconomic gains that such integration could bring. The analysis focuses specifically on seven Latin American economies: Brazil, Chile, Colombia, Mexico, Panama, Peru, and Uruguay (LA-7). The chapter is structured as follows. The first section defines the concept of financial integration and describes the various indices of financial integration constructed and used in our analysis. The second section examines whether there is a deficit of global and regional integration in Latin America compared with other regions and compared with the countries' own socioeconomic fundamentals. The third section lays out the pros and cons of greater financial integration in Latin America and quantifies the potential macroeconomic gains from integration.

DEFINITION AND MEASUREMENT OF FINANCIAL INTEGRATION

This section defines the concept of financial integration and proposes a number of indicators to measure it, based on a principal component analysis. These indicators are used in the two analytical sections that follow.

Defining the Concept of Financial Integration

Financial integration is the process through which the financial markets of two or more countries or regions become more connected to each other. Financial integration can take many forms, including cross-border capital flows (for example, firms raising funds in foreign capital markets), foreign participation in domestic markets (for example, a parent bank's ability to set up a subsidiary abroad), sharing of information and practices among financial institutions, or unification of market infrastructures. Financial integration can have a regional or global dimension, depending on whether a country's financial market is more closely connected to neighboring countries or to global financial centers/institutions.

Financial integration is a multifaceted concept with no universally accepted definition. From a theoretical point of view, integration may be signaled by the convergence of the prices of assets with the same characteristics (law of one price). Perfect integration exists if similar assets have the same price even if they are traded on different markets. To work with a more tractable indicator, we define financial integration by two main criteria:

- The first criterion is the degree of *cross-border financial activity*. In this sense, the concept of integration is very close to that of financial globalization, defined as "the extent to which countries are linked through cross-border financial holdings, and proxied by the sum of countries' gross external assets and liabilities relative to GDP" (IMF 2008). According to this criterion, any barrier to exchange or market access impedes the free movement of capital and limits integration.
- The second criterion is the degree of *convergence and consolidation across markets*. Financial openness and free access are not sufficient conditions for integration. Two markets can be perfectly open to each other but still imperfectly integrated because, for example, they retain very distinct market structures.[1] In their definition of an integrated financial market, Baele and others (2004, 6) include the feature that market participants "face a single set of rules when they decide to deal with financial instruments and/or services." According to this criterion, a single (common and fully harmonized) market is the ultimate form of financial integration.

These two criteria are interconnected. The convergence of market structures facilitates and creates incentives for cross-border capital flows, while financial openness offers opportunities to import financial institutions and know-how from abroad, paving the way for greater harmonization across markets.

In practice, financial integration is always imperfect. Segmentation stems from various sources, including capital flow restrictions (some of which have a prudential purpose), technical constraints hindering cross-border flows, insufficient

[1] For instance, the discussion on financial fragmentation in the euro area (and its implications for the transmission of the European Central Bank's monetary policy) has focused at least as much on the absence of common firewalls (resolution and deposit insurance funds and supervisory mechanisms) as on the need to revive bilateral financial flows.

harmonization of financial regulations, cultural barriers, and country-specific risks that deter foreign investors.

Building Indicators of Financial Integration

Building on the foregoing definition, this chapter constructs a number of composite indicators of financial integration that combine information from various dimensions of the concept (Table 2.1).

Our *baseline* composite index combines financial openness and financial convergence. The first component is the de facto openness of the financial account measured by the sum of stocks of foreign assets and liabilities as a share of GDP. The second component is the regional dispersion of stock market returns measured by the standard deviation of returns of Morgan Stanley Capital International indices across countries of the same region (lower standard deviations would imply greater convergence). Although this indicator of regional convergence is widely used in the literature (Baele and others 2004), it presents obvious drawbacks (in particular, that differences in returns may be related to idiosyncratic risks), but the analysis is limited by data availability. To combine the two indicators, a principal component analysis (PCA) is used, in which the weights of the standardized variables are the squared factor loadings.[2]

The analysis also uses three *alternative* integration indices:

- The first alternative index replaces the traditional broad indicator of external openness (stock of external assets plus liabilities as a ratio of GDP) with the narrower external liability-to-GDP ratio. Indeed, some countries may hold large proportions of financial assets abroad, while having a low level of de facto integration. These assets, which may coexist with capital controls, could reflect past capital outflows (for example, Argentina) or large current account surpluses (for example, China). Limiting the measure of openness to include only external liabilities is one way to circumvent this problem.
- In the second alternative indicator, the first two components are identical to those used in the baseline index but a third component is added, which is the ratio of private sector credit provided by banks to GDP. There are two reasons why a measure of financial depth may enter the integration index. First, since financial integration allows savers to invest in a broader range of investment and risk-sharing instruments while enabling borrowers to tap a broader range of financing and risk management instruments at home and abroad, the concepts of integration and depth are closely related. Second, to reap the full benefits of integration and be a meaningful contributor to an integrated playing field, individual markets need to have a certain size. Thus, the depth criterion excludes markets that are too small, even if they meet the other two criteria.

[2] The objective of the PCA is to reduce the number of variables of interest into a single factor, which captures most of their variances (for the indices constructed in this exercise, the first component explains more than 50 percent of the total variance).

TABLE 2.1

Principal Components for Financial Integration (FI) Indicators

	FI: baseline	FI: alternate 1	FI: alternate 2	FI: alternate 3.1	FI: alternate 3.2	FI: alternate 3.3	FI: alternate 3.4
Measures of global financial openness							
Stock of external assets plus liabilities vis-à-vis the rest of the world, ratio to GDP	✓		✓	✓	✓	✓	
Stock of external liabilities vis-à-vis the rest of the world, ratio to GDP		✓					✓
Measures of regional convergence							
Eight-region world: Standard deviation of equity returns among countries of the same region[1]	✓	✓	✓	✓		✓	✓
Four-region world: Standard deviation of equity returns among countries of the same region[2]					✓		
Financial system depth							
Banking system credit to the private sector, ratio to GDP			✓				
Measures of regional financial openness							
Eight-region world: Stock of external assets plus liabilities vis-à-vis countries of the same region, (eight regions) share of total external position[1]				✓			
Four-region world: Stock of external assets plus liabilities vis-à-vis countries of the same region, (four regions) share of total external position[2]					✓		
Proximity based: weighted average distance vis-à-vis all other countries of the world: weighted by reporting country's share of external assets plus liabilities to each partner[3]						✓	
Proximity based: weighted average distance vis-à-vis all other countries of the world, weighted by reporting country's share of external liabilities to each partner[3]							✓

Source: IMF staff compilation.

[1] Divides the world into one "region" of advanced economies and seven emerging market regions: Africa, Asia, Europe, Latin America, Middle East and North Africa, Commonwealth of Independent States, and other small states.

[2] Captures the integration of both emerging market and advanced economies within one of four large geographic regions: Asia, Europe, the Western Hemisphere, and other countries.

[3] Observes the degree to which international financial partner countries are geographically close or distant. First, distances between country pairs are normalized as one minus the distance divided by the global maximum such that near countries are scored close to 1 and far countries are scored close to zero. Distances are normalized by dividing all distances by the maximum distance between any two countries. Next, normalized distances are weighted by the reporting country's share of either external assets + external liabilities or just the external liabilities vis-à-vis each of its partners.

- The third alternative index provides a better picture of regional integration by including a measure of relative regional openness (ratio of regional assets and liabilities to total foreign assets and liabilities of a given country) alongside global financial openness and regional convergence. The theory is that countries are regionally integrated in a meaningful way when they fulfill three conditions: they have to (1) be open globally, (2) be relatively more open to their neighbors, and (3) present signs of financial convergence. We include global openness (defined in absolute terms) in addition to the regional openness measure (defined in relative terms) to ensure that the concept of regional integration is meaningful and captures both the scale and the direction of financial flows. For example, a country could be a closed economy with the exception of small linkages with one neighbor. If we did not include the global openness measure, this country would appear to be highly regionally integrated despite the fact that it is a de facto closed economy.

Several variants of the relative regional openness concept are developed, as defining regions can be challenging. The first variant is an eight-region world (advanced economies, Africa, Asia, emerging Europe, Latin America and the Caribbean, the Middle East and North Africa, the Commonwealth of Independent States, and other small states), based on IMF *World Economic Outlook* classifications, which emphasize regionalism among emerging market/developing economies. The second approach consolidates the world into just four regions (Asia, Europe, the Western Hemisphere, and the rest of the world) and captures the observed behavior that emerging market/developing countries tend to integrate with nearby advanced economies (for instance, Mexico with the United States or eastern with western Europe). The third variant replaces predetermined regions with distance-based weights whose values rise when countries are geographically close. Bilateral financial positions (using external assets and liabilities) are then weighted with this distance, so that the regional openness indicator increases continuously when countries are more financially open to geographically close partners. Finally, the fourth variant uses the same methodology as the third, but focuses solely on external liabilities.

IS THERE A DEFICIT OF FINANCIAL INTEGRATION IN LATIN AMERICA?

This section assesses the dearth of global and regional integration in Latin America, based on a descriptive comparison to other regions and an econometric analysis to estimate an integration gap relative to what would be predicted by countries' (or regions') own macroeconomic fundamentals.

How Does Integration in Latin America Compare with That in Other Regions?

By the turn of the century, most countries in Latin America had embarked on a process of financial liberalization. This process has been characterized by a reduction of impediments to cross-border financial transactions, increased participation of foreign banks in the local banking systems, and greater cross-border capital market activity. Today most Latin American countries have fewer de jure restrictions on capital flows than Asian economies do (Galindo, Izquierdo, and Rojas-Suárez 2010).

However, de facto integration of Latin America with the rest of the world remains low. To assess the degree of financial integration, Figures 2.1 and 2.2 use three measures of cross-border capital flows:[3]

- The first, and most common, is international investment positions (IIPs), presented here as the sum of foreign asset and liability stocks outstanding. Although the dollar value of international assets and liabilities among all Latin American countries has grown over the past decade, the region has not increased its international exposure (foreign assets plus liabilities in percent of regional GDP). Nor has the region's relative importance as a partner in international finance improved, unlike the allocation of international financial positions vis-à-vis emerging Asia, which doubled between 2004 and 2013 (Figure 2.1).
- The second measure looks at cross-border claims held by Bank for International Settlements (BIS)-reporting banks. These data include not only traditional loans (across borders) but also portfolio equity and debt holdings of BIS-reporting banks. Here again, the broad group of all Latin American countries has garnered a relatively low 3 percent to 5 percent of BIS claims over the past 10 years (Figure 2.2, panel 1).
- The third indicator uses the data sets of bilateral portfolio and foreign direct investment (FDI) stocks outstanding reported in the IMF's Coordinated Portfolio Investment Survey and Coordinated Direct Investment Survey.[4] Although technically these are components of the IIP data, their bilateral nature permits investigation of regional integration. This indicator reiterates the relatively low (and potentially declining) participation of the Latin American region while highlighting the importance of FDI flows relative to portfolio investments (Figure 2.2, panel 2).

Intraregional integration in Latin America also seems less advanced than in other emerging market regions. Figure 2.3 shows that there is greater intraregional investment, through FDI and portfolio flows, among the Association of Southeast Asian Nations countries, reflecting both the fruits of long trade and financial negotiations and the important presence of a large, diversified trade and financial center (Singapore). Regarding the evolution of regional integration over time, the available indicators of financial regionalism show different trends, depending on how it is measured. For portfolio assets, there is an apparent diversification

[3] In principle, the best measures of financial integration should be price-based. However, in light of the difficulty of adequately identifying homogeneous assets across countries, this section relies on quantity-based indicators.

[4] Data available at http://cdis.imf.org and http://cpis.imf.org.

Figure 2.1 Global Financial Integration in Latin America and the Caribbean: International Investment Positions (IIPs)

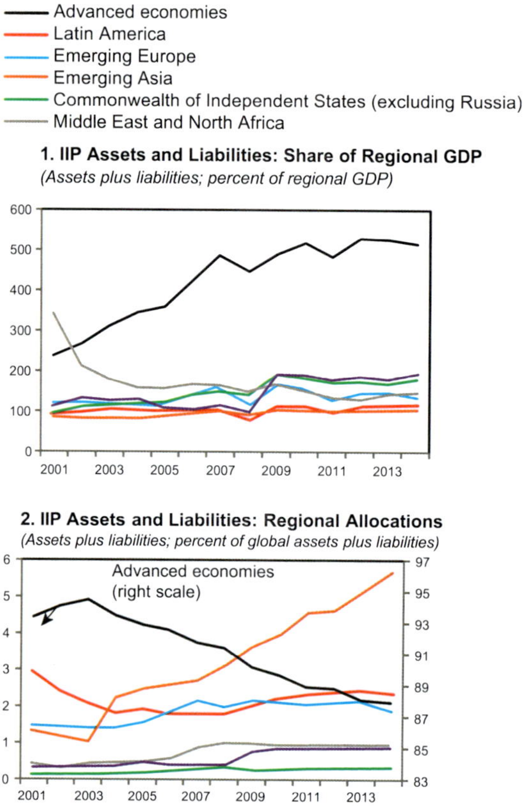

Sources: IMF, Balance of Payments Statistics.
Note: Values are not consolidated for intraregional trade.

away from regional assets in Latin America, as the intraregional share has fallen from over 10 percent to under 5 percent since 2008 (Figure 2.4, panel 1). The data for FDI, available only since 2009, suggest a declining trend (Figure 2.4, panel 2). However, indicators of cross-border bank lending do point to some momentum in Latin America. Table 2.2 highlights the expanding positions that Latin BIS-reporting banks are taking in neighboring countries.[5] Since 2005, the share of claims on other LA-7 countries has risen most dramatically in Chile and Brazil.

[5] BIS bank lending data are available for only four Latin American countries.

Figure 2.2 Global Financial Integration in Latin America and the Caribbean (LAC): International Bank Claims, Portfolio, and Foreign Direct Investment

1. Consolidated International BIS Bank Claims on Selected Regions[1]
(Percent of total consolidated BIS international claims)

2. LAC: Portfolio and FDI Stocks Outstanding[2]
(Billions of U.S. dollars)

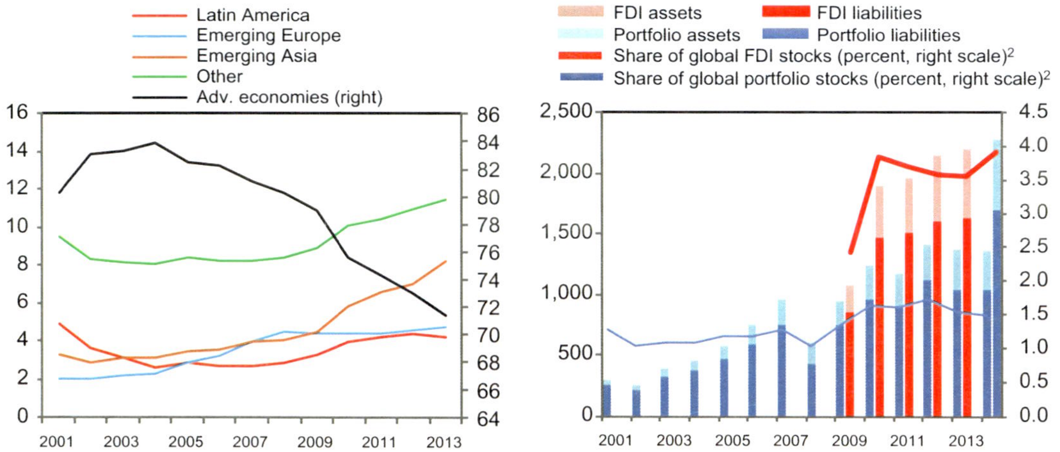

Sources: Bank for International Settlements, Consolidated Banking Statistics; IMF, Balance of Payments Statistics; Coordinated Portfolio Investment Survey and Coordinated Direct Investment Survey.

Note: Values are not consolidated for intraregional trade. BIS = Bank for International Settlements; FDI = foreign direct investment.

[1] BIS bank lending, immediate borrower basis. Foreign claims include cross-border lending, holdings of debt and equity securities, and local currency lending to residents.

[2] Aggregate assets plus liabilities of Latin America, in percent of aggregate assets plus liabilities of all reporting countries.

Figure 2.3 Intraregional Component of Global Integration: Portfolio and Foreign Direct Investments, 2014

1. International Portfolio Stocks Outstanding[1]
(Positions outstanding, percent of group GDP)

2. International FDI Stocks Outstanding[1]
(Positions outstanding, percent of group GDP)

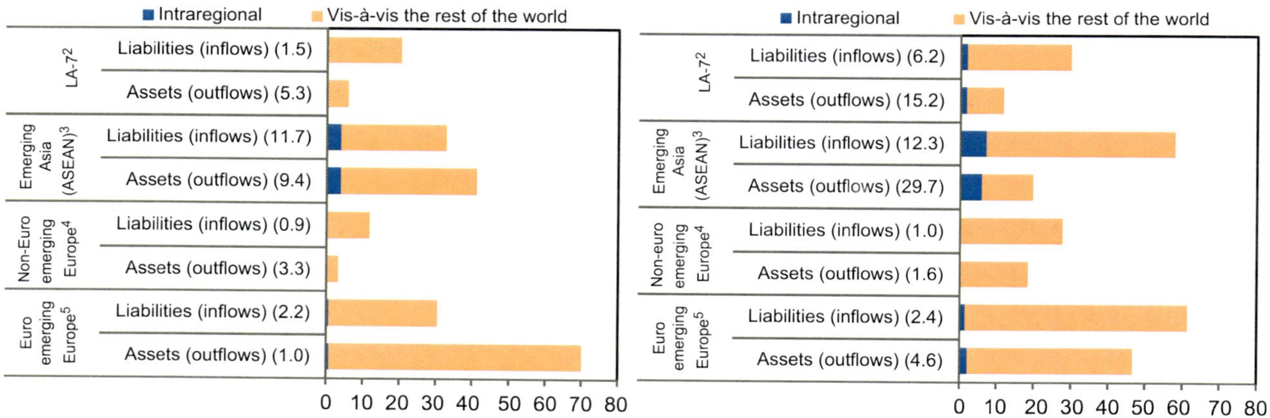

Sources: IMF, Coordinated Portfolio Investment Survey and Coordinated Direct Investment Survey.
[1] Numbers in parentheses report the share of intraregional assets or liabilities in total assets or liabilities of the region.
[2] LA-7 Includes Brazil, Chile, Colombia, Mexico, Panama, Peru, and Uruguay.
[3] Emerging Asia includes Brunei, Cambodia, Indonesia, Lao P.D.R., Malaysia, Myanmar, the Philippines, Singapore, Thailand, and Vietnam. ASEAN = the Association of Southeast Asian Nations.
[4] Non-euro emerging Europe includes Bulgaria, Hungary, Poland, Romania, and Russia.
[5] Euro emerging Europe includes Cyprus, Estonia, Greece, Latvia, Malta, Slovak Republic, and Slovenia.

Figure 2.4. Evolution of Intraregional Integration
(Stocks outstanding, percent of group GDP)

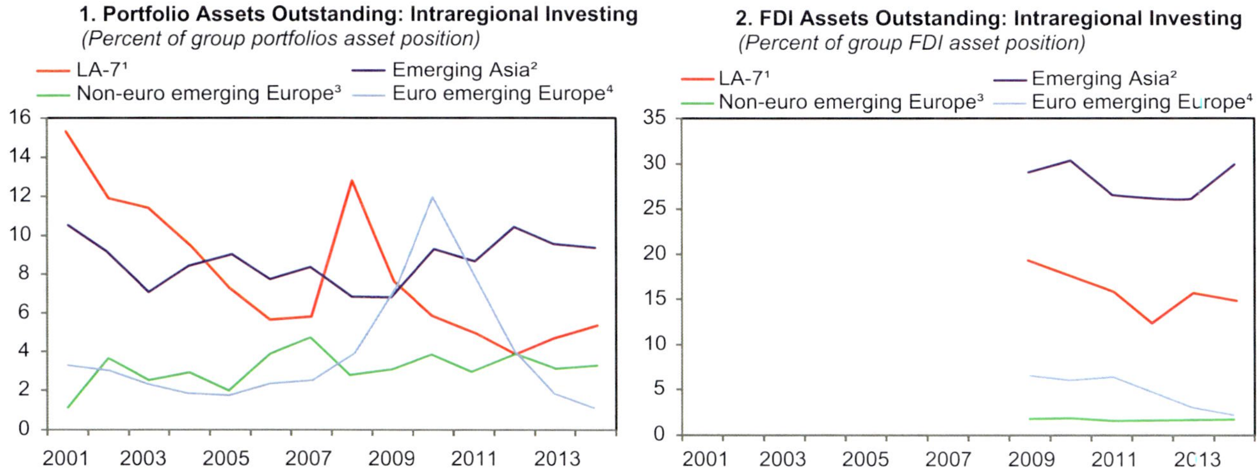

Source: IMF, Coordinated Direct Investment Survey.
[1] LA-7 Includes Brazil, Chile, Colombia, Mexico, Panama, Peru, and Uruguay.
[2] Emerging Asia includes Brunei, Cambodia, Indonesia, Lao P.D.R., Malaysia, Myanmar, Philippines, Singapore, Thailand, and Vietnam.
[3] Non-euro emerging Europe includes Bulgaria, Hungary, Poland, Romania, and Russia.
[4] Euro emerging Europe includes Cyprus, Estonia, Greece, Latvia, Malta, Slovak Republic, and Slovenia.

TABLE 2.2

Consolidated Foreign Claims on the World by BIS-Reporting Banks in Four Latin American Countries *(Percent of GDP)*

	2005	2006	2007	2008	2009	2010	2011	2012	2013
Brazil	3.3	2.7	3.1	2.5	3.2	3.7	3.4	4.1	5.0
of which: claims on other LA-7	*0.0*	*0.1*	*0.1*	*0.1*	*0.4*	*0.5*	*0.5*	*0.7*	*0.8*
Chile	2.4	2.1	2.1	1.7	1.9	1.9	2.6	5.2	4.8
of which: claims on other LA-7	*0.6*	*0.4*	*0.5*	*0.6*	*0.7*	*0.6*	*0.7*	*2.9*	*2.3*
Mexico	0.6	0.5	0.6	0.7	0.9	0.6	0.4	0.4	0.5
of which: claims on other LA-7	*0.0*	*0.0*	*0.0*	*0.0*	*0.0*	*0.0*	*0.0*	*0.0*	*0.0*
Panama	66.2	48.1	51.7	48.3	47.0	44.5	44.9	42.0	42.7
of which: claims on other LA-7	*11.7*	*12.5*	*14.0*	*10.9*	*10.8*	*12.0*	*12.4*	*10.6*	*11.6*

Source: Bank for International Settlements, Consolidated Banking Statistics.

Cross-border mergers and acquisitions provide anecdotal evidence of global fragmentation and increased regional integration after the global financial crisis. Although the trend in Latin America seems less pronounced than in emerging Europe or emerging Asia, several global banks have withdrawn from Latin America since the global financial crisis to refocus on their core markets and activities, and regional or domestic banks have taken over their activities. For example, in 2015 Grupo Financiero Inbursa of Mexico purchased the banking operations of Standard Chartered in Brazil, and in 2012 Corpbanca (Chile) acquired Santander's banks in Colombia. LA-7 institutions are also seizing the opportunity to expand into Central America: Grupo Aval, the largest conglomerate in Colombia, acquired BBVA activities in Panama, and the Ficohsa group of Panama purchased Citibank's operations in Honduras and Nicaragua. Nonbank financial institutions have also been subject to advanced country divestitures. One of the largest moves was the BBVA sale of its pension fund management firms in Chile, Colombia, Mexico, and Peru to regional and local buyers.

Another dimension of regional integration is the MILA initiative that began in 2011. Unlike the Pacific Alliance, whose agenda for integration is set by the political leadership of the member countries (Chile, Colombia, Mexico, and Peru), MILA is a private sector initiative of the four Pacific Alliance stock exchanges and custodians/depositories, which seek to mutually increase trading volumes by facilitating cross-border trading. Early accomplishments include the cross-listing of share prices on all exchanges and the full cross-listing of initial public offers.[6] Furthering integration will require agreement on facilities for

[6] Share prices on the secondary market are quoted for all firms listed on all MILA exchanges in the currency of the home exchange, but this is not considered full cross-listing, as cross-border trades are conducted via correspondent brokers and settlement is often conducted via the back offices. An intermediary achievement in the pursuit of full integration is the treatment of initial public offerings, which are simultaneously and fully listed on all exchanges and so do not require correspondent brokers for trading.

direct trading across exchanges, payment and settlement facilities to mitigate counterparty risks, and broadening of securities to include fixed-income instruments. Beyond the MILA framework, regional exchanges are also integrating through ownership agreements. In 2009 the Bolsa Mexicana purchased an ownership stake in Bolsa de Lima, and in 2015 BM&F Bovespa bought into the Santiago Exchange. Through cross-ownership relationships, exchanges can explore synergies in trading platforms, settlement, and cross-listing.

Measuring the Extent of Financial Integration of Latin American Countries

The measurement of financial integration can be refined further. Simple cross-country comparisons may paint a distorted picture of the degree of integration of Latin American markets relative to other regions, for instance, because countries that are less advanced economically often have shallower financial markets. This section attempts to quantify the extent to which Latin American markets are underintegrated *given their economic fundamentals* by controlling for factors such as the level of economic development (proxied by GDP per capita in purchasing power parity dollars), trade openness (exports plus imports divided by GDP), countries' past history of financial crises (as compiled by Reinhart and Rogoff[7]), the public-debt-to-GDP ratio (which, as a stock variable, cannot be easily modified by the government), and the quality of the institutional framework (measured by the investment profile subcomponent of the PRS Group's International Country Risk Guide Index[8]). Variables that are more directly and immediately affected by economic policy—such as the extent of capital controls—are not included, as the purpose of our econometric analysis is not to provide the best fit for the data but to control for exogenous factors.

The models relate financial integration to a set of control variables. In each specification, a measure of financial integration is regressed (either the baseline or to the alternative composite indices of financial integration presented earlier or their subcomponents) on its macroeconomic determinants and fixed effects. The degree of under- or overintegration is then calculated as the difference between the estimated country (or region) fixed effect and the sample average of all country (or region) fixed effects. Because the purpose of the regressions is to filter out the effect of certain fundamentals and not to interpret a causal model, the endogeneity problem inherent in this type of analysis is less of a concern. The following equation is estimated over a sample of 67 countries between the mid-1980s and 2014:

$$FI_{it} = \beta.X_{it} + \alpha_i + \varepsilon_{it}$$

where FI_{it} denotes the financial integration indicator, X_{it} is a vector of control variables, and α_i are the country fixed effects.

[7] Data available at http://www.reinhartandrogoff.com/data.

[8] Data available at http://www.prsgroup.com/about-us/our-two-methodologies/icrg.

The econometric results (shown in Annex Tables 2.1 to 2.5) confirm that the LA-7 countries are underintegrated as a whole, although there are important differences between countries and across the various dimensions of financial integration. In each model, the sign of the control variables is consistent with prior results. The main result is that although the LA-7 countries do not appear underintegrated from the perspective of international cross-border capital flows, once broader measures of integration are used through the composite integration indices, these countries *do* appear to be underintegrated on the whole, even after controlling for fundamentals. The extent of integration varies across the LA-7, with Panama appearing more integrated than the rest in most specifications, likely owing to its sizable offshore financial sector and its role as a regional hub for Central American countries.

- Annex Table 2.1 shows the outcomes of various models explaining the degree of global financial openness (measured either as the ratio of gross external assets and liabilities to GDP or as the liability ratio, both in logarithm). The results of Annex Table 2.1 suggest that LA-7 countries are relatively well integrated from an openness perspective compared with the sample average, but this result is partly driven by Panama and Chile, which show a greater degree of openness than the other countries.
- Annex Table 2.2 presents the results using the baseline consolidated index of financial integration described earlier. After combining the dimensions of financial openness and financial convergence, it appears that the LA-7 countries are indeed underintegrated, with the exception of Panama, which shows a level of integration in line with the sample average after controlling for fundamentals. This result suggests that the relatively high degree of global openness of countries such as Chile and Peru is more than offset by the lack of regional convergence exhibited by their financial markets.
- Results using the first alternative consolidated index of financial integration, which combines the ratio of convergence and external liabilities to GDP as a measure of openness, are shown in Annex Table 2.3. The results using this narrower measure of openness (which helps preclude cases in which large external assets do not correspond to integration) corroborate the findings of the baseline index. With the exception of Panama, LA-7 countries show a degree of underintegration virtually identical to the baseline results presented in Annex Table 2.2. In this case, Panama stands out as the one LA-7 country whose level of integration is above the sample average.
- Annex Table 2.4 presents the findings using the second alternative consolidated index of integration, incorporating three components: openness, convergence, and depth. The results support the outcomes shown in Annex Tables 2.2 and 2.3, confirming that even with the added dimension of depth, the LA-7 countries—excluding Panama—are underintegrated relative to the sample average, after controlling for fundamentals. An interesting nuance of these results is that after adding depth, the integration outcomes for the LA-7 worsened relative to the two-component indices, with

the exception of Panama and Chile. Panama's result was not only above the sample average but significantly stronger than its outcomes using the two-component indices of integration. Regarding Chile, although the integration outcome was still negative (indicating underintegration), the magnitude of underintegration was halved relative to previous results, suggesting a relatively deep market. Combined with Chile's positive result in the openness models presented in Annex Table 2.1, one could conjecture that Chile's underintegration comes largely from a lack of convergence with the region rather than a lack of global openness or financial depth. For the remaining five LA-7 countries, only the results shown in Table 2.1—gauging global openness—were positive, putting the onus of their underintegration on the lack of regional convergence and depth of their financial markets.

- Annex Table 2.5 displays the findings of the third alternative consolidated index of integration, which includes a measure for relative regional openness in addition to the measure for global financial openness and regional convergence. The results including the regional measure stand out from the previous findings in that all LA-7 countries, including Panama, exhibit underintegration relative to the sample average. That said, Panama still shows the lowest degree of underintegration among the LA-7 countries. This may suggest that Panama's high degree of financial integration, demonstrated in the other findings, largely reflects extra- rather than intraregional integration. Another interesting finding that emerges using this index is that Brazil, Colombia, Peru, and Uruguay are less underintegrated relative to the sample than Chile and Mexico. Mexico's result may reflect its higher degree of integration with the United States (which is not included in the same regional grouping as Mexico for this exercise) compared with its integration with the region. In the case of Chile, which showed a relatively high degree of openness and depth compared to other LA-7 countries in the previous indices, the results confirm our theory that the interconnections of its relatively deep financial markets principally stem from outside the region rather than within.

BENEFITS OF FURTHER INTEGRATION IN LATIN AMERICA

This section describes the benefits of greater financial integration and provides a quantitative estimate of these benefits on growth using econometric analysis.

The Pros and Cons of Greater Financial Integration

By expanding possible financing options and vehicles for saving in a country, *global financial integration* can enhance financial development, which in turn has been linked to higher economic growth (Sahay and others 2015). There are at least three key channels of transmission to growth. First, integration may stimulate capital accumulation through financial deepening in the host country. If capital is brought from outside, competition among financial institutions can be enhanced, particularly when the domestic financial sector contains few institutions and maintains high spreads between borrowing and lending rates, and economies of scale can be exploited by pooling larger amounts of savings. The monetary transmission mechanism can also be enhanced if the banking sector becomes more competitive. All these factors are likely to lower borrowing costs and stimulate investment. Second, better resource allocation and importation of technology and knowledge may create opportunities for efficiency gains and boost productivity, which is another source of growth. Third, financial integration can promote growth indirectly by exposing policy decisions and corporate actions to greater financial market scrutiny.

In addition to raising the growth trend, financial integration may foster economic resilience and reduce volatility around the trend. Output volatility can be mitigated through two main factors. First, financial integration is likely to increase the depth of financial markets, leading to greater market liquidity: possibilities to buy and sell securities will increase with the emergence of new players and new instruments. Second, financial integration offers new opportunities for risk-sharing and intertemporal consumption smoothing through the diversification of portfolios across asset classes, sectors, and countries. Overall, this stabilization effect should be particularly beneficial in Latin American countries, where production bases are concentrated and there is a heavy dependence on agricultural activities or the extraction of natural resources (IMF 2015b).[9]

On top of these overarching advantages of integration, *regional financial integration* can bring a number of additional benefits for both the home and host countries:

- Cross-border financial activity (bank and nonbank) both follows and can be followed by cross-border trade and thus could help foster wider regional economic integration. A larger common market creates new growth opportunities, which may be influential in Latin America in a context of lower commodity prices and tighter global financial conditions.
- Regional banks (robustly supervised with sufficient high-quality capital to support their cross-border operations) and regional markets may have a better understanding than global institutions of the needs of the region. They may be able to provide expertise particularly suited to the host country, such as in the area of improving financial inclusion. The homogeneous importance of commodity exports across the region is also fertile ground for transplanting expertise in trade and industrial credit.
- At the regional level, capital market integration creates scope for economies of scale, especially when individual markets are relatively small. In many Latin American countries, the small size of national markets (in some cases owing partly to domestic regulatory factors) constrains financial sector

[9] It should be noted that the scope for mutual benefits from regional risk-sharing may be limited by the synchronization of economic cycles in commodity-exporting countries.

growth and efficiency, contributing to higher costs, a narrower range of financial products, and the exclusion of many from formal financial services. Addressing regulatory limitations and facilitating regional integration could help loosen these constraints by allowing governments, financial intermediaries, and corporations to access a regional market with greater depth and liquidity. In addition, larger inflows of foreign capital to the region may follow, as a larger and more liquid regional market may be more attractive to international investors.

- Regional banks can fill the hole left by retrenching global banks. Since the global financial crisis, financial pressures and increased regulatory oversight have led some global institutions to reduce their cross-border activities and pull back into their core markets (IMF 2015a). Responding to the withdrawal of these banks, intraregional acquisition activity has been growing rapidly in a number of emerging markets, particularly in Asia and emerging Europe (BIS 2014). This trend has so far been less pronounced in much of Latin America, where it has been more common for domestic institutions to absorb the assets of departing global banks. Regional integration could help avoid increased consolidation of domestic financial sector activity and mitigate a possible credit squeeze if North American and Spanish banks were to continue reducing their presence in the region. Although this strategy could lead to the emergence of large regional banks and bring the risk of concentration at a regional level, it would nonetheless foster greater competition and diversification of risks within domestic markets.
- Regional integration can also alleviate the pressure on domestic markets arising from the significant growth of the nonbank financial sector (particularly pension funds) in Latin American countries in recent years. Current regulations governing pension fund investments in Latin American countries compel the funds to invest the vast majority of their portfolios in domestic assets. Given the relatively small size of many Latin American financial markets, the investment options available to these pension funds are severely limited, and most end up overweighted in domestic government securities. Although the motivation behind these investment restrictions is the preservation of savings and financial stability, the development of domestic financial markets in most Latin American countries has not kept up with the growth of their pension funds, and the restrictions may paradoxically lead to the creation of bubbles and instability. If regional integration—through the harmonization of regulations and more coordinated supervision—were to widen pension funds' permissible investment options to include other countries in the region, this could be a solution.
- Almost all Latin American countries currently face the urgent need to improve their physical infrastructure. However, upgrades to logistics and transport infrastructure typically require sizable investments, necessitating deep and well-developed financial markets. While pension funds in some Latin American countries have invested in domestic infrastructure projects,

the caps on their permissible investments in such projects are dwarfed by the size of the projects. Thus, given the absence of deep domestic markets, the need for economies of scale is yet another reason to carefully assess the possibility of advancing regional financial integration in Latin America. Investment vehicles could then be established at a regional level to pool resources for infrastructure projects around the region.

Financial integration has its fair share of critics, and the aforementioned advantages of global and regional integration are not assured unless accompanying measures are in place, particularly enhanced supervision. Cross-border financial activity also brings risks, including adverse spillovers if there is insufficient official capacity to exercise necessary oversight. Critics of financial integration point to financial crises following capital account liberalizations in Mexico (1994), east Asia (1997), and Russia (1998). In fact, efforts to identify empirically positive results from financial integration often struggle to generalize results and must narrow the findings to selected forms of integration (FDI and equity are statistically favored over debt instruments) or acknowledge necessary preconditions such as high levels of economic development, institutional quality, or financial development. Greater integration could also render countries' macroprudential policies less effective and easier to circumvent through cross-border leakages and provision of credit (IMF 2014).

One particular concern is that increased cross-border banking sector integration may adversely affect financial stability through the transmission of international shocks. Giannetti and Laeven (2012) and Jeon, Olivero, and Wu (2013) describe how stresses in the home country of parent banks widen the funding spreads in subsidiary and branch markets and even pit operations in different emerging market countries against each other for liquidity from parent banks.[10] Degryse and others (2009) find that foreign banks tend to reinforce credit segmentation whether they enter via greenfield investment and target the most transparent and creditworthy borrowers or via merger/acquisition, in which case the composition of loan portfolio credit quality changes little. Furthermore, evidence of financial integration and foreign bank presence leading to enhanced financial inclusion and depth is mixed: several studies—including Detragiache, Gupta, and Tressel (2008) and Claessens and van Horen (2014)—associate the prominence of foreign banks with lower credit-to-GDP ratios in developing countries.

Nonetheless, proponents of integration maintain that although integration brings both costs and benefits, the latter outweigh the former, particularly when preconditions for successful integration, such as consolidated supervision and enhanced cross-border information sharing, are in place. For example, Rancière, Tornell, and Westermann (2006, 2008) show that the direct effects of financial

[10] Dependence on local funding and lending in local currency, as is common in Latin America, can insulate domestic credit by subsidiaries from crises in the home countries of parent banks (Kamil and Rai 2010).

liberalization on growth outweigh the negative indirect effect of higher propensity to crises. In their analysis of the costs and benefits of financial globalization, Kose and others (2006, 1) also recognize the existence of conflicting results but conclude that the empirical literature "lends some qualified support to the view that developing countries can benefit from financial globalization, but with many nuances. On the other hand, there is little systematic evidence to support widely-cited claims that financial globalization by itself leads to deeper and more costly developing country growth crises."

How Large Could the Potential Macroeconomic Gains from Greater Financial Integration in Latin America Be?

To quantify the benefits of further integration in Latin America, a model relating financial integration to economic growth is estimated. The specification, which follows Beck and Levine (2004) and Sahay and others (2015), includes the standard control variables of growth equations: initial income per capita, trade openness, inflation, government expenditure-to-GDP ratio, investment-to-GDP ratio, population growth, and several measures of institutional framework quality (proxied by the International Country Risk Guide [ICRG] indicators of country risk). The sample is similar to the one used earlier and includes 76 countries between the mid-1980s and 2014.

In light of the endogeneity of the integration variable with respect to growth, the baseline model uses an instrumental variable (IV) panel estimator with the following instruments: the first lag of the integration variable; the capital controls indicator by Fernández and others (2015); the occurrence of a banking crisis 10 years earlier; and a subcomponent of the ICRG political risk index, which describes the extent to which profits can be transferred or repatriated out of a country. All the instruments are assumed to impact integration directly but affect growth indirectly. Admittedly, it is very difficult to find fully exogenous instruments in a macroeconomic setting. This chapter assumes that the institutional framework (capital controls, profit repatriation rules) is exogenous with respect to growth, which may be justified by the fact that these variables are slow-moving.

The estimated equation is therefore:

$$y_{it} = \alpha_i + \beta_1 \times FI_{it} + \beta_2.X_{it} + \varepsilon_{it}$$

where y_{it} denotes GDP growth, FI_{it} the financial integration indicator defined earlier, X_{it} the control variables, and α_i the fixed effect. Time dummies are also included in some specifications.

After correcting for endogeneity, financial integration—proxied by the baseline index of Table 2.1—is found to be positively correlated with growth. In models without this correction, integration is either statistically insignificant or negatively correlated to growth. With the IV correction, the elasticity is clearly positive, regardless of the number of control variables (shown in Annex Table 2.6, columns 1–3), whether the equation is saturated with time dummies (column 4), or whether real growth or real growth per capita is used as a dependent variable (column 5). Results are also robust to removing the banking crisis instrument, the inclusion of which presents the disadvantage of reducing the sample size, as the variable denotes the existence of a crisis 10 years earlier and is not available for some countries (column 6). The results of a dynamic model estimated by the Arellano–Bond generalized method of moments (GMM—see Bond, Hoeffler, and Temple 2001), with lagged GDP growth as the explanatory variable, are also presented, and the financial integration variable coefficient is broadly unchanged (column 7).[11]

Another potential issue is that the lagged GDP-per-capita level is generally endogenous in growth equations (Bond, Hoeffler, and Temple 2001). To circumvent this problem, an equation is presented that excludes the variable and finds that the integration coefficient is broadly unchanged (column 8). The endogeneity of both the integration variable and the lagged GDP level are corrected by rewriting the growth regression as a dynamic model in levels[12] and estimating it with the first-differenced Arellano–Bond GMM estimator; alongside the lagged (first-differenced) variables, the additional instruments mentioned above (capital controls indicator, occurrence of a banking crisis 10 years earlier, and profit repatriation rule) are included. The effect of financial integration is again positive and significant (column 9), but the regression suffers from the traditional GMM shortcomings, including a high sensitivity to the number of lags used for the instruments. Finally, the possibility of nonlinear relationships was accounted for through interaction terms and a quadratic form of the integration indicator. However, the nonlinear models did not produce robust results.

Annex Table 2.7 shows the results of specifications with the alternative measures of integration. The following indicators (described earlier and in Table 2.1) are used: a two-component index with the ratio of external liabilities to GDP (column 1); a three-component index that adds a measure of financial depth (column 2); and variants of the three-component index including regional openness (columns 3–6). Column 3 measures regional integration as the ratio of a country's regional assets and liabilities to total foreign assets and liabilities in an eight-region framework. Column 4 replicates the indicator with a four-region split. Column 5 measures regional integration by weighting the sum of assets and liabilities with the distance between countries. Column 6 measures regional integration by weighting liabilities with the distance between countries. In all these specifications, the effect of financial integration remains positive and significant.

As a last sensitivity exercise, we conduct regressions with simpler measures of financial integration. The last three columns show that simple financial openness ratios are positively related to growth. Column 7 reports the results of a regression

---

[11] In this case, the elasticity of the financial integration variable cannot be directly compared with the other specifications because of the lagged dependent variable term. This coefficient should first be multiplied by 1 over 1 minus the coefficient of the lagged GDP growth to get the long-term elasticity.

[12] See Bond, Hoeffler, and Temple (2001), equation 16. By rewriting a growth model as a dynamic model in level (with the GDP level on the left-hand side), the control variable on the right-hand side becomes the lagged level of GDP rather than the lagged level of GDP per capita.

with global openness measured as financial assets plus financial liabilities in percent of GDP. Columns 8 and 9 replicate the results with regional openness indicators—defined in a similar way (ratio of regional assets plus regional liabilities to GDP), with an eight- or four-region split.

Overall, financial integration and economic performance are found to be positively correlated. The various specifications return elasticities of 0.01–0.02 for the regional integration variable. Using the measure of underintegration calculated earlier, it is possible to estimate the effect of closing the integration gap in the LA-7 countries. Specifically, combining the two steps, the analysis predicts a growth effect in the range of 1/4 to 3/4 percentage point on average if the gap is fully closed.[13] (The growth dividend would be lower if progress is partial.) These results should be treated with caution, as most variables in growth regressions are endogenous, creating potential estimation biases that IV and GMM estimators cannot always correct.

CONCLUSION

There has seldom been a better moment to advance regional financial integration in Latin America. The aftermath of the global financial crisis has brought significantly tighter banking regulations and a trend of de-risking. Consequently, global banks have been withdrawing from Latin America and other emerging markets to return home. At the same time, the commodity boom is over, and with slower growth foreseen in China over the medium term, Latin America's commodity producers will face hard times unless they are able to establish alternative avenues of growth. These avenues would require investment and deep capital markets. This is not a juncture at which Latin American countries can comfortably afford to see their financial markets contract. Enhanced financial integration within the region provides one possible solution. Providentially, initiatives to promote regional financial integration, such as the Pacific Alliance and MILA, are currently enjoying political support.

The analysis in this chapter finds strong evidence of financial underintegration in the LA-7, from both a descriptive and an econometric perspective. Moreover, this integration gap applies to both global and regional financial integration. Other emerging market regions, such as east Asia and eastern Europe, seem to be more integrated with each other and with the outside world compared with our Latin American sample. Furthermore, the LA-7 countries appear to be underintegrated given their own macro- and socioeconomic fundamentals. Latin America would benefit greatly from reducing this degree of financial underintegration. Our econometric results suggest that the positive impact on growth of closing the integration gap could be 1/4 to 3/4 percentage point, on average. Of course, given the traditional challenges involved in estimating causal effects with

---

[13] In the first step, the difference between the country fixed effect and the sample average is used to estimate the degree of underintegration. In the fixed effect models, this gap averages 0.3–0.4 in LA-7 countries. With an elasticity of 0.01–0.02, the growth effect is therefore 0.3–0.8 percentage points.

macroeconomic data, our results, although robust to alternative specifications, should be treated with caution.

To move the baton of enhanced regional financial integration forward and realize the macroeconomic benefits, the following chapters suggest a number of concrete steps that could be taken by the Latin American countries in question. While there has been considerable political traction for projects such as MILA, to get the process effectively rolling would require the logistical and economic nuts and bolts to be firmly in place. In particular, the countries would need to harmonize their accounting, regulatory practices, and taxation schemes, and establish coordinated and consolidated supervision, enhanced cross-border information sharing, and macroprudential policies. All this would require substantial investment, but without it the risks of integration could outweigh the benefits by undermining the resilience of financial systems. The case for enhanced regional financial integration in Latin America is clear. If all stakeholders are brought on board and the requisite regulatory and supervisory innovations instituted, success is well within grasp.

ANNEX 2.1. ECONOMETRIC RESULTS

ANNEX TABLE 2.1

Financial Market Integration: Financial Openness

	Stock of Gross External Assets + Liabilities/GDP			Stock of Gross External Liabilities/GDP	
	OLS (1)[1]	OLS (2)[1]	FE[2]	OLS[1]	FE[2]
Log of GDP per capita	0.31***	0.43***	0.62***	0.25***	0.54***
Purchasing power parity	*8.44*	*8.20*	*3.85*	*4.94*	*3.69*
Government debt/GDP		0.37***	0.48***	0.34***	0.52***
		5.20	*6.28*	*4.40*	*6.85*
Trade openness		0.66***	0.43***	0.68***	0.43***
		6.53	*2.86*	*6.30*	*2.90*
Institutional quality[3]		0.04***	0.05***	0.04***	0.05***
		2.77	*4.38*	*2.96*	*4.01*
History of bank crises (t – 10)[4]		–0.14**	–0.06	–0.11*	–0.07*
		–2.38	*–1.66*	*–1.98*	*–1.82*
LA-7 dummy[5]	–0.13***	0.16***		0.20***	
	–6.18	*5.98*		*3.83*	
Non-LA-7 dummy[5]	0.01***	–0.02***		–0.02***	
	8.44	*–7.17*		*–4.74*	
Brazil dummy[5]			–0.34***		–0.19***
			–3.55		*–3.54*
Chile dummy[5]			0.54***		0.62***
			3.11		*3.10*
Colombia dummy[5]			–0.01***		0.10***
			–3.50		*3.50*
Mexico dummy[5]			–0.65***		–0.48***
			–3.84		*–3.85*
Peru dummy[5]			0.12***		0.33***
			3.50		*3.43*
Panama dummy[5]			0.89***		0.79***
			3.03		*3.13*
Uruguay dummy[5]			–0.19***		–0.30***
			–3.56		*–3.74*
Number of observations	5,681	1,336	1,336	1,336	1,336
R-squared	0.23	0.71	0.91	0.57	0.85

Note: Time dummies have been incorporated in all specifications. Robust T-statistics are in italics. LA-7 = Brazil, Chile, Colombia, Mexico, Panama, Peru, and Uruguay.

*** $p < 0.01$, ** $p < 0.05$, * $p < 0.1$.

[1] The OLS regressions are ordinary least squares regressions with standard errors adjusted for clustering at the country level for a panel of 67 countries from 1986 to 2011. Selected country and/or regional dummies are included.

[2] The FE regressions estimate country fixed effects for all countries in the sample, but only the LA-7 results are reported in this table.

[3] The investment profile subcomponent of the International Country Risk Guide political risk index is used to gauge institutional quality.

[4] Indicator of past banking crises following Reinhart and Rogoff (2009). Data available at http://www.reinhartandrogoff.com/data.

[5] Demeaned estimates: fixed effect estimates minus a sample average of fixed effects.

ANNEX TABLE 2.2

Baseline Financial Integration Index with Two Components, Openness and Convergence

	OLS (1)[1]	OLS (2)[1]	OLS (3)[1]	FE[2]
Log of GDP per capita	0.27***	0.27***	0.38***	0.79***
Purchasing power parity	*5.20*	*5.20*	*4.26*	*3.18*
Trade openness			0.63***	0.58**
			3.36	*2.34*
Government debt/GDP			0.22***	
			3.59	
Institutional quality[3]			0.04**	0.06***
			2.34	*2.86*
History of bank crises (t – 10)[4]			–0.11	–0.21***
			–1.57	*–2.88*
LA-7 dummy[5]	–0.71***		–0.02***	
	–6.46		*–4.56*	
Non-LA-7 dummy[5]	0.08***	0.08***	0.00***	
	5.42	*5.41*	*4.40*	
Brazil dummy[5]		–0.93***		–0.07***
		–7.00		*–3.11*
Chile dummy[5]		–0.81***		–0.85***
		–6.68		*–3.61*
Colombia dummy[5]		–0.85***		–0.09***
		–7.06		*–3.29*
Mexico dummy[5]		–0.92***		–0.78***
		–6.83		*–3.52*
Peru dummy[5]		–0.72***		0.04***
		–6.97		*3.36*
Panama dummy[5]		–0.05***		0.07***
		–5.29		*3.32*
Uruguay dummy[5]		–0.76***		–0.51***
		–6.62		*–3.42*
Number of observations	3,901	3,901	1,289	1,601
R-squared	0.13	0.14	0.42	0.61

Note: Time dummies have been incorporated in all specifications. The dependent variable is a principal component from two variables: openness (external assets + liabilities as a ratio of GDP) and convergence. This is the baseline indicator described in Table 2.1. LA-7 = Brazil, Chile, Colombia, Mexico, Panama, Peru, and Uruguay.

Robust T-statistics are in italics.

*** $p < 0.01$, ** $p < 0.05$, * $p < 0.1$.

[1] The OLS regressions are ordinary least squares regressions with standard errors adjusted for clustering at the country level for a panel of 67 countries from 1986 to 2011. Selected country and/or regional dummies are included.

[2] The FE regression estimates country fixed effects for all countries in the sample; only LA-7 results are reported.

[3] The investment profile subcomponent of the International Country Risk Guide political risk index is used to gauge institutional quality.

[4] Indicator of past banking crises following Reinhart and Rogoff (2009).

[5] Demeaned estimates: fixed effect estimates minus a sample average of fixed effects.

ANNEX TABLE 2.3

Alternative Financial Integration Index with Two Components, External Liabilities and Convergence

	OLS (1)[1]	OLS (2)[1]	OLS (3)[1]	FE[2]
Log of GDP per capita	0.21***	0.21***	0.36***	0.81***
Purchasing power parity	*4.03*	*4.03*	*3.88*	*3.18*
Trade openness			0.65***	0.53**
			3.58	*2.23*
Government debt/GDP			0.23***	
			3.78	
Institutional quality[3]			0.01	0.03
			0.78	*1.25*
History of bank crises (*t* – 10)[4]			–0.11	–0.20***
			–1.65	*–2.83*
LA-7 dummy[5]	–0.67***		0.02***	
	–5.25		*3.98*	
Non-LA-7 dummy[5]	0.08***	0.08***	0.00***	
	4.18	*4.18*	*3.89*	
Brazil dummy[5]		–0.90***		–0.17***
		–5.87		*–3.08*
Chile dummy[5]		–0.74***		–0.76***
		–5.48		*–3.50*
Colombia dummy[5]		–0.85***		–0.17***
		–5.96		*–3.25*
Mexico dummy[5]		–0.86***		–0.76***
		–5.68		*–3.43*
Peru dummy[5]		–0.66***		0.06***
		–5.70		*3.27*
Panama dummy[5]		0.10***		0.22***
		3.85		*3.18*
Uruguay dummy[5]		–0.76***		–0.53***
		–5.55		*–3.36*
Number of observations	3,901	3,901	1,289	1,601
R-squared	0.09	0.10	0.42	0.62

Note: Time dummies have been incorporated in all specifications. The dependent variable is the principal component from two variables: external liabilities as a ratio of GDP and convergence.

This is the financial integration, alternate 1, described in Table 2.1. LA-7 = Brazil, Chile, Colombia, Mexico, Panama, Peru, and Uruguay. Robust T-statistics are in italics.

*** $p < 0.01$, ** $p < 0.05$, * $p < 0.1$.

[1] The OLS regressions are ordinary least squares regressions with standard errors adjusted for clustering at the country level for a panel of 67 countries from 1986 to 2011. Selected country and/or regional dummies are included.

[2] The FE regression estimates country fixed effects for all countries in the sample; only LA-7 results are reported.

[3] The investment profile subcomponent of the International Country Risk Guide political risk index is used to gauge institutional quality.

[4] Indicator of past banking crises following Reinhart and Rogoff (2009).

[5] Demeaned estimates: fixed effect estimates minus a sample average of fixed effects.

ANNEX TABLE 2.4

Alternative Financial Integration Index with Three Components, Including Financial Depth

	OLS (1)[1]	OLS (2)[1]	OLS (3)[1]	FE[2]
Log of GDP per capita	0.63***	0.63***	0.85***	1.28***
Purchasing power parity	*8.02*	*8.01*	*6.52*	*3.78*
Trade openness			0.70***	
			2.93	
Government debt/GDP			0.29***	
			3.02	
Institutional quality[3]			0.09***	0.07**
			3.43	*2.53*
History of bank crises (t – 10)[4]			–0.34***	–0.28***
			3.63	*3.57*
LA-7 dummy[5]	–0.54***		–0.20***	
	–8.20		*–7.10*	
Non-LA-7 dummy[5]	0.06***	0.06***	0.02***	
	8.59	*8.57*	*7.08*	
Brazil dummy[5]		–0.80***		–0.69***
		–8.89		*–4.26*
Chile dummy[5]		0.19***		–0.37***
		7.15		*–4.01*
Colombia dummy[5]		–0.73***		–0.41***
		–9.1		*–4.33*
Mexico dummy[5]		–1.20***		–1.33***
		–9.25		*–4.42*
Peru dummy[5]		–0.67***		–0.17***
		–9.29		*–4.38*
Panama dummy[5]		0.69***		0.88***
		7.06		*3.88*
Uruguay dummy[5]		–0.78***		–0.81***
		–8.86		*–4.33*
Observations	3,271	3,271	1,160	1,456
R-squared	0.33	0.34	0.57	0.77

Note: Time dummies have been incorporated in all specifications. The dependent variable is the principal component from three variables: openness, convergence, and depth. This is the financial integration alternate 2 described in Table 2.1. LA-7 = Brazil, Chile, Colombia, Mexico, Panama, Peru, and Uruguay. Robust T-statistics are in italics.

*** $p < 0.01$, ** $p < 0.05$, * $p < 0.1$.

[1] The OLS regressions are ordinary least squares regressions with standard errors adjusted for clustering at the country level for a panel of 66 countries from 1986 to 2011. Selected country and/or regional dummies are included.

[2] The FE regression estimates country fixed effects for all countries in the sample; only LA-7 results are reported.

[3] The investment profile subcomponent of the International Country Risk Guide political risk index is used to gauge institutional quality.

[4] Indicator of past banking crises following Reinhart and Rogoff (2009).

[5] Demeaned estimates: fixed effect estimates minus a sample average of fixed effects.

ANNEX TABLE 2.5

Alternative Financial Integration Index with Three Components, Including Regional Openness

	OLS (1)[1]	OLS (2)[1]	OLS (3)[1]	FE[2]
Log of GDP per capita	0.36***	0.36***	0.28***	0.41**
Purchasing power parity	*6.25*	*6.23*	*4.56*	*2.45*
Trade openness			0.63***	0.48***
			3.81	*3.37*
Government debt/GDP			0.24***	
			2.83	
Institutional quality[3]			0.07***	
			2.78	
LA-7 dummy[4]	–0.61***		–0.35***	
	–7.11		*–6.94*	
Non-LA-7 dummy[4]	0.03***	0.03***	0.01***	
	6.65	*6.63*	*6.59*	
Brazil dummy[4]		–0.77***		–0.21**
		–7.39		*–2.36*
Chile dummy[4]		–0.63***		–0.58**
		–6.95		*–2.60*
Colombia dummy[4]		–0.66***		–0.25**
		–7.41		*–2.48*
Mexico dummy[4]		–0.85***		–0.69***
		–7.40		*–2.67*
Peru dummy[4]		–0.59***		–0.31**
		–7.41		*–2.59*
Panama dummy[4]		–0.29***		–0.22**
		–6.58		*–2.46*
Uruguay dummy[4]		–0.51***		–0.31**
		–6.88		*–2.46*
Observations	1,816	1,816	1,428	1,814
R-squared	0.17	0.18	0.30	0.65

Note: Time dummies have been incorporated in all specifications. The dependent variable is the principal component from three variables: global openness, regional convergence, and regional integration based on eight regions. This is the financial integration alternate 3.1 described in Table 2.1. Robust T-statistics are in italics. LA-7 = Brazil, Chile, Colombia, Mexico, Panama, Peru, and Uruguay.

*** $p < 0.01$, ** $p < 0.05$, * $p < 0.1$.

[1] The OLS regressions are ordinary least squares regressions with standard errors adjusted for clustering at the country level for a panel of 66 countries from 1986 to 2011. Selected country and/or regional dummies are included.

[2] The FE regression estimates country fixed effects for all countries in the sample; only LA-7 results are reported.

[3] The investment profile subcomponent of the International Country Risk Guide political risk index is used to gauge institutional quality.

[4] Demeaned estimates: fixed effect estimates minus a sample average of fixed effects.

ANNEX TABLE 2.6

Impact of Financial Integration on GDP Growth

Variables	(1) Real GDP Growth	(2) Real GDP Growth	(3) Real GDP Growth	(4) Real GDP Growth[1]	(5) Real GDP Growth per Capita	(6) Real GDP Growth	(7) GMM: Real GDP Growth	(8) Real GDP Growth	(9) GMM: Log of Real GDP
Financial integration indicator: baseline[2]	0.02*	0.02**	0.02**	0.01*	0.02**	0.01**	0.01***	0.02**	0.01**
	(0.01)	(0.01)	(0.01)	(0.01)	(0.01)	(0.01)	(0.00)	(0.01)	(0.00)
Log of trade openness[3]		0.04***	0.03**	0.02	0.03**	0.03***	0.05***	0.02	0.04***
		(0.01)	(0.01)	(0.01)	(0.01)	(0.01)	(0.01)	(0.01)	(0.01)
Log of GDP per capita (t – 1)	–0.05***	–0.05***	–0.02*	–0.11***	–0.02*	–0.02**	–0.09***		
Purchasing power parity	(0.01)	(0.01)	(0.01)	(0.04)	(0.01)	(0.01)	(0.00)		
Log of investment-to-GDP ratio[4]	0.14***	0.14***	0.08***	0.09***	0.08***	0.07***	0.02***	0.07***	0.09***
	(0.02)	(0.02)	(0.01)	(0.01)	(0.01)	(0.01)	(0.00)	(0.01)	(0.01)
Log of public-expenditures-to-GDP ratio[5]		–0.08***	–0.05**	–0.05**	–0.05**	–0.06***	–0.05***	–0.06***	–0.03***
		(0.02)	(0.02)	(0.02)	(0.02)	(0.02)	(0.01)	(0.02)	(0.01)
Log change in population		–0.83**	–0.61*	–0.51*	–1.62***	–0.33	0.51***	–0.61*	–0.90***
		(0.39)	(0.36)	(0.28)	(0.36)	(0.23)	(0.13)	(0.33)	(0.25)
CPI inflation rate		–0.08*	–0.02	0.03	–0.02	–0.04	0	–0.01	–0.03*
		(0.05)	(0.04)	(0.03)	(0.04)	(0.03)	(0.00)	(0.04)	(0.02)
ICRG composite index[6]			0.00***	0.00***	0.00***	0.00***	0.00***	0.00***	0.00***
			(0.00)	(0.00)	(0.00)	(0.00)	(0.00)	(0.00)	(0.00)
Dummy year 2009			–0.03***		–0.03***	–0.03***	–0.02***	–0.03***	–0.03***
			(0.00)		(0.00)	(0.00)	(0.00)	(0.00)	(0.00)

(Continued)

Impact of Financial Integration on GDP Growth (*Cont.*)

Variables	(1) Real GDP Growth	(2) Real GDP Growth	(3) Real GDP Growth	(4) Real GDP Growth[1]	(5) Real GDP Growth per Capita	(6) Real GDP Growth	(7) GMM: Real GDP Growth	(8) Real GDP Growth	(9) GMM: Log of Real GDP
Real GDP growth (t – 1)							0		
							(0.02)		
Log of real GDP (t – 1)									0.96***
									(0.01)
Constant							0.61***		0.52***
							(0.04)		(0.10)
Number of observations	716	678	678	678	678	864	2,705	678	677
R-squared	0.19	0.32	0.44	0.58	0.44	0.47		0.44	
Number of countries	59	59	59	59	59	76	124	59	59
Robust standard errors in parentheses									

Note: All specifications estimated with instrumental variable panel estimator except for specifications 7 and 9, which use the generalized method of moments (GMM). CPI = consumer price index; ICRG = International Country Risk Guide.

*** $p < 0.01$, ** $p < 0.05$, * $p < 0.1$.

[1] This specification is saturated with time dummies, which are not reproduced in the table.

[2] Principal component of two variables: global openness and regional asset price convergence. This is the baseline described in Table 2.1.

[3] Exports plus imports as a ratio of GDP.

[4] Private and public investment as a ratio of GDP.

[5] Current and capital expenditures of the general government as a ratio of GDP.

[6] ICRG composite index of political, economic, and financial country risks.

ANNEX TABLE 2.7

Impact of Financial Integration on Growth, Using Alternative Financial Integration Indicators

Variables	Real GDP Growth (1)	Real GDP Growth (2)	Real GDP Growth (3)	Real GDP Growth (4)	Real GDP Growth (5)	Real GDP Growth (6)	Real GDP Growth (7)	Real GDP Growth (8)	Real GDP Growth (9)
Financial integration (FI) indicator: alternative 1[1]	0.02**								
	(0.01)								
FI: alternative 2[2]		0.01***							
		(0.00)							
FI: alternative 3.1[3]			0.03*						
			(0.01)						
FI: alternative 3.2[4]				0.02*					
				(0.01)					
FI: alternative 3.3[5]					0.09*				
					(0.05)				
FI: alternative 3.4[6]						0.06**			
						(0.03)			
FI: global openness ratio[7]							0.01***		
							(0.00)		
FI: regional openness ratio (eight regions)[8]								0.01*	
								(0.01)	
FI: regional openness ratio (four regions)[9]									0.01**
									(0.01)
Log of trade-openness-to-GDP ratio[10]	0.03**	0.05***	0.06***	0.03**	0.02	0.02	0.02***	0.06***	0.05**
	(0.01)	(0.01)	(0.01)	(0.01)	(0.03)	(0.02)	(0.01)	(0.02)	(0.02)
Log of GDP per capita (t – 1)	–0.02*	–0.03**	–0.04**	–0.03***	–0.04**	–0.04***	–0.04***	–0.09***	–0.10**
Purchasing power parity	(0.01)	(0.01)	(0.01)	(0.01)	(0.02)	(0.01)	(0.01)	(0.03)	(0.04)
Log of investment-to-GDP ratio[11]	0.08***	0.07***	0.09***	0.11***	0.11***	0.11***	0.03***	0.05***	0.06***
	(0.01)	(0.01)	(0.01)	(0.01)	(0.03)	(0.02)	(0.01)	(0.01)	(0.01)

(Continued)

Impact of Financial Integration on Growth, Using Alternative Financial Integration Indicators (*Cont.*)

Variables	Real GDP Growth (1)	Real GDP Growth (2)	Real GDP Growth (3)	Real GDP Growth (4)	Real GDP Growth (5)	Real GDP Growth (6)	Real GDP Growth (7)	Real GDP Growth (8)	Real GDP Growth (9)
Log of fiscal-expenditures-to-GDP ratio[12]	−0.05**	−0.08***	−0.07***	−0.06***	−0.01	−0.03	−0.03*	−0.05**	−0.04*
	(0.02)	(0.02)	(0.02)	(0.02)	(0.03)	(0.02)	(0.02)	(0.02)	(0.02)
Log of change of population	−0.57*	−0.52	−0.73*	−0.67**	−0.50	−0.42	0.74***	0.23	0.17
	(0.32)	(0.33)	(0.44)	(0.30)	(0.67)	(0.44)	(0.20)	(0.23)	(0.23)
Consumer price index inflation rate	−0.03	−0.01	−0.31*	−0.32***	0.03	−0.01	−0.00	−0.14***	−0.18***
	(0.04)	(0.03)	(0.17)	(0.11)	(0.09)	(0.08)	(0.00)	(0.05)	(0.07)
ICRG composite[13]	0.00***	0.00***	0.00***		0.01***	0.01***	0.00***	0.00***	0.00***
	(0.00)	(0.00)	(0.00)		(0.00)	(0.00)	(0.00)	(0.00)	(0.00)
Year 2009 dummy	−0.03***			−0.03***				−0.03***	−0.03***
	(0.00)			(0.00)				(0.00)	(0.01)
Number of observations	678	601	624	634	624	624	2,949	1,181	1,153
R-squared	0.45	0.41	0.23	0.40	−1.09	−0.09	0.15	0.26	0.21
Number of countries	59	59	59	59	59	59	124	120	117

Note: All equations are estimated with instrumented variable estimation. Robust standard errors in parentheses.

*** $p < 0.01$, ** $p < 0.05$, * $p < 0.1$.

[1] Principal component of two variables: global integration of external liabilities and asset price convergence within an eight-region world.

[2] Principal component of three variables: global integration of external assets and liabilities, banking system credit to the private sector, and asset price convergence within an eight-region world.

[3] Principal component of three variables: global integration of external assets and liabilities, asset price convergence, and integration of external assets and liabilities within an eight-region world.

[4] Principal component of three variables: global integration of external assets and liabilities, asset price convergence, and integration of external assets and liabilities within a four-region world.

[5] Principal component of three variables: global integration of external liabilities, asset price convergence within an eight-region world, and average proximity of external asset and liability partners.

[6] Principal component of three variables: global integration of external liabilities, asset price convergence within an eight-region world, and average proximity of external liability partners.

[7] Global openness is measured as the log of external assets plus liabilities in percent of GDP.

[8] Regional openness (eight regions) is measured as the log of external regional assets plus liabilities (vis-à-vis narrow regional partners) as a ratio of GDP.

[9] Regional openness (four regions) is measured as the log of external regional assets plus liabilities (vis-à-vis broad regional partners) as a ratio of GDP.

[10] Exports plus imports as a ratio of GDP.

[11] Private and public investment as a ratio of GDP.

[12] Current and capital expenditures of the general government as a ratio of GDP.

[13] International Country Risk Guide (ICRG) composite index of political, economic, and financial risks.

REFERENCES

Baele, L., A. Ferrando, P. Hördahl, E. Krylova, and C. Monnet. 2004. "Measuring European Financial Integration." ECB Occasional Paper 14, European Central Bank, Frankfurt, Germany.

Bank for International Settlements (BIS). 2014. "EME Banking Systems and Regional Financial Integration." Committee on the Global Financial System (CGFS) Publications 51, Basel, Switzerland.

Beck, T., and R. Levine. 2004. "Stock Markets, Banks and Growth: Panel Evidence." *Journal of Banking and Finance* 28 (3): 423–42.

Bond, S., A. Hoeffler, and J. Temple. 2001. "GMM Estimation of Empirical Growth Models." CEPR Discussion Paper 3048, Center for Economic and Policy Research, Washington.

Claessens, S., and N. van Horen. 2014. "Foreign Banks: Trends and Impact." *Journal of Money, Credit and Banking* 46 (1): 295–326.

Degryse, H., O. Havrylchyk, E. M. Jurzyk, and S. J. Kozak. 2009. "Foreign Bank Entry and Credit Allocation in Emerging Markets." IMF Working Paper 09/270, International Monetary Fund, Washington.

Detragiache, E., P. Gupta, and T. Tressel. 2008. "Foreign Banks in Poor Countries: Theory and Evidence." *Journal of Finance* 63 (October 5): 2123–60.

Fernández, A., M. W. Klein, A. Rebucci, M. Schindler, and M. Uribe. 2015. "Capital Control Measures: A New Dataset." NBER Working Paper 20970, National Bureau of Economic Research, Cambridge, Massachusetts.

Galindo, A., A. Izquierdo, and L. Rojas-Suárez. 2010. "Financial Integration and Foreign Banks in Latin America: How Do They Impact the Transmission of External Financial Shocks?" IDB Working Paper Series, IDB-WP-116, Inter-American Development Bank, Washington.

Giannetti, M., and L. Laeven. 2012. "Flight Home, Flight Abroad and International Credit Cycles." *American Economic Review: Papers & Proceedings* 102 (3): 219–24.

International Monetary Fund (IMF). 2008. "Reaping the Benefits of Financial Globalization." IMF Policy Paper, Washington.

———. 2014. "Staff Guidance Note on Macroprudential Policy." Washington. http://www.imf.org/external/np/pp/eng/2014/110614.pdf.

———. 2015a. "International Banking after the Crisis: Increasingly Local and Safer?" *Global Financial Stability Report*. Washington, April.

———. 2015b. "Long-Run Growth in Latin America and the Caribbean: The Role of Economic Diversification and Complexity." *Regional Economic Outlook: Western Hemisphere*. Washington, April.

Jeon, B. N., M. P. Olivero, and J. Wu. 2013. "Multinational Banking and the International Transmission of Financial Shocks: Evidence from Foreign Bank Subsidiaries." *Journal of Banking & Finance* 37 (3): 952–72.

Kamil, H., and K. Rai. 2010. "The Global Credit Crunch and Foreign Banks' Lending to Emerging Markets: Why Did Latin America Fare Better?" IMF Working Paper 10/102, International Monetary Fund, Washington.

Kose, A., E. Prasad, K. S. Rogoff, and S. Wei. 2006. "Financial Globalization: A Reappraisal." NBER Working Paper 12484, National Bureau of Economic Research, Cambridge, Massachusetts.

Rancière, R., A. Tornell, and F. Westermann. 2006. "Decomposing the Effects of Financial Liberalization: Crises vs. Growth." *Journal of Banking & Finance* 30: 3331–48.

———. 2008. "Systemic Crises and Growth." *Quarterly Journal of Economics* 123 (1): 359–406.

Reinhart, C. M., and K. S. Rogoff. 2009. *This Time Is Different: Eight Centuries of Financial Folly*. Princeton, New Jersey: Princeton University Press.

Sahay, R., M. Čihák, P. N'Diaye, A. Barajas, R. Bi, D. Ayala, Y. Gao, A. Kyobe, L. Nguyen, C. Saborowski, K. Svirydzenka, and S. R. Yousefi. 2015. "Rethinking Financial Deepening: Stability and Growth in Emerging Markets." IMF Staff Discussion Note 15/08, International Monetary Fund, Washington.

CHAPTER 3

Barriers to Integration in Banking

IULIA RUXANDRA TEODORU

Banking systems are the largest financial intermediaries in the LA-7 countries (Brazil, Chile, Colombia, Mexico, Panama, Peru, and Uruguay), amounting to about 100 percent of LA-7 GDP. Brazil's banking system is by far the largest in absolute terms, while Panama and Chile have the largest as a share of GDP (Figure 3.1). Since the liberalization of financial systems in the 1990s, most assets in the LA-7 countries are with private banks (about 60 percent of LA-7 GDP), while assets in public banks remain high only in Brazil and Uruguay. Foreign banks also hold important market shares in some of the LA-7 countries (27 percent of LA-7 GDP). However, the integration of regional banking systems remains low. Despite liberalization, most banking systems are characterized by high concentration and, in some cases, high bank interest rate spreads.

OVERVIEW

Robust bank asset growth has led to an increased prominence of banking sectors in the LA-7 countries, resulting in greater macrofinancial linkages. Supported by solid economic growth, banking assets grew on average by 14 percent over the past decade, with the highest growth in Brazil and Peru, closely followed by Uruguay. In terms of size of assets, Brazil accounts for nearly two-thirds of Latin America's banking assets, while Mexico contributes one-tenth (Table 3.1). Brazil's share of private banks (45 percent) is closer to its share in regional GDP. Although banks are the largest financial intermediaries in the LA-7, there is still significant scope for growth, given relatively low levels of intermediation compared to advanced and other emerging market economies.

Credit expansion in recent years has been fostered by economic growth, stable macroeconomic policies, and reforms to deepen financial markets. Credit growth in Uruguay has been high, albeit from low levels, driven by economic growth as well as official attempts to increase financial access (Figure 3.2). Credit growth in Brazil decelerated to 11 percent in 2014 from a high rate of about 30 percent in 2010,[1] driven by a slowdown in credit expansion by public banks, while private bank credit has continued to expand at a moderate pace (Figure 3.3). This slower

[1] The high credit growth rate in 2010 was due to both demand (high economic growth—7 percent—and increasing financial inclusion) and supply factors, such as changes in regulations for housing loans, collateral, and payroll deductible loans.

Figure 3.1 LA-7 Indicators of Banking Sector Growth, Size, and Concentration

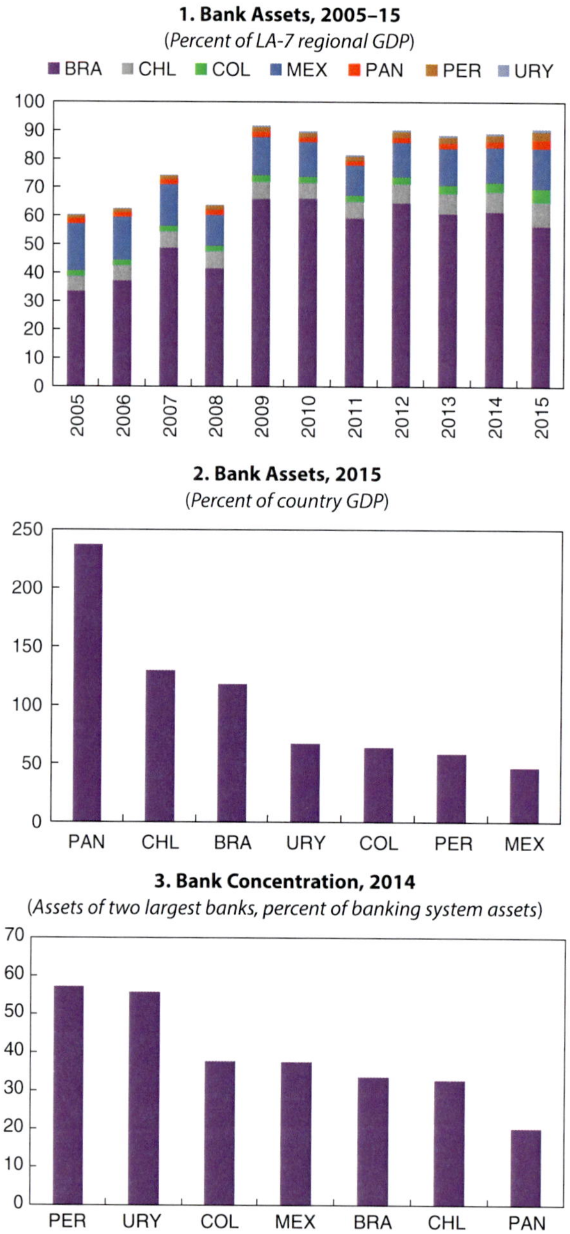

Sources: Bureau van Dijk; IMF, International Financial Statistics; national authorities; and IMF staff calculations.
Note: BRA = Brazil; CHL = Chile; COL = Colombia; MEX = Mexico; PAN = Panama; PER = Peru; URY = Uruguay.

TABLE 3.1

Size of the Regional Market *(Total assets in millions of U.S. dollars, public and private assets in percent of GDP)*

	LA-7	Brazil	Mexico	Colombia	Chile	Peru	Uruguay	Panama
Total bank assets	4,058,018	2,736,535	617,149	190,639	286,485	97,532	39,483	90,195
Public bank assets	36	62	9	4	18	1	32	17
Private bank assets	62	69	43	55	100	49	39	178

Sources: National authorities; and IMF staff calculations.
Note: Data are as at year-end 2014 or latest available.

Figure 3.2 Credit Growth, 2010–15
(Percent, annual average)

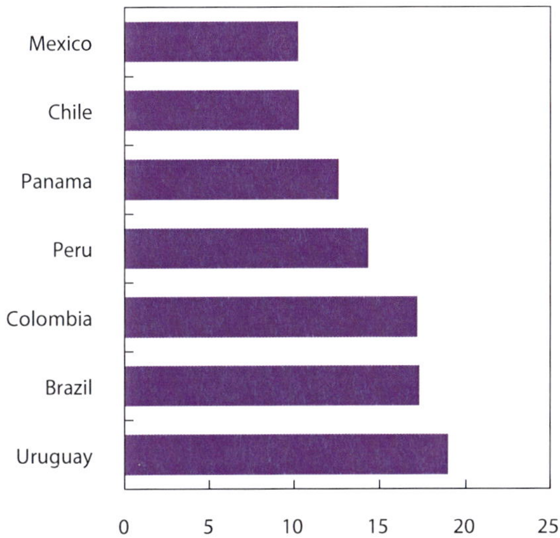

Source: IMF, International Financial Statistics.

credit growth likely reflects lower demand, given weaker economic activity. Since 2011, credit in Peru has been slowing gradually as a result of macroprudential measures, but growth rates still average about 15 percent. Credit growth in Mexico moderated to below 10 percent in 2014 from 17 percent in 2011, driven in part by a deceleration in construction lending after financial difficulties surfaced among the three largest builders. At the same time, lending by the publicly owned development banks is growing rapidly, given a new mandate of promoting microfinance and lending to underserved sectors. Credit growth in Colombia was also buoyant during this period and will likely continue to outpace nominal GDP growth, in line with the government's financial inclusion policy.

Financial intermediation in the LA-7 remains limited compared with advanced economies and other emerging market economies; however, important heterogeneity exists. Chile has the highest credit-to-private-sector ratio among the LA-7,

Figure 3.3 Breakdown of the Largest Private Banking Assets
(Percent)

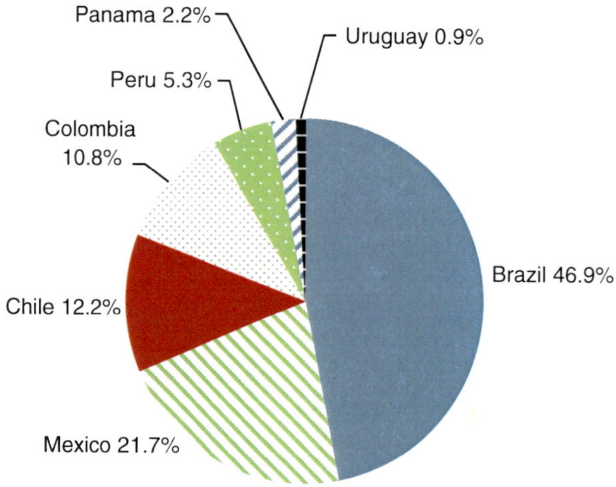

Sources: Country Superintendencies; and IMF, World Economic Outlook database.

while banking sector intermediation in Mexico, Peru, and Uruguay remains relatively low. Chile's credit to the private sector has more than doubled since 1995 (from 50 percent to more than 100 percent of GDP in 2014), while it has remained about 35 percent of GDP in Mexico, Peru, and Uruguay for the past two decades. Moreover, Chile is the only LA-7 country whose credit to the private sector is comparable to that of emerging Asia and G7 economies (that is, Canada, France, Germany, Japan, Italy, the United Kingdom, and the United States). Even Brazil's credit-to-GDP ratio remains relatively low compared with those in emerging Asia and the G7. In terms of deposits, Brazil and Panama lead with ratios of 60 percent of GDP, although these ratios are much lower than in emerging Asia. Peru has the lowest ratio. Although Mexican financial institutions exhibit a low deposit ratio, they have access to other financial funding through corporate bond issuance and capital markets. Financial access in terms of number of branches per capita is lowest in Uruguay and Mexico.

Dollarization in some of the LA-7 countries has slowed in recent years. High dollarization was a response to hyperinflation episodes and past crises and consequent loss of purchasing power of domestic deposits (Figure 3.4). Dollarization slowed—and even reversed—after policy initiatives that included the adoption of inflation-targeting frameworks, macroprudential measures (including differential reserve requirements on local currency versus foreign currency deposits and capital requirements on foreign exchange loans), and the development of local currency capital markets. In Peru, foreign exchange corporate loans have decelerated sharply since de-dollarization measures were introduced at the end of 2014: new repos in domestic currency to support the growth of credit in local currency and encourage the substitution of foreign currency loans with local currency loans, higher reserve requirements on foreign currency deposits, and reserve requirements for banks that do not meet certain de-dollarization targets for credits.

Figure 3.4 Foreign Currency Loans and Liabilities

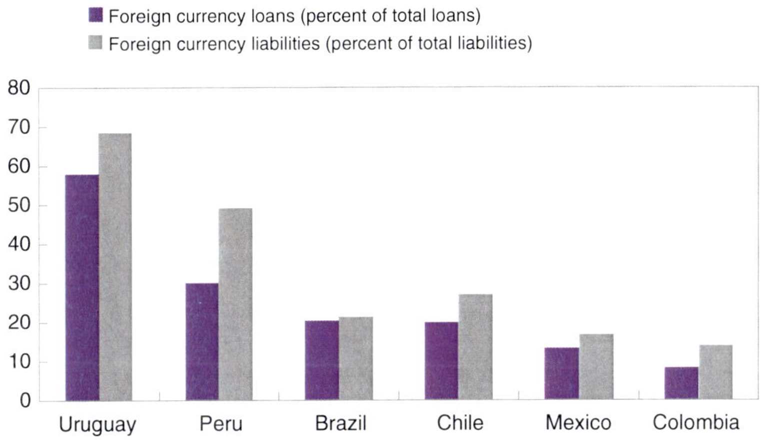

Source: IMF, Financial Soundness Indicators.

Uruguay, on the other hand, still has a highly dollarized financial sector, possibly associated with inflation persistently above the target range, with foreign exchange loans accounting for 60 percent of total loans and foreign exchange liabilities close to 80 percent of total liabilities. At the other end, Mexico and Colombia have much lower foreign exchange lending and foreign exchange liabilities. Mexico saw a significant reduction in dollarization recently, while dollarization in Brazil has been increasing.

Most banking systems in the LA-7 are characterized by high concentration, which likely impacts loan rates and spreads. In Peru and Uruguay, the three largest banks account for about 70 percent of banking system assets, and in Uruguay, 40 percent of banking system assets are controlled by one government-owned bank. In Brazil, Chile, Colombia, and Mexico, the three largest banks hold 50 percent of banking system assets. Brazil also stands out with 45 percent of banking system assets controlled by public banks, with a high degree of earmarked and subsidized lending.

Bank spreads in several LA-7 countries are high compared with spreads in other regions (Figure 3.5). Brazil has the highest spreads at over 15 percent,[2] and return on equity is reported to be about 20 percent for the largest banks. At the same time, Brazilian banks show high operating expenses owing to entrenched

[2] The rate for Brazil averages spreads for nonfinancial corporations (10 percent) and households (26 percent). Jorgensen and Apostolos (2013), in "Brazil's Bank Spread in International Context: From Macro to Micro Driver," use the net interest margin to measure the bank spread and derive a pure spread (or margin) that is comparable across banks in a given country. This pure spread varies across countries and over time according to the extent of bank competition and macroeconomic (interest rate) volatility in each country. While their study looks only at the period 1995–2009, their measure could suggest lower spreads for Brazil in recent years.

Figure 3.5 Interest Rate Spread, 2014
(Lending minus deposit rate, percent)

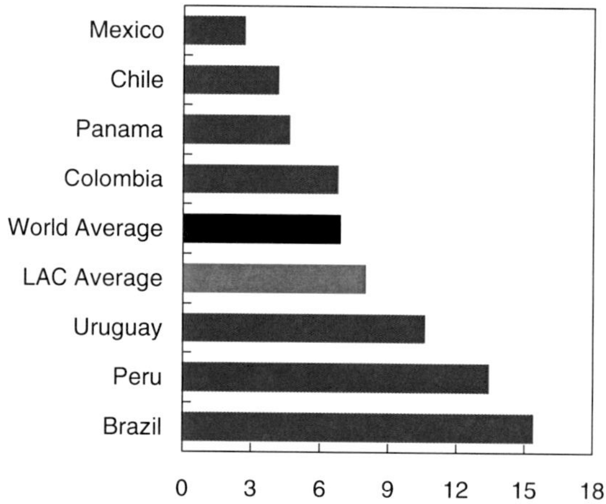

Source: IMF, International Financial Statistics.
Note: LAC = Latin America and the Caribbean.

inefficiencies,[3] especially in state-owned banks, which have a high share of directed lending and social projects. Brazil ranks poorly in terms of ease of doing business, and high administrative costs also increase overall costs for private banks. Uruguay too has high interest rate spreads and operating expenses. Although spreads are also high in Peru, the country benefits from one of the lowest rates for operating expenses. Spreads have been coming down in Colombia, Mexico, and Panama, hinting at increased competition in those markets.

STATE OF PLAY

Banking systems in the LA-7 countries have been liberalized since the 1990s. This liberalization process involved deregulation and opening to foreign bank entry and privatization. The market share of foreign banks is high in some of the LA-7 countries, but the cross-border share of regional banks remains minute (Figure 3.6). Panama is the only exception: regional banks hold 33 percent of bank assets in Panama (22 percent are held by Colombian banks). Foreign ownership of banks is highest in Mexico, with most bank assets held by North American and European banks. Seventy percent of bank assets are foreign-owned: 18 percent are owned by U.S. banks and 37 percent by Spanish banks. At the same time, Mexican banks, such as Banco Azteca, have a very small cross-border regional

[3] See, for instance, the Organisation for Economic Co-operation and Development (OECD 2011) Economic Surveys and Tecles and Tabak (2010). According to the OECD, operating costs are three times higher in Brazil than the average for OECD countries and 40 percent above the average in Latin America (see also Beck and Demirgüç-Kunt 2009).

Figure 3.6 Commercial Bank Ownership
(Bank assets in percent of GDP)

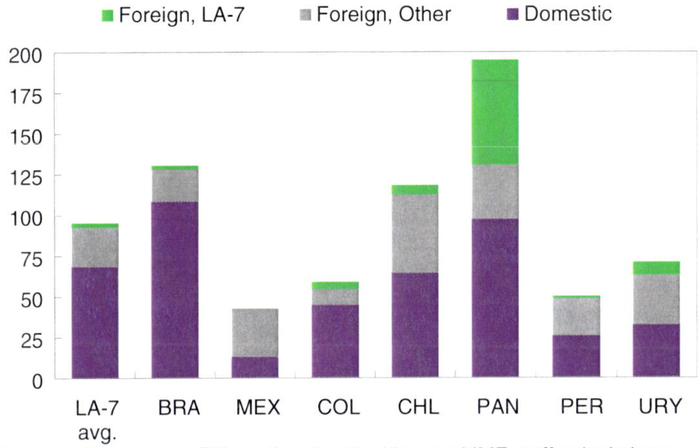

Sources: Bureau van Dijk; national authorities; and IMF staff calculations.
Note: Data are as at year-end 2014 or latest available. LA-7 = Brazil (BRA), Chile (CHL), Colombia (COL), Mexico (MEX), Panama (PAN), Peru (PER), and Uruguay (URY).

presence. Brazil and Colombia lie at the other end of the range, with bank assets predominantly held by domestic banks—mostly government-owned banks in Brazil and private banks in Colombia.

Foreign claims of some Bank for International Settlements (BIS)-reporting Latin American banks in the region provide some evidence of increasing regional integration since 2005.[4] Claims on the region by Chilean banks represent 50 percent of total claims, the highest among BIS-reporting banks in Latin America, while Panama's claims account for 30 percent of total claims (Table 3.2). Foreign claims by Brazilian banks on other LA-7 countries, although they have increased significantly since 2005, are still only about 13 percent of total claims: $18 billion, of which 12 percent are on Chile. Most foreign claims are on the United States and the United Kingdom. Foreign claims by Mexican banks on other LA-7 countries are small—only 3 percent of total claims.

Mergers and acquisitions by Latin American banks of assets of international banks withdrawing from the region suggest a trend toward greater regional integration (see Annex Table 3.1). Regional banks, especially Colombian banks,

[4] The Consolidated Banking Statistics (CBS) of the BIS capture the worldwide consolidated positions of internationally active banking groups headquartered in reporting countries. The data include the claims of reporting banks' foreign affiliates but exclude intragroup positions; this approach is similar to that followed by banking supervisors. The CBS are designed to analyze the exposure of internationally active banks of different nationalities to individual countries and sectors. Exposures can take many forms; for example, cross-border claims, local claims of banks' foreign affiliates, derivatives, guarantees, or credit commitments. Colombia, Peru, and Uruguay do not report to the BIS; thus, total foreign claims of the LA-7 on the region are likely underestimated.

TABLE 3.2

Consolidated Foreign Claims on the World by BIS-Reporting Banks in Four Latin American Countries *(Percent of domestic GDP)*

	2005	2006	2007	2008	2009	2010	2011	2012	2013
Brazil	3.3	2.7	3.1	2.5	3.2	3.7	3.4	4.1	5.0
Claims on other LA-7 countries	*0.0*	*0.1*	*0.1*	*0.1*	*0.4*	*0.5*	*0.5*	*0.7*	*0.8*
Chile	2.4	2.1	2.1	1.7	1.9	1.9	2.6	5.2	4.8
Claims on other LA-7 countries	*0.6*	*0.4*	*0.5*	*0.6*	*0.7*	*0.6*	*0.7*	*2.9*	*2.3*
Mexico	0.6	0.5	0.6	0.7	0.9	0.6	0.4	0.4	0.5
Claims on other LA-7 countries	*0.0*	*0.0*	*0.0*	*0.0*	*0.0*	*0.0*	*0.0*	*0.0*	*0.0*
Panama	66.2	48.1	51.7	48.3	47.0	44.5	44.9	42.0	42.7
Claims on other LA-7 countries	*11.7*	*12.5*	*14.0*	*10.9*	*10.8*	*12.0*	*12.4*	*10.6*	*11.6*

Source: Bank for International Settlements (BIS), Consolidated Banking Statistics.
Note: LA-7 = Brazil, Chile, Colombia, Mexico, Panama, Peru, and Uruguay.

acquired businesses of HSBC, Santander, BBVA, and Citibank, which were withdrawing particularly from Central America but also from Paraguay and Peru. The assets of Colombian banks' subsidiaries abroad reached $50 billion, accounting for 24 percent of the total assets of the Colombian banking system. Colombian banks have attained a significant market position in Central America: 22 percent of assets on average. The share of Colombian bank assets in Panama has reached 23 percent; in El Salvador it is more than 50 percent. These regional integration trends can spur enhancements to supervisory, resolution, and tax system frameworks.

Citibank's plan to sell its retail banking and credit card operations in Argentina, Brazil, and Colombia will open opportunities for acquisitions by regional players. In comparison with its U.S. competitors, Citibank used to get more profits from abroad than from its home market, and it had a presence in Latin America for more than 100 years. In light of the ongoing global regulatory changes and possibly the rather small scale of its business in markets such as Brazil, the bank is now increasingly focusing on corporate and institutional clients in an attempt to cut costs and boost profits from niche markets. At the end of 2015, Citibank had scaled back its global operations from 40 countries in 2012 to 24 and reduced its consumer lending in 11 markets, including Peru, Costa Rica, and four other countries in Central and South America. In Argentina, Banco Macro and BBVA are frontrunners for buying Citibank's assets; in Brazil, private banks Itaú and Bradesco, and public bank Banco do Brasil are likely to be among the interested parties. The total deal value in the three countries could rise to as much as $400 million. Although the sale of Citibank's consumer business brings opportunities for regional acquisitions, competition may be hurt through the likely consolidation of market shares by the acquiring bank. The acquisition of HSBC's retail business by Bradesco in Brazil attracted a deeper review by the antitrust regulator, which ordered the disclosure of all offers the bank received in the past two years and an explanation of why it picked Bradesco.

The aim of the expansion of Colombian banks was to follow Colombian clients abroad as a first step and then diversify their portfolios to serve other clients too. The high capitalization of the banks and the acquisition opportunities arising from the withdrawal of foreign banks from Central America supported this expansion. Banco de Bogotá, based in Bogotá, has a very different loan portfolio in Colombia (leadership in corporate banking) than it has in its BAC subsidiary in Central America/Panama—much more emphasis on consumer credit and mortgage lending. This has enabled it to have a more diversified portfolio overall, as well as to benefit from cross-complementarities: bringing credit card technology from Panama to Colombia and exporting corporate lending know-how from Colombia to Panama. Bancolombia (based in Medellin) has a portfolio in Central America/Panama that includes all core banking products (corporate lending as well as consumer credit and mortgage lending); in Colombia, its portfolio is mostly corporate banking. Davivienda (based in Bogotá) has a portfolio in Central America/Panama that is increasingly focusing on consumer lending, while withdrawing from corporate lending (which had been HSBC's main portfolio focus); its loan portfolio in Colombia has a high share of corporate lending and smaller shares of consumer and mortgage lending.

Corpbanca, based in Santiago, was the first Chilean bank to expand abroad. The bank invested in Colombia as a result of the high banking penetration rates and low opportunities to continue growing profitably in Chile. The bank had a 5 percent market share after 10 years in the Chilean market; the large difference between the profitability and cost of funding of the three biggest banks and the rest of the market made it hard for a bank with a smaller market share to sustain profits. After searching for a jurisdiction with policies similar to Chile's, it bought Santander Colombia (which had a market share of 3 percent) and then Colombian Helmbank, as it felt it would be hard to have a profitable operation with such a small market share. Both banks were retail-focused, and together achieved a 6.5 percent market share in the Colombian market.

Banco de Credito del Peru, based in Lima, has a small presence regionally. The bank had older retail businesses only in Bolivia and Central America, and entered Chile and Colombia after the global financial crisis as an investment bank (with a microcredit business in Colombia), because it did not have the capital to expand to those markets as a universal bank.

PROSPECTS FOR FURTHER REGIONAL FINANCIAL INTEGRATION

Two Brazilian banks (one of which is an investment bank) have a regional perspective and have established a significant presence across Latin America. Bank Itaú, based in São Paolo, has the strength and the ambition to become the major regional player. The size of the bank is close to that of the entire Mexican banking system ($420 billion in assets). It has expanded regionally mainly through mergers and acquisitions, but through a few greenfield investments in Colombia and Mexico as well. The bank is in corporate and investment banking in Colombia, Peru, and Mexico, and in retail and wholesale banking in Argentina, Chile, Paraguay, and Uruguay. With its most recent acquisition of Chilean Corpbanca[5] (and merger with Corpbanca Colombia), the share of Itaú's cross-border business will reach 13 percent, up from 7 percent in 2011. Its strategy is to diversify its retail and corporate portfolio to other markets. It considers it more challenging to develop a retail business abroad, given the need for funding, while following corporate clients abroad. Its ultimate corporate vision is to go global. Itaú encountered difficulties developing its credit card business in Mexico, so it is trying to develop an investment banking business using broker-dealers. In Colombia, given the consolidated banking market, the bank will try to develop in investment banking.

Similarly, investment bank BTG Pactual, based in São Paolo, aspires to be the investment bank of the region. Investment banks are likely to be more able than retail banks to establish operations abroad, owing to the lower cost structure and initial investment involved in their operations. BTG Pactual started expanding throughout much of Latin America after the global financial crisis, when global banks were seen to be withdrawing. It merged with Celfin Capital—a brokerage and asset manager with operations in Chile, Colombia, and Peru—and set up a greenfield brokerage in Mexico. It sees profit opportunities in these countries because of their underdeveloped capital markets and the capital markets integration initiative within the Pacific Alliance (PA). As a 100 percent wholesale funding bank, BTG Pactual sees its expansion through Latin America as providing a more diversified wholesale funding base; owing to high funding costs, it does not plan to enter into retail.[6] However, other Brazilian banks focus on the domestic market. They see potential to expand domestically and appear to be consolidating their positions at home.

Conditions in other countries have so far precluded much regional integration. The large presence in Mexico of U.S. and Spanish banks means that any decisions on expansion to the Latin American region from Mexico are made by headquarters rather than by the Mexican subsidiaries. Among domestic banks, only Bank Azteca has decided to expand regionally, with a small presence in Brazil, Guatemala, Panama, and Peru, among others. Also, the more important real economy ties with North America and Europe have so far dampened pressures for regional financial integration. Furthermore, from a financial stability perspective (at least until the global financial crisis), global banks were considered by most countries to have advantages that made them preferable to regional Latin

[5] Corpbanca had expanded its operations to Colombia, in part owing to the very low spreads and profitability and the high banking intermediation rates in Chile; however, it became vulnerable to takeover as a result of problems in the nonfinancial part of the conglomerate.

[6] Since the arrest of its CEO on corruption charges in November 2015, however, BTG Pactual has experienced bouts of market pressure. Risk emanates from its relatively heavy reliance on wholesale funding, which has translated into noticeable swings in wholesale deposits. This could hinder the bank's ability to further expand its operations in the region over the near term.

American banks: they were considered easier to discipline, less politically connected, and more accountable.

Although the Chilean, Mexican, and Peruvian banking systems are very open, equity prices appear to be a deterrent for acquisitions. Chile, Mexico, and Peru liberalized their banking systems in the 1990s, and they all attracted foreign capital, especially from North America and Europe. Only a few large Latin American banks can afford entry to these markets, given high equity prices compared with valuations. Large Colombian banks find these markets attractive, but prices of assets can be prohibitive, and concentrated markets represent a barrier to entry. Of the Colombian banks, GNB Sudameris acquired HSBC's operations in Peru, while Brazil's Bank Itaú and BTG Pactual entered the market as investment banks. Banco de Crédito del Peru has entered Chile and Colombia as an investment bank. In addition, Bank Itaú acquired Corpbanca in Chile and merged with Corpbanca Colombia.

In some countries, such as Brazil, high bank concentration and size of the market are potential barriers to regional bank entry. High bank concentration is likely due to the role played by family-owned and publicly owned banks. The power of incumbents, including financial conglomerates with linkages to the real sector, could be a strong deterrent to entry. The Brazilian banking system has been consolidating, and Bradesco, the second largest private bank, is acquiring the retail business of HSBC, increasing its market share from 11 percent to 14 percent. In addition, the three large government-owned banks have grown significantly since the global financial crisis. BNDES, the development bank, lends to large conglomerates at subsidized rates. The legal regime for entry by foreign banks in Brazil is relatively opaque, and entry requires presidential approval, which may have a chilling effect on potential entrants. In Uruguay, BROU has had a legal monopoly on public employee accounts, which has given the public bank a majority share of the peso deposit market. Since Banco do Brasil's exit in 2005 after 20 years, the only regional bank in the Uruguayan market is Bank Itaú. Banking fees and rates in Uruguay are high compared with the rest of the region because banks' operating costs are very high while profits are relatively low. Uruguayan banks have consolidated in an attempt to gain scale economies: in 2002, there were 20 private banks; today there are only nine.

Ease of doing business (getting credit, protecting investors, and enforcing contracts) is hampered by institutional and regulatory factors and lack of competition. For example, in Brazil there is no full depth of or access to credit information, especially distribution of positive data (repayment of loans and loans due performance) to build positive credit files for borrowers so they can benefit from lower interest rates. On the other hand, Mexico has achieved the highest rating in terms of full depth of credit information (see World Bank 2015). Colombia also has a high rating in terms of depth of credit information. All financial institutions supervised by the Financial Superintendency of Colombia, including small banks, have access from and report data to the credit bureau and must have well-defined credit-granting criteria; for example, they must take into account information on the debtor's current and past payment performance, pay timely attention to his or her liabilities, and consider financial and credit history from credit bureaus and rating agencies. While supervised entities provide credit information to determine asset quality in monthly and quarterly financial statements, some credit exposures are not covered, such as off-balance-sheet exposures, letters of credit, and bank collateral and sureties.

High concentration and lack of competition are a likely explanation for high loan spreads in some of the LA-7 countries. Competition, low taxation and reserve requirements, strong creditor rights and legal framework, availability of information on borrowers, and a stable macro environment would reduce bank spreads. While some of the LA-7 banking systems have similar levels of concentration, they have diverging interest rate spreads, explained in part by institutional and regulatory factors,[7] competition, level of foreign bank participation, and technological spillovers from foreign banks that lower costs and improve efficiency in the market. These factors, combined with a more stable macro environment, could help explain lower spreads in Mexico.

Another impediment to safer cross-border regional banking integration is the fact that countries are moving at different speeds to adopt the new regulatory agendas. There are big differences in the speed of adoption of enhanced supervisory and regulatory frameworks—such as a consistent capital definition (Basel III) and the International Financial Reporting Standard—which make it hard to establish a level playing field across countries during the (possibly protracted) transition period. Brazil and Mexico lead the region in the implementation of Basel III, closely following the international timeline. Peru is next, while Chile and Colombia have taken a more gradual approach. Colombia has enhanced its capital measure, bringing it closer to the Basel III definition.

A bank's ownership structure could also be an impediment to regional acquisitions. When HSBC tried to sell its operations to GNB Sudameris (Colombian) in Uruguay, the deal fell apart reportedly because the banks owned by the owner of GNB Sudameris do not have the same holding structure in different jurisdictions, a situation that the Uruguayan supervisor considered inappropriate. The SFC affirmed that it performs supervision on a consolidated basis over its supervised entities and therefore requires GNB Sudameris to fulfill prudential regulations such as capital requirements, but this was not considered sufficient.

GLOBAL FINANCIAL DE-INTEGRATION

Regulations in the home countries of global banks aimed at strengthening banks' resilience have reduced the profitability of subsidiaries. These measures have discouraged bank subsidiaries from playing an active role in markets as intermediaries or liquidity providers. Liquidity in sovereign debt markets has fallen as certain big banks (mainly from the United Kingdom and the United States) have

---

[7] Jorgensen and Apostolos (2013) found that institutional and regulatory factors were the most significant factors in determining spreads in Brazil during the period 1995–2009.

substantially reduced their presence in regional markets. Consolidation rules applied globally by parent banks on their subsidiaries appear in some cases to have come into conflict with the legal regulations in Latin American host countries and raised the costs of doing business in those countries, not only vis-à-vis previous requirements but also relative to local banks. Vigorous application of these regulations could further the deglobalization trend. In the new regulatory environment, the costs and benefits of subsidiaries operating in emerging markets are likely to shift, possibly initiating further downsizing or withdrawal from these markets.[8]

Bilateral and multilateral initiatives to increase the transparency of the international financial system have also contributed to a loss of correspondent banks in Latin America. U.S. agencies' enforcement actions against breaches of compliance with domestic regulations on trade and economic sanctions, tax evasion, and anti-money laundering/combatting the financing of terrorism, as well as other post–global financial crisis developments, have led international banks operating under U.S. regulations to withdraw from activities seen as high risk. This has had a particular impact on correspondent banking relationships. A small number of large international banks dominate the provision of correspondent banking services for banks in the region, and some of them have been ending or reducing the provision of these services for local banks. For example, in Mexico, JPMorgan is maintaining its wholesale business but is withdrawing from providing correspondent bank services to small and medium-sized banks. For some local banks, Bank of America is the only major U.S. bank still offering correspondent banking facilities. This evolution overall is intended to increase transparency in financial transactions and financial institutions' risk management policies; however, authorities in the region have raised concerns about these developments in various forms. They report the withdrawal of lines to medium-sized banks, which cater to small and medium-sized enterprises, raising the cost of finance for these enterprises and in some cases causing loss of access to credit from U.S. exporters, who fear for the safety of their payments in the future.

REGIONAL FINANCIAL INTEGRATION AS A ROUTE TOWARD GLOBAL INTEGRATION

Opening domestic economies could favorably position Latin American countries for further global integration in the future. BBVA, based in Madrid, sees room for expansion in Latin America, given opportunities for profit and low banking intermediation rates. BBVA already has a well-diversified portfolio across Latin America, and 50 percent of the bank's profits are derived from its business in Mexico (30 percent) and South America. BBVA's business model is retail banking, with market shares of 22 percent in Mexico and Peru, and 9.4 percent and 6.7

[8] Chapter 2 of the IMF's April 2015 *Global Financial Stability Report* documents the decline in cross-border lending and finds that it can be explained by a combination of regulatory changes, weaknesses in bank balance sheets, and macroeconomic factors.

percent in Colombia and Chile, respectively. BBVA is the only bank that operates in all four countries of the PA, which it views as a huge opportunity for growing its business. Its model is to establish subsidiaries autonomous in capital and liquidity, which would limit contagion risk among the group's units and reduce systemic risk. The bank could be affected by the special ring-fencing rules issued in Mexico in 2014, according to which Mexican authorities can not only request full information on parent companies but can also stop dividends if they believe the parent company is in trouble. A further impediment for operating in Latin America is that, in consolidation with the parent bank in Europe, home country assets might receive a lower rating (for example, because they are in Mexican pesos). In general, more regulatory stringency by the European supervisory authorities may constrain BBVA's regional activities.

Similarly, Santander, based in Madrid, has been diversifying its portfolio in the region: 38 percent of the bank's profits are derived from its business in Brazil (19 percent), Mexico (8 percent), and the rest of South America (11 percent). In 2012, Santander sold a 24.9 percent stake in its Mexican bank through an initial public offering, following a similar sale in 2009 of part of its Brazilian subsidiary. The proceeds of these sales were used to reinforce the group's core capital. Santander's business model is mainly retail banking, focused on a few countries where it aims to reach at least a 10 percent market share (current market share is 17 percent in Chile, 14 percent in Mexico, and 8 percent in Brazil). In Brazil, the objective is to grow both its retail and corporate businesses. In Mexico, the objective is to grow more than the market, particularly with high-income clients and small and medium-sized enterprises, and to become one of the leading banks in financing the government's infrastructure plans. Santander and BBVA seem to have largely divided the Latin American markets between themselves: where Santander is present, BBVA generally is not. Santander's subsidiaries are completely autonomous in capital and liquidity, which limits contagion risk. There is also limited cross-funding among subsidiaries in Latin America, and excess liquidity cannot be moved easily (deposits cannot be shared across countries). Santander Brazil is not allowed to lend in dollars to Brazilian corporates, so the branch in the Cayman Islands is used for foreign currency lending to Brazilian firms.

POLICY RECOMMENDATIONS

- Move forward to harmonize regulatory frameworks across the region, as well as the legal framework for bank restructuring and resolution, toward international standards and best practices, with a view to promoting financial stability and establishing a level playing field across countries as well as across banks operating cross-border in the region.
- Strengthen consolidated supervision. Supervisory agencies should have adequate powers over nonbank holding companies of banks, both domestically and cross-border.

- Increase transparency regarding entry of foreign banks. To increase competition and lower the cost of financing, foreign banks should be allowed to enter the banking system through an explicit, open, objective, and nondiscriminatory statutory and regulatory framework.[9] At this point, regional banks seem to be more likely than global banks to respond to such opening.
- In dollarized economies, strengthen prudential requirements on dollar lending and encourage the private sector to hedge its foreign currency exposures, while further supporting the de-dollarization process and deepening financial and capital markets. Deepening financial markets has proven to be an effective way to achieve de-dollarization, including through an active policy of de-dollarizing public debt, deepening local currency bond markets, and promoting the development of markets for foreign exchange derivatives along with foreign exchange flexibility. When market conditions and financial stability considerations permit, Brazil and Colombia could consider relaxing the constraints on foreign exchange activities and adjusting net open foreign exchange position limits for settlements in other currencies where present limits are low.
- Continue to promote best efforts to ensure strong direct home and cross-border supervision, including measures to ensure effective customer due diligence. Countries should work with key international financial center regulators and international bodies, such as the Financial Stability Board and the Financial Action Task Force, to ensure a clear understanding of regulations and policies relevant to their financial institutions. Countries should also be encouraged to assess the need to adapt their financial systems to the new regulatory environment and to consider public sector support in case of market failure.

[9] For instance, the process for meeting the requirement of presidential approval for a foreign bank to enter the Brazilian market could be made fully transparent.

ANNEX 3.1. DIVESTMENTS FOLLOWING THE GLOBAL FINANCIAL CRISIS

ANNEX TABLE 3.1

Retrenchment from Emerging Markets by Global Banks since 2009

Year	Value (Millions of U.S. dollars)	Banking Operations/Assets for Sale: Name	Banking Operations/Assets for Sale: Country	Selling Firm: Name	Selling Firm: Country
Latin America and the Caribbean					
2009	n.a.	Credit card portfolio	Argentina	Citigroup Inc	USA
2012	n.a.	Banco Suquia SA	Argentina	Credit Agricole SA	France
2011	n.a.	JP Morgan Vastera Argentina SRL	Argentina	JP Morgan Chase & Co	USA
2011	76.8	CIBC Bank & Trust Co Cayman Ltd, CIBC Trust Co Bahamas Ltd	Bahamas	Canadian Imperial Bank of Commerce/Canada	Canada
2015	45.0	Banco Standard de Investimentos SA	Brazil	Standard Bank Group Ltd	S. Africa
2009	18.7	Credit portfolio	Chile	Banco Santander SA	Spain
2010	n.a.	Corporate and Commercial Banking Operations	Chile	Royal Bank of Scotland Group PLC	Britain
2010	n.a.	Scotiabank Colombia SA	Colombia	Royal Bank of Scotland Group PLC	Britain
2012	1,229.0	Banco CorpBanca Colombia SA	Colombia	Banco Santander SA	Spain
2012	801.0	Banco Davivienda Salvadoreno SA, Banco HSBC Costa Rica SA, Banco HSBC Honduras SA	Costa Rica, Honduras	HSBC Holdings PLC	Britain
2010	25.0	Ecuadorian Branch Assets and Liabilities	Ecuador	Lloyds Banking Group PLC	Britain
2013	2,233.8	HSBC Bank Panama SA	Panama	HSBC Holdings PLC	Britain
2009	85.1	ABN AMRO Paraguay	Paraguay	Banco Santander SA	Spain
2010	n.a.	Credit Uruguay Banco	Uruguay	Credit Agricole SA	France
2012	n.a.	Uruguayan Operations	Uruguay	Lloyds Banking Group PLC	Britain
2013	0.3	Galval Agente de Valores SA	Uruguay	Grupo Financiero Galicia SA	Argentina
2009	1,050.0	Banco de Venezuela SA Banco Universal	Venezuela	Banco Santander SA	Spain
Middle East, Africa, and the Commonwealth of Independent States					
2015	n.a.	Egypt loan and deposit portfolio	Egypt	Bank of Nova Scotia/The	Canada
2014	n.a.	Banking business/Jordan	Jordan	HSBC Holdings PLC	Britain

(Continued)

ANNEX TABLE 3.1

Retrenchment from Emerging Markets by Global Banks since 2009 (*Continued*)					
	Value	**Banking Operations/Assets for Sale**		**Selling Firm**	
Year	**(Millions of U.S. dollars)**	**Name**	**Country**	**Name**	**Country**
2009	324.6	Societe Ivoirienne de Banque SA, Union Gabonaise de Banque SA, Credit du Congo, Societe Camerounaise de Banque, Credit du Senegal	Senegal	Credit Agricole SA	France
2013	2,106.4	Barclays Africa Ltd	South Africa	Barclays PLC	Britain
2014	177.0	United Arab Emirates retail banking operations	U.A.E.	Barclays PLC	Britain
2011	16.5	Royal Bank of Scotland NB Uzbekistan CJSC	Uzbekistan	Royal Bank of Scotland Group PLC	Britain
Emerging Europe					
2014	n.a.	Credit Agricole Bulgaria	Bulgaria	Credit Agricole SA	France
2014	18.9	Banco Popolare Croatia dd	Croatia	Banco Popolare SC	Italy
2011	69.1	Equa Bank AS	Czech	Banco Popolare SC	Italy
2013	n.a.	ATF Bank JSC	Kazakhstan	UniCredit SpA	Italy
2011	n.a.	Banque Societe Generale Vostok, DeltaCredit Bank, Rusfinans Bank	Russia	Societe Generale SA	France
2011	n.a.	Expobank LLC	Russia	Barclays PLC	Britain
2012	158.0	Cetelem Bank LLC	Russia	BNP Paribas SA	France
2013	n.a.	Certain Russian assets	Russia	Societe Generale SA	France
2010	84.9	Millennium Bank AS	Turkey	Banco Comercial Portugues SA	Portugal
2012	3,542.5	DenizBank AS	Turkey	Dexia SA	Belgium
2013	n.a.	Turkey Consumer Banking Business	Turkey	Citigroup Inc	USA
2012	n.a.	Bank Forum JSC	Ukraine	Commerzbank AG	Germany
Emerging Asia					
2015	n.a.	Banking business in India	India	HSBC Holdings PLC	Britain
2010	50.5	Royal Bank of Scotland Ltd/ Pakistan	Pakistan	Banco Santander SA, RBS Group PLC, Kingdom of the Netherlands	
2012	n.a.	Banking Business/Pakistan	Pakistan	HSBC Holdings PLC	Britain
2014	n.a.	Banking Business in Pakistan	Pakistan	HSBC Holdings PLC	Britain
2010	n.a.	RBS Philippines Inc	Philippines	Royal Bank of Scotland Group PLC, RFS Holdings BV	
2014	n.a.	Trust business of Deutsche Bank Manila Branch	Philippines	Deutsche Bank AG	Germany
2012	113.3	Retail Banking and Wealth Management business	Thailand	HSBC Holdings PLC	Britain

Source: Bloomberg, L.P.

REFERENCES

Beck, T., and A. Demirgüç-Kunt. 2009. "Financial Institutions and Markets across Countries and over Time: Data and Analysis." Policy Research Working Paper 4943, World Bank, Washington.

International Monetary Fund. 2015. "International Banking after the Crisis: Increasingly Local and Safer?" Chapter 2 in *Global Financial Stability Report: Navigating Monetary Policy Challenges and Managing Risks.* Washington, April.

Jorgensen, O. H., and A. Apostolos. 2013. "Brazil's Bank Spread in International Context: From Macro to Micro Drivers." Policy Research Working Paper 6611, World Bank, Washington.

Organisation for Economic Co-operation and Development. 2011. *OECD Economic Surveys: Brazil 2011.* Paris: OECD.

Tecles, P., and B. M. Tabak. 2010. "Determinants of Bank Efficiency: The Case of Brazil," Working Paper Series 210, Central Bank of Brazil, Brasilia.

World Bank. 2015. *Doing Business Report.* Washington: World Bank.

CHAPTER 4

Barriers to Integration in the Insurance Sector

ALLA MYRVODA AND BENNETT SUTTON

In the countries that make up the LA-7 (Brazil, Chile, Colombia, Mexico, Panama, Peru, and Uruguay), insurance penetration (measured by premiums in percent of GDP) remains low, ranging from 1 to 4 percentage points of GDP, although the sector has expanded at a significant rate over the past decade. In 2014, assets totaled almost 10 percent of regional GDP, influenced in many cases by changes in the domestic regulatory frameworks. Broadening of formal sectors and larger nominal losses from natural disasters are likely to fuel the non-life segment, whereas purchases of life and retirement products have been growing the life portion of the insurance sector for some time now. The sector's growth is partly stymied by the limited availability of long-term financial instruments denominated in the domestic currency, given that their demand is often crowded out by pension funds.

OVERVIEW

The insurance sector in Latin America has grown significantly over the past decade. Insurance premiums quadrupled between 2003 and 2013, reaching almost $160 billion by 2013 (Figure 4.1), owing largely to resilient economic performance and strong employment growth but also supported by the entrance of vigorously expanding foreign firms, regulatory reform implementation, and improvements to the business environment in the region. Robust vehicle sales have contributed to expansion of the non-life insurance sector, while sales of pension-related products have fueled life insurance segments in many countries (Figure 4.2). Market maturity varies greatly by country, with Chile and Brazil having the longest maturities, as indicated by larger contributions of life premiums. In Latin America, compulsory insurance has played a number of roles; for example, life insurance in Chile is strongly driven by mandatory products, while the absence of compulsory federal auto insurance in Mexico has limited non-life insurance sector penetration.[1] The size and growth of the insurance sector is often

[1] Compulsory auto insurance in Mexico is being phased in; it began to apply to certain cars in September 2014.

Figure 4.1 Insurance Market Size, Penetration, and Density
(Premiums in U.S. dollars and percent of GDP, 2013)

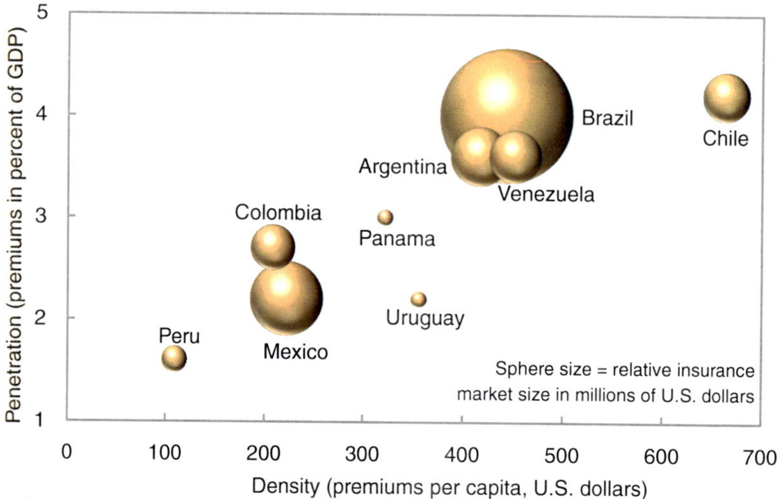

Source: SIGMA Swiss Re.

Figure 4.2 Premium Distribution
(Share of total, 2013)

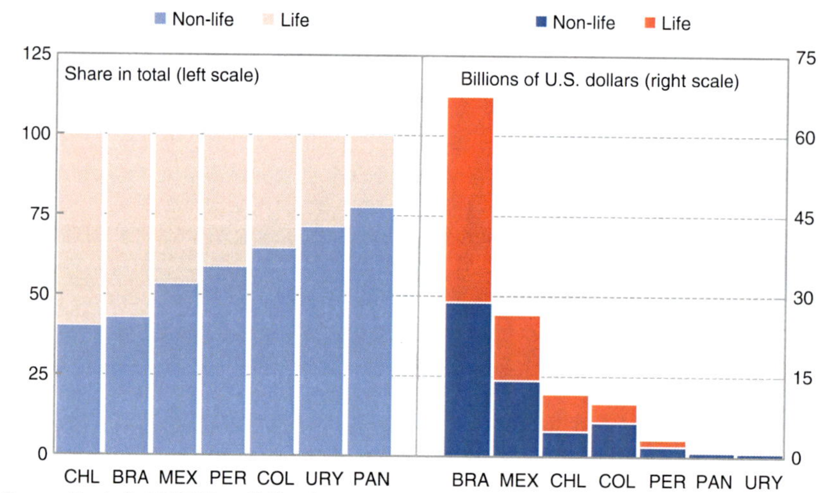

Sources: Fundación MAPFRE; and IMF staff estimates and calculations.

shaped by a number of characteristics, including those related to market competition, business specification, and regulatory environment. Thus, in the LA-7 countries the main insurance distribution channels often include agents, brokers, and banks, which vary by type of insurance sold. Many companies specializing in life insurance, for example, create their own networks of agents, who sell only the home company's products. This distribution channel can be very costly owing to the large resource requirements for agent management, remuneration, training, and supervision.

Insurance market concentration varies by country but remains elevated on average. In Uruguay, for example, the large state-owned insurance company controls 80 percent of the market, while the two largest companies in Peru manage about 60 percent of total premiums. Colombia's 10 largest companies account for almost 80 percent of the market share. In Brazil, although there are more than 110 companies, the largest 10 companies account for about 65 percent of the sector premiums. Chile's market concentration also appears to be somewhat lower: the 10 largest companies account for about 60 percent of market share.

The size of the market and the rate of market growth are also influenced by the regulatory environment, which is at different stages of development across the region. Some countries are setting the stage for implementing risk-based capital models, with Brazil and Mexico at the forefront in meeting Solvency II equivalent standards (Box 4.1). Chile is also expected to adopt frameworks similar to Solvency II in the coming years. Other countries, however, continue to operate under regimes similar to Solvency I, with Colombia and Peru considering comprehensive regulatory reforms as they continue to implement risk capital requirements.

Insurance companies' growth patterns are also shaped in part by investment opportunities and regulatory investment limits. Thus, given the relatively small size of the equity markets, LA-7 insurers largely choose to invest in debt securities. In Colombia, Mexico, Peru, and Uruguay, about three-quarters of investment portfolio allocations of life insurers are held in bonds. In Panama, on the other hand, only about a quarter of the portfolio is allocated toward bonds. While companies in Mexico and Uruguay tend to hold mostly government bonds, in Chile, Colombia, Panama, and Peru, companies appear to favor private debt securities. The rest of the portfolio usually includes equity shares, real estate investments, and other instruments. Real estate investments are typically small, with the largest share (about 10 percent) observed for Chile. Equity shares are also relatively low, except in the case of Panama, where the majority of the portfolio is invested in equities.

In general, the prospects for future growth of the insurance sector are promising. The low insurance penetration of the LA-7 market in comparison with penetration in advanced and other emerging markets suggests a sizable unrealized potential. The relatively young population across the region provides an expectation of future purchases of life and retirement products, while rising income levels are likely to stimulate automobile sales and drive non-life insurance growth. Regional susceptibility to natural disasters is likely to feed property and casualty market expansion, while the authorities' efforts to increase the level of formalization of the economies of the LA-7 countries are also likely to contribute to future growth.

Box 4.1 What Is Solvency II and What Is Its Impact on Insurance Regulation in Latin America?

Solvency II is a comprehensive insurance sector regulatory framework introduced by the European Commission in 2009. It introduces risk-sensitive capital requirements (similar to the principles in Basel banking agreements) and establishes rules for risk management and governance, including the categorization of assets and liabilities. Solvency II also strives to improve transparency in reporting to the public and to supervisors. Although Solvency II is not a global mandate, many emerging market countries are embracing its tenets as best practices for their own regulatory reforms.

The Latin American insurance industry has been undergoing significant regulatory reforms designed to strengthen stability, improve transparency, generate efficiency, and align with the worldwide trend of more rigorous rules. While most countries continue to strive to improve insurance industry regulation, the pace and extent of development varies across the region. Brazil, Chile, and Mexico are leading the way in the introduction of Solvency II-type frameworks in Latin America, with regulations set to be implemented by 2017.

Regulatory changes are expected to tighten prudential requirements, encourage product diversification, promote transparency, and strengthen linkages with foreign countries through higher reinsurance. The impact of the regulatory changes is expected to vary by country, but some general effects are likely. More advanced regulatory frameworks that incorporate risk-based charges will likely generate higher overall capital requirements, in particular under Solvency II-type regimes. This may encourage insurers to diversify their business and product portfolios. Efforts to decrease capital requirements may also translate into higher demand for reinsurance, essentially strengthening links with other countries—including the European Union (EU), as a large portion of reinsurance is done through European companies. New regulations will also impose tougher rules governing the process of risk identification and monitoring, and will set strict disclosure standards.

Stricter regulatory frameworks may generate mergers and acquisitions in the region, as smaller companies may face difficulties complying with tougher guidelines. Smaller single-line insurers may find it hard to operate under new guidelines that include changes in governance, risk management, capital requirements, and reporting. This situation could lead to mergers and acquisitions and higher industry concentration. In Chile, Colombia, and Mexico, more stringent regulatory frameworks are increasing transparency and efficiency, and making the insurance companies more streamlined.

Further convergence of Latin American and European regulation via the implementation of Solvency II-type regimes will even the playing field for foreign subsidiaries and empower Latin American insurers to access EU markets. For large multinational insurance groups that have their home offices in the European Union (such as MAPFRE, for example), Solvency II-type regulation largely extends to their subsidiaries in Latin America and Asia-Pacific. Thus, while the subsidiary structure of foreign companies operating in Latin America compels them to comply with host country regulations, they may also be required to conform to the tougher Solvency II regulations of the parent country in the European Union, including higher capital reserves. Domestic insurers in Latin America—those without operations in the European Union but who compete with EU rivals in their home markets—could retain some competitive advantage as long as the Solvency II-type rules are still being implemented. Once implemented, these rules are likely to even the playing field for domestic and foreign insurance market players, making some Latin American markets—particularly in Brazil, Chile, and Mexico—more attractive to foreign entities.

Figure 4.3 Insurance Firm Ownership, 2014
(Insurance sector assets in percent of GDP)

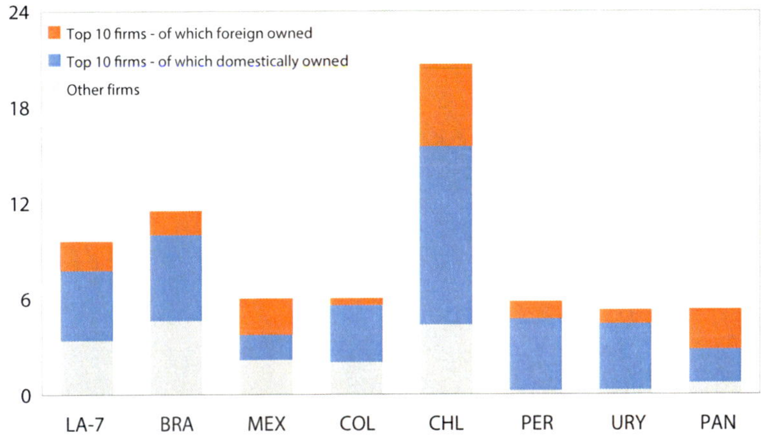

Sources: Bureau van Dijk; national authorities; and IMF staff calculations.
Note: Data are as at year-end 2014 or latest available. LA-7 = Brazil (BRA), Chile (CHL), Colombia (COL), Mexico (MEX), Panama (PAN), Peru (PER), and Uruguay (URY).

STATE OF PLAY

Cross-border financial integration, both regional and global, has been primarily observed in the form of cross-border company ownership and more relationships with large international reinsurance firms (Figure 4.3) rather than investments in foreign assets. Latin America has seen a notable shift in the ownership structure of the 10 largest insurance groups, which account for almost half of the market share (Figure 4.4). Among these 10 groups, the market share of regional companies has increased from 32 percent to 54 percent since 2003.[2] This upsurge is mainly driven by the life insurance segment: the share of regional companies in this segment more than doubled over the past decade, rising from 32 percent to 68 percent of the market (see Table 4.1). This reordering was brought on by the fast expansion of Brazilian giants Bradesco, Itaú/Unibanco, and Brasilprev, as well as the Colombian conglomerate Suramericana. Bradesco has been the leading insurance group in the region since 2004, largely fueled by domestic market growth. But the region has also witnessed a number of mergers and acquisitions that have pushed up the size and ranking of the largest regional companies. In the non-life segment, the growth of regional insurance groups (while still exceeding

[2] Based on estimates by Fundacion MAPFRE and IMF staff calculations.

Figure 4.4 Insurance Market Premiums

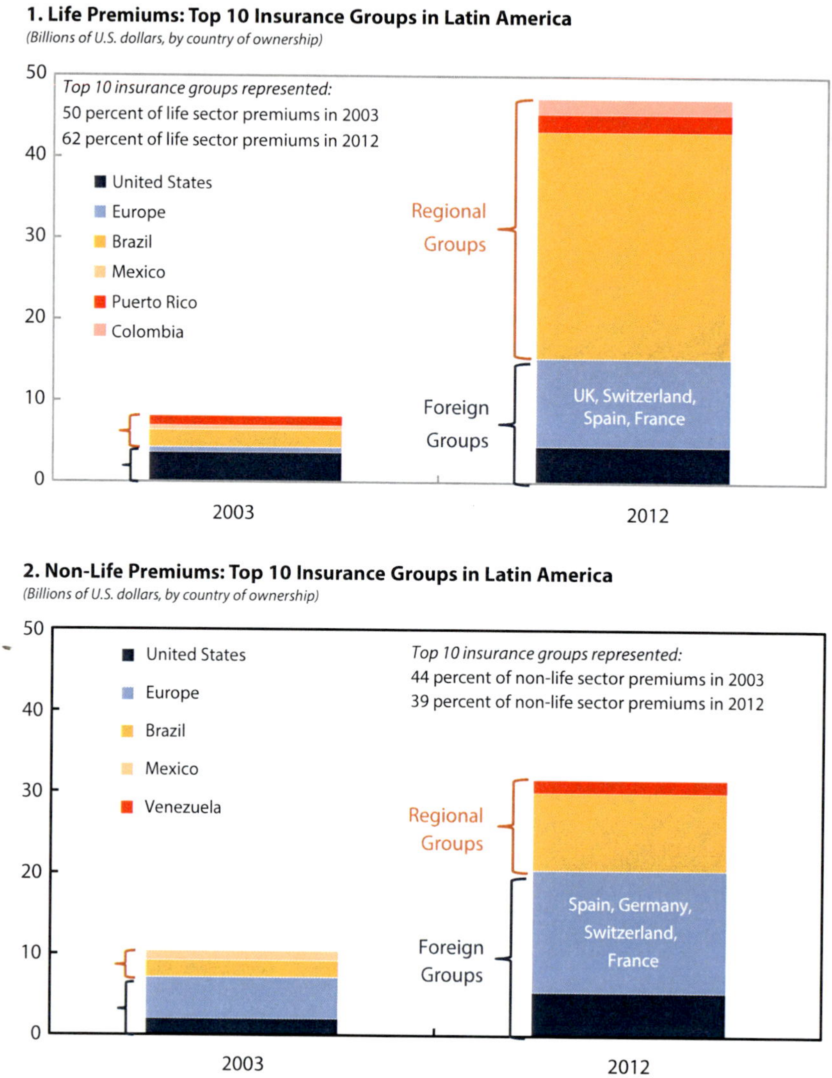

Sources: Fundacion MAPFRE; and IMF staff estimates and calculations.

the segment of companies operated by managers from elsewhere in the world) has been less pronounced, with both regional and global companies doubling in size.

Reinsurance has become particularly important in the property and casualty segment of non-life insurance, particularly as rapid economic development has increased the value of losses from natural disasters such as earthquakes and hurricanes, which are all too common in the region. However, reinsurance strategies are not widely pursued, as the proportion of ceded premiums often reported to remain relatively low.

TABLE 4.1

Ranking of Top 10 Insurance Groups in Latin America (2003 and 2012)

2003				2012			
Group	Country	Premiums (Millions of U.S. dollars)	Market Share (Percent)	Group	Country	Premiums (Millions of U.S. dollars)	Market Share (Percent)
Total Insurance							
ING	Netherlands	2,996	7.5	BRADESCO	Brazil	13,540	8.7
BRADESCO	Brazil	2,328	5.8	ITAÚ/UNIBANCO	Brazil	11,620	7.4
METLIFE	United States	1,977	5.0	MAPFRE	Spain	10,625	6.8
AIG	United States	1,927	4.8	BRASILPREV	Brazil	8,030	5.1
GNP	Mexico	1,720	4.3	ZURICH	Switzerland	6,689	4.3
MAPFRE	Spain	1,484	3.7	METLIFE	United States	5,090	3.3
TRIPLE-S	Puerto Rico	1,335	3.3	PORTO SEGURO	Brazil	4,435	2.8
ITAÚ	Brazil	1,256	3.1	LIBERTY MUTUAL	United States	4,020	2.6
ALIANZ	Germany	894	2.2	CNP	France	3,119	2.0
ZURICH	Switzerland	880	2.2	ALLIANZ	Germany	2,952	1.9
Top 10 groups		16,797	42.1	Top 10 groups		70,120	44.8
of which Latin American[1]		5,304	31.6	of which Latin American[1]		37,625	53.7
Total sector		39,897	100.0	Total sector		156,449	100.0

(Continued)

TABLE 4.1 *(Continued)*

Ranking of Top 10 Insurance Groups in Latin America (2003 and 2012)

2003				2012			
Group	Country	Premiums (Millions of U.S. dollars)	Market Share (Percent)	Group	Country	Premiums (Millions of U.S. dollars)	Market Share (Percent)
Non-Life Insurance							
ING	Netherlands	2,368	10.0	MAPFRE	Spain	7,763	9.5
AIG	United States	1,415	5.9	PORTO SEGUROS	Brazil	4,198	5.1
MAPFRE	Spain	1,275	5.4	LIBERTY MUTUAL	United States	3,817	4.7
GNP	Mexico	1,187	5.0	BRADESCO	Brazil	2,882	3.5
BRADESCO	Brazil	891	3.7	ZURICH	Switzerland	2,880	3.5
ALLIANZ	Germany	744	3.1	ALLIANZ	Germany	2,475	3.0
ZURICH	Switzerland	718	3.0	ITAÚ/UNIBANCO	Brazil	2,423	3.0
LIBERTY MUTUAL	United States	621	2.6	AXA	France	1,901	2.3
ITAÚ	Brazil	589	2.5	MERCANTIL	Venezuela	1,642	2.0
PORTO SEGUROS	Brazil	563	2.4	ACE	United States	1,623	2.0
Top 10 groups		10,371	43.6	Top 10 groups		31,604	38.7
of which Latin American[1]		3,230	31.1	of which Latin American[1]		11,145	35.3
Total sector		23,791	100.0	Total sector		81,580	100.0

(Continued)

TABLE 4.1 *(Continued)*

Ranking of Top 10 Insurance Groups in Latin America (2003 and 2012)

2003				2012			
Group	Country	Premiums (Millions of U.S. dollars)	Market Share (Percent)	Group	Country	Premiums (Millions of U.S. dollars)	Market Share (Percent)
Life Insurance							
METLIFE	United States	1,794	11.1	BRADESCO	Brazil	10,659	14.2
BRADESCO	Brazil	1,437	8.9	ITAÚ/UNIBANCO	Brazil	9,189	12.3
TRIPLE-S	Puerto Rico	1,207	7.5	BRASILPREV	Brazil	8,030	10.7
ITAÚ	Brazil	667	4.1	METLIFE	United States	4,512	6.0
ING	Netherlands	628	3.9	ZURICH	Switzerland	3,808	5.1
GNP	Mexico	533	3.3	MAPFRE	Spain	2,862	3.8
AIG	United States	511	3.2	CNP	France	2,245	3.0
MCS	United States	504	3.1	TRIPLE-S	Puerto Rico	2,223	3.0
HUMANA	United States	433	2.7	HSBC	UK	1,898	2.5
NEW YORK LIFE	United States	425	2.6	SURAMERICANA	Colombia	1,873	2.5
Top 10 groups		8,139	50.5	Top 10 groups		47,299	63.2
of which Latin American[1]		2,637	32.4	of which Latin American[1]		31,974	67.6
Total sector		16,106	100.0	Total sector		74,869	100.0

Sources: Fundacion MAPFRE; and IMF staff estimates and calculations.
[1] In percent of top 10 premiums.

The majority of the reinsurance activity is provided by foreign (primarily European) companies.

ANALYSIS

Regional integration is more likely to occur through merger and acquisition activity than through greenfield investment and organic growth, which reflects characteristics of the LA-7 insurance market rather than regulatory regimes. Growth potential and market stability make LA-7 countries appealing for new entrants. The insurance sectors are still comparatively small and, in some cases, populated by many small underwriters and brokers, so firm valuations are modest enough that firms can find opportunities to grow market shares by mergers and acquisitions. Organic growth could take much longer, especially in the more competitive markets of Brazil, Chile, and Mexico. Yet the market power of the larger firms is often cited as a key deterrent to cross-border expansion—much more so than regulatory barriers. Among the companies specializing in life insurance, the distribution channel is a potential obstacle to greenfield investment: setting up a network of agents can translate into a sizable up-front fixed cost, and developing a sound agent base can take several years. Relative product complexity in many markets (usually in the form of bundled products to attract a larger customer base) is another obstacle to entry. Market deepening is also depressed by slow progress in building trust in insurance companies and their products, as well as by limited product awareness. Insurance products remain unaffordable for a large fraction of the population of the region, and the lack of products for these segments contributes to low insurance penetration.

Financial integration through investments in regional assets is currently quite limited and unlikely to expand in any meaningful way. Demand for foreign currency assets is most often driven by shortages of domestic securities, forcing some firms to maintain persistent maturity and currency mismatches. Investment portfolio allocation decisions are largely directed by regulatory limits and insurance product specialization. Portfolio allocations of life and non-life insurance companies differ on the basis of the currency and maturity composition of their liabilities. The composition of country portfolios continues to shift toward life insurance, driven largely by the flow of funds from people who are retiring and converting their pensions into annuities. Within the LA-7, Chile, Peru, and Uruguay have the largest contributions of private pensions to life insurance growth,[3] some of which is driven by legal and regulatory frameworks. In Chile, for example, life annuities are growing at low double-digit rates owing to the participation of life insurance companies in the social security system. An insurance company selling annuities generally must be able to begin paying out a stream of payments denominated in domestic currency soon after the annuities

[3] In Brazil, the fastest-growing market has been the life free benefits generator, a product with all the characteristics of a pension but classified as life insurance. It is currently the largest segment in Brazil.

are purchased and over an extended period, thus requiring currency and maturity hedging of its assets and liabilities. Some insurance companies find it difficult to match the currency and maturity of their assets and liabilities, primarily because of the limited supply of liquid domestic securities and a shortage of long-term assets in the domestic markets. Tapping foreign markets is also complicated by the scarcity of foreign exchange derivatives of sufficiently long duration in all countries. Thus, firms often elect to live with maturity mismatches as large as three or even five years. Chilean life insurers with annuity liabilities, for example, show a systematic maturity mismatch of assets and liabilities owing to the shortage of assets with durations similar to those of liabilities.

As insurers strive to minimize maturity and currency mismatches, holdings of foreign securities remain well below the regulatory limits in many countries. In Mexico, for example, the share of foreign securities remains below 3 percent, even though the regulatory limit is 10 percent. Mexican companies that do offer insurance products denominated in foreign currency tend to have slightly higher shares of foreign securities holdings.

POLICY RECOMMENDATIONS

Binding regulatory restrictions on pension funds' foreign investment decisions often have an indirect impact on investment opportunities of insurance companies in the LA-7 region, and this effect can be exacerbated by the limited availability of financial instruments in domestic capital markets. Pension funds, unable to invest a larger share of their assets abroad, often adhere to buy-and-hold practices of domestic securities, crowding out domestic investment opportunities for the insurance companies. This in turn generates balance sheet mismatches between the assets and liabilities of many insurance companies. A number of policies could address these constraints and improve portfolio diversification and risk coverage of insurance companies, including these:

- Harmonize financial infrastructure and operational practices across the LA-7 countries. Maintaining widely disparate regulatory frameworks increases the burden of compliance, which acts as a disincentive to movement across borders. Converging on the best practices suggested in Solvency II would ease this burden and promote greater integration, although it might require legal changes in a number of countries.
- Relaxing regulatory foreign asset limits for pension funds would also ease the burden of optimal portfolio allocation for insurance companies. Limited domestic investment opportunities have led to a number of challenges for the insurance companies in the region. The short supply of domestic securities is magnified by the overwhelming presence of pension funds, which increasingly hold securities to maturity and crowd out investment opportunities for the insurance sector. Insurance companies are in need of better domestic options in local currency and of long-term maturity. Relaxing foreign investment limits for pension funds would not only ease the

difficulty of optimal pension fund portfolio allocation but would also provide additional investment opportunities for the insurance sector.

- Simplifying new product development policies would foster capital market expansion and increase investment opportunities. Authorities should also review regulatory requirements to ease the process of creating new products in the domestic capital markets. Infrastructure product development, for example, could provide a valuable instrument for portfolio diversification for pension funds and insurance companies alike.
- Data quality and provisions need further improvements to support industry monitoring and diagnosis of vulnerabilities. The availability of high-quality data on insurance companies varies by country, and the heterogeneity of publicly available information on insurance companies in many cases prevents proper comparison of industry performance across countries. Harmonization and improved quality and availability of data would not only support monitoring by the authorities but also increase transparency in the sector.

CHAPTER 5

Barriers to Integration for Pension Funds

ALLA MYRVODA

Pension funds are becoming increasingly important in financial markets in the LA-7 (Brazil, Chile, Colombia, Mexico, Panama, Peru, and Uruguay). The size of these pension funds has surpassed 17 percent of GDP in assets under management, largely driven by growing participation following legal changes in most of the region. Brazil dominates LA-7 pension fund assets in value terms, while the Chilean pension fund industry—whose framework has often been used as a model in the region—remains the largest in relation to the country's size. Despite the rapid growth, total assets and participation rates within the LA-7 remain below those of advanced country averages, thus strengthening expectations that LA-7 pension fund growth will continue to outstrip that of regional GDP. Countries' regulatory frameworks restrict most pension funds to largely domestic investments, although in many cases Latin American pension funds have outgrown domestic capital markets.

OVERVIEW

For more than a decade, domestic pension funds have been among the largest institutional investors in many Latin American countries, increasingly expanding their importance in the capital markets. Pension fund participation in government securities markets increased significantly over the past decade; for example, pension funds' share of the sovereign debt market almost doubled in Colombia and tripled in Peru. Brazilian Previ, Chilean AFP Provida, and Mexican Afore XXI Banorte are now ranked among the largest 100 pension funds in the world.[1]

Overall assets under management in LA-7 pension funds have reached almost $700 billion through the combination of healthy returns and rising contributions that reflect higher incomes and a growing participation base as younger, more urban population segments enter the formal workforce. Authorities have also promoted private pension participation as a means to build domestic savings and stem the growth of public pensions. As a result, pension fund asset accumulation has well outpaced regional economic growth, significantly increasing their importance in the regional financial systems and domestic capital markets. Between 2008 and

[1] Towers Watson (2014) ratings of the largest pension funds.

Figure 5.1 Pension Fund Assets
(Percent of GDP, index 2008 = 100)

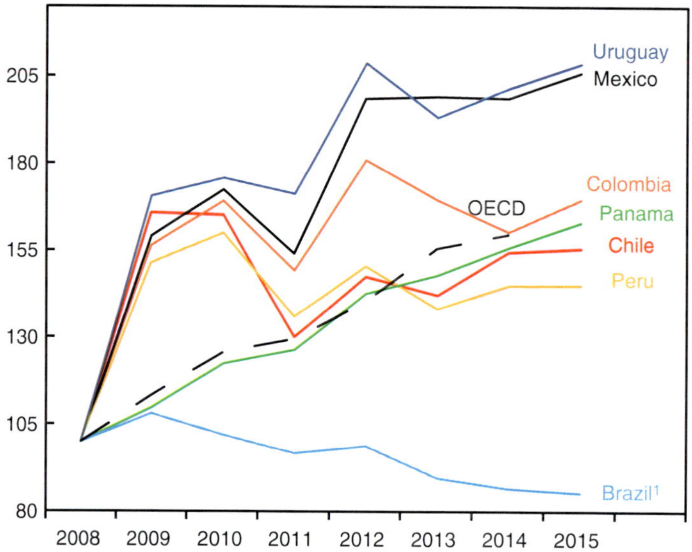

Sources: Brazilian Association of Closed Pension Funds; Brazilian National Superintendent of Pension Funds; International Association of Bodies Supervision of Pension Funds; Organisation for Economic Cooperation and Development; and IMF staff estimates and calculations.
Note: Data for some countries may include partial estimates depending on availability. Data for Panama are from the Superintendencia del Mercado Valores (Superintendency of Securities).
[1] Estimates for Brazil reflect total assets of the Brazilian closed pension funds system.

2015, LA-7 pension assets experienced growth rates that ranged between 40 percent and 110 percent, in many cases outpacing their counterparts in Organisation for Economic Co-operation and Development (OECD) member countries (Figure 5.1). Pension fund assets in many LA-7 countries now rank as the second largest among financial intermediaries, trailing only the banking system.

Given their relatively recent establishment, LA-7 pension funds have ample room for growth, as their size remains well below developed country averages. At the end of 2015, pension fund assets in LA-7 were well below the OECD average of 37 percent of GDP for every country except Chile (Figure 5.2).[2] The majority of the current pension fund systems in the LA-7 countries trace their origin to the introduction of mandatory participation in defined contribution pension systems in the 1990s, following the example of Chile in 1981. Brazil has an organization-sponsored pension system that is largely of a defined benefit nature, but many organizations are transitioning to a defined contribution system. The public sector pension plan is also transitioning from defined benefit to defined contribution. Chile, Colombia, Mexico, Peru, and Uruguay have implemented various forms of a multifund system, in which younger participants are steered

[2] Based on simple average of OECD countries reported in OECD Global Pension Statistics.

Figure 5.2 Pension Fund Assets, 2015
(Percent of GDP)

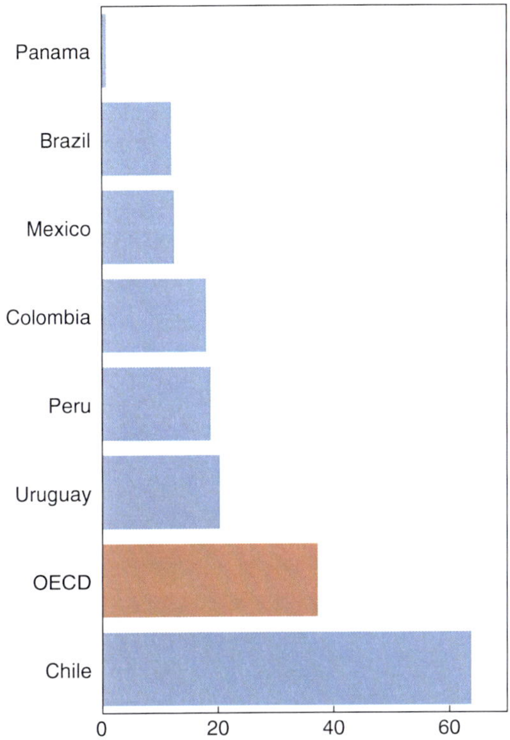

Sources: Brazilian Association of Closed Pension Funds; Brazilian National Superintendent of Pension Funds; International Association of Bodies Supervision of Pension Funds; and IMF staff estimates and calculations.
Note: Data are for year 2015 or latest available. Some countries may include partial estimates depending on availability. Data for Panama are from the Superintendencia del Mercado Valores (Superintendency of Securities); data for Brazil cover Entidades Fechadas de Previdência Complementar, segundo patrocínio predominante. 2014 simple average for Organisation for Economic Co-operation and Development (OECD).

toward more aggressive funds while older contributors deposit into safer portfolios. Panama has retained its single-fund system. Another distinguishing characteristic of Latin American pension funds is the highly elevated levels of industry concentration. The two largest pension funds in Colombia, Peru, and Uruguay manage more than 70 percent of the industry accounts and assets; the total number of pension fund administrators in each country is four. In Chile, Mexico, and Brazil, by contrast, the two largest pension funds manage about 50 percent, 40 percent, and 30 percent of total assets, respectively. Historically, despite significant variations among the countries, pension fund performance in the LA-7 region largely remained on par with performance of other financial intermediaries. However, profitability in 2015 and early 2016 declined in real and nominal terms.

STATE OF PLAY

Regional integration of pension fund markets in the LA-7 remains quite limited. Financial integration of pension funds—regional and with the rest of the world—has historically occurred through two main channels: the internationalization of pension fund management firms and cross-border investments of pension fund assets. Although the first channel has seen some activity in recent years, the second continues to be limited by low regulatory investment limits. Cross-border management of pension fund assets has increased as a result of consolidation trends and the withdrawal of a number of global institutions, and regional asset managers are beginning to assert themselves. Currently, the largest pension funds and the majority of assets are controlled by domestic asset managers (except in Chile); however, foreign asset managers have sizable market shares in Chile, Mexico, Peru, and Uruguay (Figure 5.3). In recent years, there have been mergers and acquisitions in many LA-7 countries, involving both domestic and foreign asset management firms. Several foreign institutional investment groups (such as BBVA, ING, and HSBC, among others) have withdrawn from the pension fund industry in the region; they have been partially replaced by others, including Principal Financial Group and MetLife. At the same time, Latin American financial groups, such as Grupo Suramericana de Inversiones (Colombia) and its affiliates, have acquired

Figure 5.3 Pension Fund Assets under Management
(Billions of U.S. dollars, 2014)

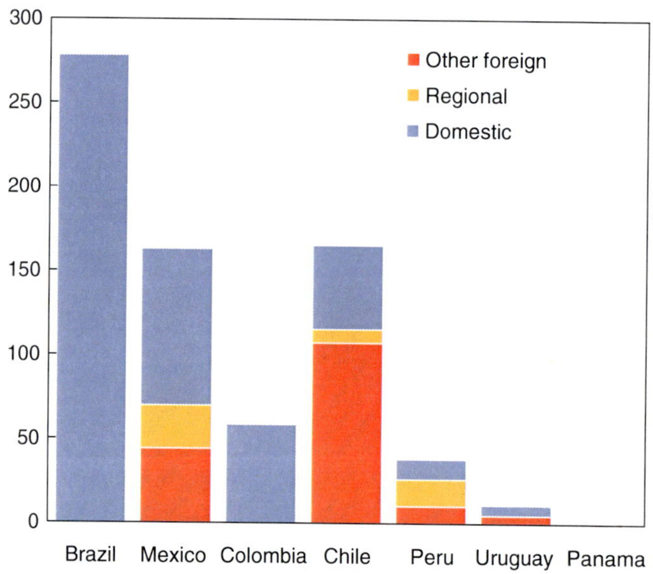

Sources: Bureau van Dijk; national authorities; and IMF staff calculations.
Note: Data are as at year-end 2014 or latest available. Data for some countries may include partial estimates depending on availability. Data for Panama are from the Superintendencia del Mercado Valores (Superintendency of Securities). Estimates for Brazil reflect total assets of the Brazilian closed pension funds system.

interests or controlling positions in Chile, Colombia, Mexico, Peru, and Uruguay. This trend, largely accomplished through mergers and acquisitions, has resulted in higher industry concentrations, with Colombia and Mexico as the most prominent examples. The number of pension fund administrators in Mexico fell from 21 at the end of 2007 to 11 in early 2016, while the number in Colombia fell from six in 2012 to four in the first quarter of 2016.

International investments is an important asset class for regional pension funds, although regional exposure is small. The overwhelming share of foreign holdings is invested in advanced economies, such as the euro area, Japan, and the United States, with a somewhat smaller share invested in emerging markets. Investments in other Latin American countries are relatively low; for example, some Peruvian pension managers reported LA-7 investments of just 3.7 percent of assets (9.3 percent of foreign allocations), although this share increases marginally if indirect investments through American depository receipts and Latin America–focused exchange traded funds and mutual funds are taken into account. Foreign securities investments are often allocated to debt securities, as many countries place a regulatory limit on equities in both foreign and domestic markets. Pension funds have contributed greatly to the development of domestic debt securities markets, but their role in the expansion of equity markets has been rather limited (Figure 5.4). In addition to explicit caps on foreign asset holdings,

Figure 5.4 Pension Fund: Investments, 2005–15
(Percent of total investment)

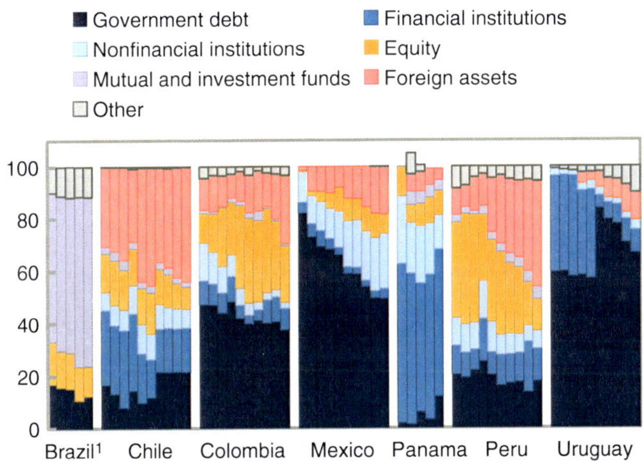

Sources: International Association of Bodies Supervision of Pension Funds; and IMF staff estimates and calculations.
Note: Data for Brazil and Panama are for 2010–14.
[1] Estimates for Brazil are from the Brazilian Association of Closed Pension Funds and the Brazilian National Superintendent of Pension Funds. Classification may vary from that of other countries. Government debt includes public bonds; other includes private loans and deposits, special purpose companies, structure investments, real estate, operations with participants, and others.

many countries in the region have regulations that indirectly discourage financial integration. For example, Uruguay not only has a foreign asset cap of just 15 percent, it has rules that limit external investments to securities from multilateral institutions. In Chile, although the regulatory limit does not appear to be binding in aggregate, foreign asset holdings are effectively constrained by additional caps on risk tolerance, as measured by sovereign ratings.[3]

ANALYSIS

Consolidation in the pension management industry has reduced the opportunities for regional firms to enter neighboring markets, which can restrain competition and prompt higher pension fund fees (see the discussion in Annex 5.1). In most cases, regulatory treatment of foreign and domestic companies is largely equivalent.[4] However, a significant impediment to new entrants is that the market is highly concentrated, and the competitive advantages[5] held by dominant, established asset managers are deemed too great for institutional investors to set up greenfield operations and grow organically. And, as with the banking industry, consolidation has increased corporate valuations beyond what foreigners are willing to pay to enter a market.

As assets under management continue to grow, pension systems in most countries of the region will have to increase their international exposures. Asset allocation strategies are likely to come under more strain as fund inflows continue to grow faster than net government borrowing, while excess allocations into bank deposits threaten to drag down returns. Issuance of corporate debt and equity can meet some of the pension fund demand for local currency investments, but in many countries these instruments can trigger volume, liquidity, and maturity concerns, as well as corporate risks. Alternative assets such as private equity and infrastructure have garnered attention in recent years—especially in Brazil, Peru, and Uruguay—but prudential limits are low and the class is generally considered too risky to expect caps to rise quickly. In the past two decades, regulators have been keener to raise caps on foreign asset holdings. While this asset class introduces foreign exchange risk, most funds have invested in highly liquid segments of advanced country markets for which currency hedging is less expensive.

The internationalization of pension assets is restrained by limits on some asset classes. Figure 5.5 shows that for LA-7 pension funds, share of investments in foreign assets is low by international standards, and is often curbed by regulatory

[3] Chilean pension funds may hold no more than 20 percent of assets in securities of countries with sovereign risk ratings lower than Chile's own (AA). This could be a complicating restriction when encouraging regional holdings, as targeted partners would all fall below this threshold.

[4] The absence of foreign asset managers in Brazil reflects regulatory limits on new investments in the Brazilian financial sector. Brazilian law allows individual residents to make investments abroad, provided that they declare the investments and the funds' origins to the local authorities.

[5] Recognized advantages include the fact that well-established institutions have greater access to securities brokers and have the first pick of the investment offerings, and the assessment among pension participants that the largest funds are the least risky.

Figure 5.5 Foreign Investments by Pension Funds Worldwide Compared with LA-7

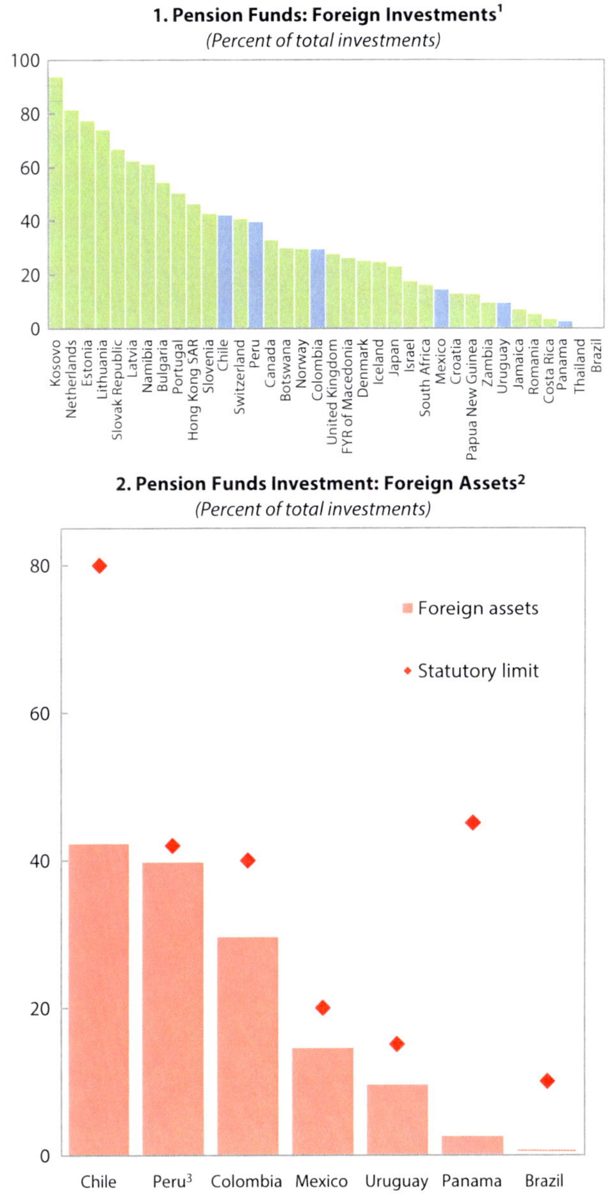

Sources: International Association of Pension Funds Supervision; Organisation for Economic Co-operation and Development; Brazilian National Superintendent of Pension Funds; and IMF staff estimates and calculations.

[1] Data for the LA-7 countries are for March 2016; 2014 or latest available for others. Estimates may be based on partial data for some countries. Hong Kong SAR data only refer to mandatory provident fund (MPF) schemes and MPF-exempted schemes registered under the Occupational Retirement Schemes Ordinance. South Africa data refer only to the funds supervised by the Pension Funds Act.

[2] Data are as of March 2016. Data for some countries may include partial estimates depending on availability.

[3] Although the statutory limit on foreign assets in Peru is 50 percent, the pension fund supervisor raises the effective limit over a period of time; at the time of writing it was set at 42 percent.

limits. Regulatory limits and restrictions on investments vary by country and generally span multiple categories, including foreign securities, equity, foreign currency, commodities, derivatives, single issuance holdings, and debt securities of lower ratings (see Annex 5.2). Limits on variable rate instruments tend to be more restrictive. Countries with a multifund system—which allows risk profile differentiation—have been able to ease their regulatory restrictions over time, permitting larger shares of investments in variable rate instruments (Chile, Colombia, Mexico, and Peru).

Pension funds in the region have outpaced the growth of domestic capital markets, complicating the task of optimal portfolio diversification and making a case for the expansion of investment opportunities through financial integration. In addition to providing retirement funding, the development of the pension fund sector has generated a number of benefits. Pension funds have contributed to higher savings rates, broadening the domestic investor base and deepening of the local securities markets. However, their asset growth has long outpaced the supply of domestic securities, triggering an array of challenges. First, pension funds now find it more difficult to achieve optimal portfolio diversification. Second, equity markets may have become more prone to asset price bubbles as pension funds pursue a limited number of securities and may exhibit herd behavior as asset managers chase the same type of securities. Third, the large size and established investment behavior of pension funds, the latter of which is based largely on a buy-and-hold strategy, combine to further diminish financial market liquidity. Trading volumes in the financial markets have declined substantially as pension funds absorb significant portions of new and existing products. And finally, pension funds' appetite for domestic instruments crowds out other financial intermediaries, such as insurance companies, from the domestic financial markets. Stronger regional integration could enable greater diversification by pension funds and enhance competition, and hence development, in financial markets.

Although the minimum return requirements enforced in some countries inspire confidence in the systems, they can create incentives for a herd mentality among asset managers and reduce diversification efforts into new foreign markets. The minimum returns requirement compels pension funds to disclose their asset composition and portfolio returns, and requires asset managers to top up returns by injecting their own cash into the fund when the return deviates significantly (generally more than 2 to 4 percentage points) below the minimum required threshold over an extended period (usually about 36 months). Typically, the industry average serves as the minimum required rate. Thus, to avoid underperforming their peer group, pension fund asset managers tend to mimic the portfolio allocation schemes of the largest pension funds, which tend to drive the reference rate. Strong homogeneity of returns across funds in a system shifts competitive pressures to management fees and marketing savvy. In such an environment—where risk taking by asset managers can be substantially limited—as negative consequences of poor returns outweigh perceived rewards of stronger performance, initial cross-border activity by market leaders would likely be followed quickly by other market participants if sufficient cross-border opportunities are available.

Against this background, it appears that it may be easier for regulators in countries with age/risk-differentiated funds to introduce new limits on asset classes with higher risk/return profiles. Softer caps on foreign assets, corporate paper, and alternative assets can be introduced in funds with the highest risk tolerances—those designed for the youngest contributors. If, over time, the changes meet regulator expectations, similar reforms can be introduced into less aggressive funds.

In an effort to diversify investments, pension funds have turned their attention to infrastructure products. So far, investments in infrastructure are reported in the range of 3 percent to 5 percent of pension fund investments, well below regulatory limits. A number of barriers prevent higher infrastructure investments, including lack of expertise in the infrastructure sector, problems of scale of pension funds, lack of transparency in the infrastructure sector, shortage of data on the performance of infrastructure projects, and lack of a benchmark. Given the unique nature of each project, investments in infrastructure, either directly or through a fund, also require significant time to complete due diligence and establish the appropriate framework for investment and risk management.[6] LA-7 pension funds see infrastructure vehicles as a promising instrument for diversification, especially as they align with the authorities' strategies for public investment and implementation of structural reform. In Mexico, for example, the recent energy reform is expected to provide a boost to the development of energy products. The long-term investment horizon of pension funds makes them natural investors in less liquid infrastructure products. While prudential limits may have contributed to preventing pension funds from investing much in such infrastructure, own risk appetite also had a part to play. Such risk appetite and internal risk controls would also help ensure that pension funds do not hold too high a share of highly illiquid infrastructure assets.

POLICY RECOMMENDATIONS

The LA-7 countries' authorities could consider several options to fine-tune their pension (funds) regulations with a view to enhance regional integration. First, higher regulatory limits on foreign security investments would ease demand pressures in domestic financial markets. The fact that Latin American pension funds have outgrown domestic securities markets provides a strong argument for an increase in regulatory limits on foreign securities, perhaps to about 50 percent in countries where they are currently set lower. Low limits can lead to suboptimal portfolio holdings and asset bubble developments in the domestic markets and may be a source of instability as they fail to accommodate portfolio reallocations

[6] Infrastructure investments of global pension funds vary greatly. Some Canadian and Australian pension funds register about 10 percent investment in infrastructure, for example, where the necessary knowledge, expertise, and resources to invest directly into infrastructure have been acquired. Other countries' infrastructure investments remain limited, largely owing to the lingering perception of risk in the sector. (Based on OECD 2011.)

in response to changes in domestic financial conditions. Relaxing limits on foreign (particularly regional) investments—subject to risk safeguards around such investments abroad and the availability of hedging instruments, plus enhancements to transparency and improvements in data—would allow pension funds to invest more across borders, easing their demand for domestic securities and allowing other financial intermediaries, such as insurance companies, greater access to financial instruments.

Given regional labor mobility among the LA-7 countries, authorities should institute pension fund portability across the region. Currently, Chile and Peru have a bilateral agreement that allows their citizens to transfer balances accumulated in their individual accounts from one country to another. Not only does this facilitate the transfer of savings, it also encourages countries to adopt best practices and harmonize asset management processes.

Authorities should simplify the process of creating infrastructure products and allow pension funds to access these instruments in other LA countries. Unrestricted access to regional infrastructure projects would provide a boost to the development of regional infrastructure products and further contribute to the development of securities markets. It would be beneficial to pension funds, as it would allow them to ensure better diversification of portfolios, as infrastructure projects are long-term investments that can match the long-term duration of their liabilities. The benefit would extend to the regional economy by facilitating infrastructure financing overall.

Countries of the region should demonstrate their commitment to integration with an understanding that in the future their pension regulators will agree to treat each other's securities as domestic. Critically, such an agreement would be preconditioned on countries' adoption of the highest standards in pension and financial system regulation and regulatory collaboration. Additionally, countries would have to harmonize their accounting standards by adopting the International Financial Reporting Standards and sign the multilateral memorandum of observance of international principles and practices relating to governance, monitoring, and mitigating financial and operational risk. A token of this commitment could be the establishment of a special category for holding bonds issued in the region that would not count against foreign asset limits. This category could have a low limit, say 5 percent, but the limit could be relaxed if asset holdings grow to the point that it becomes binding.

ANNEX 5.1. LA-7 PENSION FUNDS: OPERATING COSTS AND PENSION FEES

Pension fund fees levied on contributors directly affect the size of their retirement incomes. In a pension fund system with defined contribution arrangements, the size of retirement benefits depends not only on the contributions and the investment returns earned by such contributions but also on the fees levied by pension fund providers. Although the size of the mandatory pension fund contribution is often determined by legislation, accruing sufficient retirement benefits requires a combination of high returns and low fees (Tapia and Yermo 2008).

Comparisons with other countries indicate that LA-7 pension fund fees are higher than the level suggested by their operating costs (Annex Figures 5.1.1 and 5.1.3).[7] LA-7 pension funds on average charge higher fees than the average for Organisation for Economic Co-operation and Development (OECD) member countries as a percentage of total assets under management. Fee size is largely driven by operating costs, including fund administration expenses, marketing costs, and commissions for sales agents. Operating costs of LA-7 pension funds relative to total assets under management are comparable to the OECD country average, but average fees are higher in LA-7 countries. In fact, the fees levied on contributors by pension funds in some LA-7 countries are almost double what is needed to cover operating expenses.

Pension funds in LA-7 countries vary structurally. For example, in both Mexico and Panama, operating costs constitute less than half of income collected from fees. However, in Panama the bulk of operating expenses is for administration purposes, while in Mexico more than half of the operating costs goes toward sales commissions (Annex Figure 5.1.2).

LA-7 pension fund fees are also influenced by industry characteristics and regulatory frameworks, which largely exhibit a preference for fees levied on contributions rather than on asset balances. Pension fund fees collected from individual contributors depend on a number of factors, including the size and maturity of the system, market structure, competition, investment strategy, and regulatory framework. Less mature pension fund systems (typical in LA-7 countries) tend to have relatively higher fees. Asset allocation decisions and investment regulations also tend to influence fees, as investments in interest-bearing assets (such as debt instruments) are usually cheaper than active investments (such as equities). Thus, the higher fees in Peruvian pension funds could be partially explained by the relatively larger share of asset allocations toward equities. The structure of pension fund fees in general tends to be fairly complex. Unlike in

[7] Coverage may vary by country and by definition. Data references are based on data from the International Association of Latin American Pension Fund Supervisors, the Organisation for Economic Co-operation and Development (OECD), and IMF staff estimates and calculations. OECD country averages may not be fully comparable owing to variations in country and time period samples.

Annex Figure 5.1.1 Pension Fund Fees, 2015
(Percent of assets under management)

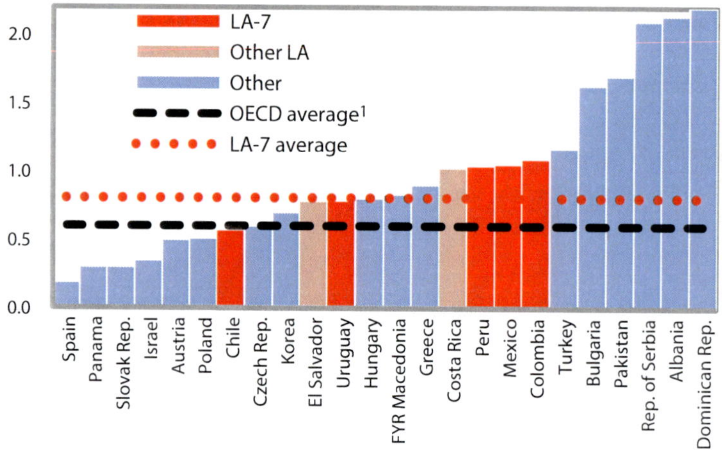

Sources: International Association of Latin American Pension Fund Supervisors; International Organization of Pension Supervisors; national authorities; World Bank; Organisation for Economic Co-operation and Development; and IMF staff estimates and calculations.
Note: Data are for 2015 or latest available. Occupational category for Spain; 2nd pillar for Slovak Republic; and voluntary plan for FYR Macedonia. LA = Latin America; LA-7 = Brazil, Chile, Colombia, Mexico, Panama, Peru, and Uruguay. OECD = Organisation for Economic Co-operation and Development.
[1] Includes selected OECD (non-Latin America and the Caribbean [LAC]) countries for which data are available. Data may not be comparable owing to differences in definitions.

central and eastern Europe, where preference is often given to fees levied on asset balances, Latin American pension funds tend to emphasize fees on contributions. Colombia, for example, levies a 16 percent fee on contributions, whereas Chile and Peru have a 10 percent fee. LA-7 pension funds also impose a fee on salary, which varies from about 1.2 percent in Peru to 3 percent in Uruguay. Mexican pension funds, on the other hand, rely on fees imposed on asset balances.

A more optimal fee structure in Latin America would cause a decline in pension fund fees without jeopardizing returns and their corresponding alignment with the managers' cost strategies. Both contribution fees and those levied on asset balances have a number of disadvantages. While contribution fees generate revenues at the start, they may not be completely aligned with the continuously changing nature of the fund managers' cost structure. On the other hand, asset management fees on balances (levied as a percentage), while responding quickly to fund costs, do not initially generate revenues. Meanwhile, performance fees tend to distort the funds' long-term goals and objectives. Against this backdrop, it may be advisable to implement annual flat fees to cover transactions carried out during each period, combined with asset management fees to absorb portfolio

Annex Figure 5.1.2 Pension Funds: Operating Costs and Fees, 2015
(Percent)

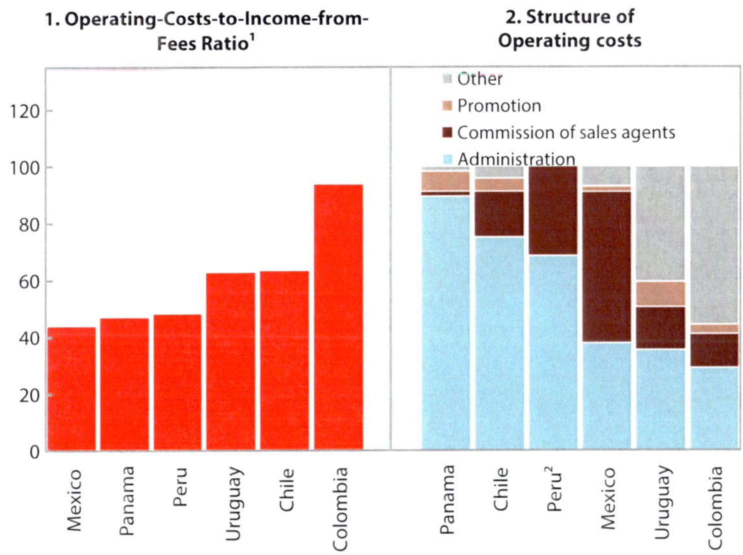

Sources: International Association of Latin American Pension Fund Supervisors; Organisation for Economic Co-operation and Development; and IMF staff estimates and calculations.
[1]Ratio of operating costs to total income from fees, implied estimate for some countries based on available data.
[2]Commission of sales agents costs for Peru may include promotion costs. Data for LA-7 cover the July–June period.

management costs. Such a strategy may be better aligned with the cost structure of the manager and cause fewer distortions of long-term investment strategies of pension providers.

Greater regional financial integration in Latin America would encourage more competition in the pension fund industry while simultaneously relieving the burden of high pension fund fees levied on customers' contributions. In some cases (such as Mexico), lower pension fund concentration might be accompanied by higher fees. This could possibly be explained by higher operating expenses incurred as a result of increased efforts by marketing and sales agents to encourage pension fund members to switch providers. Such efforts can drive up fees, as some contributors may be more responsive to marketing than to the size and structure of the fees. Increased regional integration—combined with ongoing efforts to promote financial education among contributors—would allow greater access of regional companies to domestic markets and increase competition in the pension fund industry, thus forcing managers to reduce the size of the fees they levy on their customers. Lower fees, in turn, would reinforce contributors' efforts to accumulate sufficient funds for retirement.

Annex Figure 5.1.3 Pension Funds' Operating Expenses[1]
(Percent of assets under management)

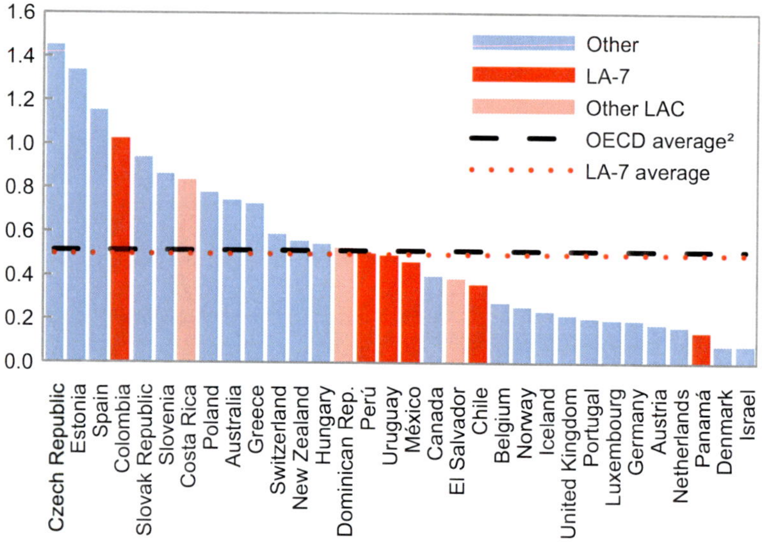

Sources: Organisation for Economic Co-operation and Development (OECD); International Association of Bodies Supervision of Pension Funds; and IMF staff estimates and calculations.
[1] For Latin and Caribbean: annual data include July 2013 to June 2014. Data for LAC countries may not be fully comparable to other economies.
[2] Includes selected OECD (non-LAC) countries for which data are available. Data may not be comparable due to differences in definition.

ANNEX 5.2. REGULATORY LIMITS ON FOREIGN INVESTMENTS BY PENSION FUNDS

ANNEX TABLE 5.2.1

Pension Funds in Latin America: Limits on Foreign Investments

Country	Legal Instrument	Foreign Investments Allowed	Foreign Investment Limit
Brazil	Banco Central do Brasil, Resolução No. 3792	Assets issued abroad belonging to the portfolios of the funds constituted in Brazil Shares of investment funds and funds classified as external debt Shares of foreign index funds admitted to trading on the stock exchange in Brazil Brazilian depositary receipts Shares issued by foreign companies based in Mercosur	10 percent
Chile	Decreto Ley No. 3500 de 1980 Banco Central de Chile, Acuerdo No. 1680-03-120517-Circular No. 3013-699	Credit instruments or negotiable securities issued or guaranteed by foreign governments, central banks, and other banks Stocks and bonds issued by foreign companies Participation shares usually traded on international markets issued by mutual funds and investment funds Debt instruments must have at least two risk ratings by international rating agencies above BBB and N-3	The law sets a maximum limit range for all funds combined (30 percent–80 percent) and a maximum limit range for each type of fund: Fund A: 45 percent–100 percent Fund B: 40 percent–90 percent Fund C: 30 percent–75 percent Fund D: 20 percent–45 percent Fund E: 15 percent–35 percent The central bank sets the limits within the above range as follows: Maximum limits for the funds combined may not exceed 80 percent of their value. Fund A: 100 percent Fund B: 90 percent Fund C: 75 percent Fund D: 45 percent Fund E: 35 percent
Colombia	Ministerio de Hacienda y Crédito Público, Decreto No. 857/2011	Debt securities issued or guaranteed by foreign governments or foreign central banks Debt securities issued, guaranteed, or originated by foreign commercial or investment banks or by foreign nonbank entities	Conservative fund: 40 percent Moderate fund: 60 percent Riskier fund: 70 percent

(Continued)

ANNEX TABLE 5.2.1

Pension Funds in Latin America: Limits on Foreign Investments (*Continued*)

Country	Legal Instrument	Foreign Investments Allowed	Foreign Investment Limit
		Debt securities issued or guaranteed by multilateral lending institutions Exchange traded funds, foreign mutual or investment funds Equity securities American depository receipts and global depository receipts Private equity funds established abroad	
Mexico		Foreign debt securities and foreign equity securities Real estate investment vehicles Bank demand deposits in foreign financial institution Derivatives with foreign equity as underlying assets	Funds 1–4: up to 20 percent for foreign debt securities At the same time, the law establishes limits per type of investment: equity, structured investments for each type of fund
Panama	Comisión Nacional de Valores, Acuerdo No 11-2005	Shares issued by foreign companies Debt securities issued by governments, central banks, foreign financial institutions, and companies of which at least 50 percent are investment grade by the country of origin or by a recognized international rating agency	Foreign investments may not exceed 50 percent per type of asset
Peru	Texto Único Ordenado de la Ley del Sistema Privado de Administración de Fondos de Pensiones Banco Central de Reserva del Perú, Circular No. 032-2014-BCRP	Financial instruments issued or guaranteed by foreign governments or central banks; shares and securities representing rights to shares registered in stock exchanges; debt securities; participation in mutual funds and hedge operations issued by foreign institutions	50 percent established by law The central bank set the operational limit at 42 percent beginning on January 1, 2015 Limits are added by category of instrument, depending on the type of fund
Uruguay	Ley 16.713	Debt securities issued by international credit organizations or foreign governments with a very high credit rating	15 percent

Source: Author's compilation.
Note: In addition to the global investment limits specified above, some countries also set limits by issuer and by issuance. Colombia, for example, sets a limit of 10 percent of the value of each fund for each issuer and a 30 percent limit for each issuance. Mexico adds a 5 percent limit of the total assets of the fund for each issuer and a 35 percent limit for each issuance.

REFERENCES

Organization for Economic Cooperation and Development (OECD). 2011. "Pension Fund Investment in Infrastructure. A Survey." OECD, Paris.

Tapia, W., and J. Yermo. 2008. "Fees in Individual Account Pension Systems: A Cross-Country Comparison." OECD Working Papers on Insurance and Private Pensions, No. 27, Paris.

Towers Watson. 2014. "The World's 500 Largest Asset Managers." https://www.towerswatson.com/en-US/Insights/IC-Types/Survey-Research-Results/2014/11/The-worlds-500-largest-asset-managers-year-end.

CHAPTER 6

Barriers to Integration in Capital Markets

ALLA MYRVODA AND BENNETT SUTTON

Market capitalizations in the LA-7 (Brazil, Chile, Colombia, Mexico, Panama, Peru, and Uruguay) are moderate in size by emerging market standards; however, continued growth and development will depend on improving liquidity conditions across the region. At the end of 2015, capitalization of LA-7 equity markets was 32 percent of regional GDP, while the value of domestically traded bonds outstanding was about 62 percent of GDP (Figure 6.1). In dollar terms, the largest bond and equity markets are in Brazil and Mexico. Despite solid market capitalizations, low trading volumes are a growing concern. Shrinking liquidity is attributed to deteriorating macroeconomic conditions, high transaction costs, and the outsized role of institutional investors and their buy-and-hold strategies.

OVERVIEW

Though most LA-7 exchanges are well-established institutions that predate the Great Depression of the 1930s, their size and importance have waxed and waned along with the macroeconomic prospects of the region. Since financial liberalization in the mid-1990s, equity markets have deepened, whether measured by capitalization, number of issuers, or types of securities traded. However, concerns remain as financial development has not kept pace with the size and activity of comparator markets in emerging Asia and Europe. Moreover, capital raised in Latin American equity markets has been somewhat limited, trading volumes are compressed, markets tend to be dominated by certain sectors, and the underdevelopment of currency and derivatives markets means that domestic instruments are mostly traded offshore (see Annexes 6.1 and 6.2). Ananchotikul and Eichengreen (2008) cite a number of factors that impair regional equity market development, including a history of high inflation, financial crises, corporate and sovereign defaults, and frequent infringement/weakening of creditor and investor rights. Financial deepening has advanced on the back of improved policy and regulatory frameworks and (more slowly) legal reforms, but the history of volatility still weighs on corporate and sovereign financing. The dominance of debt (banks, bonds, and supplier credit) and internal financing over equity reflects high direct and implicit costs of equity issuance. A World Bank study (Zervos 2004) found that in Brazil and Mexico, issuing equity was more expensive than selling

Figure 6.1 Indicators of Capital Market Growth and Size
(Percent of LA-7 GDP)

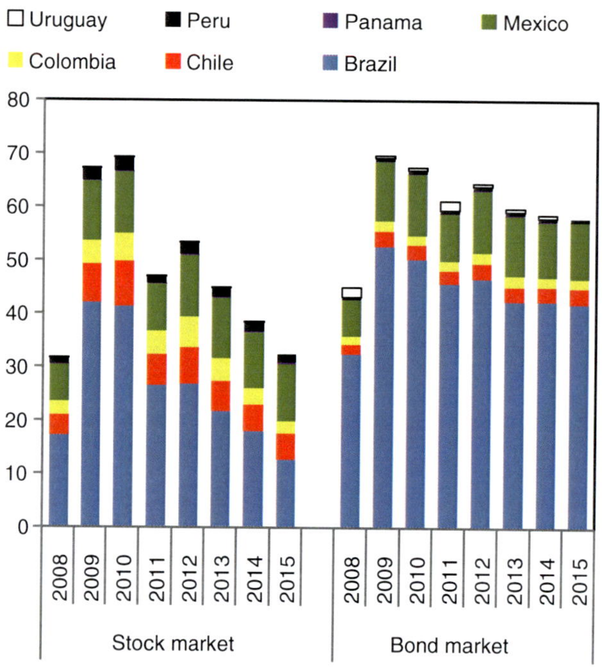

Sources: Bank for International Settlements; Federation of Ibero-American Exchanges; and Haver Analytics.

domestic bonds (200 and 275 basis points, respectively) or international bonds (217 and 170 basis points). Investors are also thought to prefer holding debt over equity holdings because of the prevalence of family and conglomerate ownership, both of which exert strong management control with less regard for the interests of minority shareholders. Latin American bond markets also bear the cost of previous profligacy. Sovereigns and corporates that issue in foreign markets generally garner larger amounts and often with lower yields or longer maturities than can be had on domestic markets. The bulk of paper in local markets is sold by sovereigns and corporations (particularly financials) with local currency assets and revenues. During the commodity boom, many producers issued internationally to take advantage of better terms and minimize currency mismatches.

STATE OF PLAY

As in other sectors of the financial system, regional financial integration among capital markets is observed in two dimensions: intraregional securities flows and the expansion of business operations across borders. With regard to the first measure, the question is to what degree are residents of the LA-7 countries buying and selling each other's financial securities? The IMF's Coordinated Portfolio

Figure 6.2 Regional and Global Integration of LA-7 Securities Markets

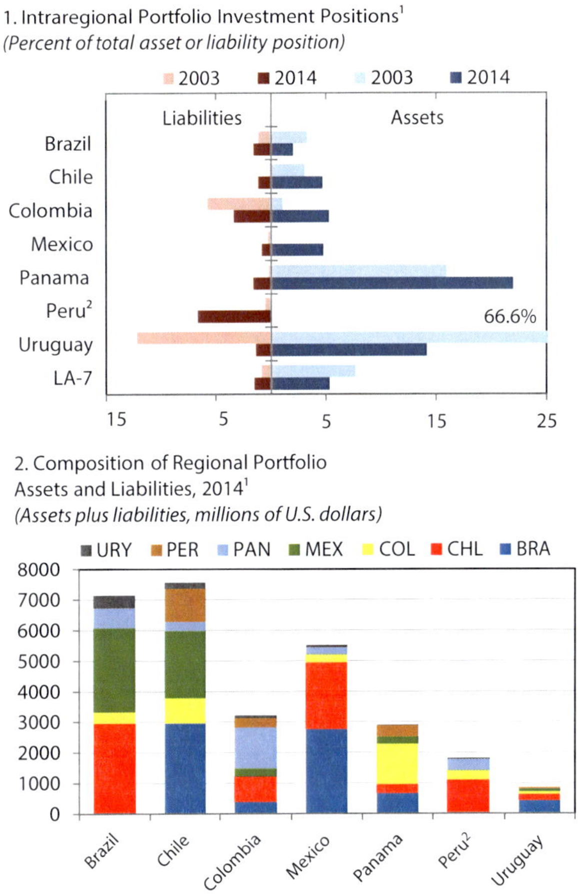

Source: IMF, Coordinated Portfolio Investment Survey.
[1] Liability data derived from partner asset positions.
[2] Derived liabilities only; asset data not available.

Investment Survey indicates that the countries of the region are increasingly open to financial opportunities (Figure 6.2, panel 1) in neighboring states. Between 2003 and 2014, five of the seven countries increased their intraregional liability financing shares, while four increased their asset exposure (although aggregate regional asset position declined on account of the drastic reallocation in Uruguay).[1] Brazil is the largest destination for intraregional assets, attracting 45 percent of investments, followed by Mexico (19 percent) and Peru (12 percent).

---

[1] In 2003, Uruguay's assets invested in the LA-7 countries accounted for 50 percent of intraregional investment; by 2014 it represented only 4.7 percent.

Chile is the largest provider of regional financing, accounting for 47 percent of liabilities, with Mexico and Panama, respectively, supplying 19 percent and 16 percent of funds. Figure 6.2, panel 2 shows the bilateral relationships between the reporting country on the horizontal axis and its regional partners.

Regional capital markets are also integrating along the operational dimension. This integration can take many forms; for example, securities exchanges reaching collaborative agreements on mutual trading rights, agreeing on post-trade clearing procedures, or adopting the same electronic trading platform. Operational integration also increases when broker-dealers purchase or establish operations abroad, facilitating the foreign trading activity of clients in both countries. Capital markets become more synergistic when they harmonize trading hours, tax treatments, supervisory practices, and international payment and settlement arrangements. Additionally, there is scope for peer reviews to assess central counterparties' (CCPs') compliance with regulatory frameworks, as well as the safety and soundness of individual CCPs, including their use of CPMI-IOSCO PFMI.[2] All these elements combined could lead to the mutual recognition of regional clearinghouses as qualified CCPs.

LA-7 exchanges are modernizing their organizational structures, trading, and settlement systems. Over the past decade the BM&F Bovespa, Bolsa Mexicana, and Bolsa de Santiago stock exchanges have fully demutualized.[3] Demutualizing increases the transparency under which exchanges are managed, because ownership stakes of the brokers in the exchange are converted into shares that are publicly traded and subject to the same reporting requirements as listed firms. Also, the right to join and trade as a broker becomes a matter of application and process rather than merely the consent of the owning brokers. Other exchanges continue to have mutualized ownership structures, though Bolsa de Lima and Bolsa de Colombia have publicly traded floats and thus must comply with financial reporting requirements that provide greater transparency of operations. The major exchanges have adopted electronic trading platforms that facilitate more cost-effective back-office support in brokerages than when over-the-counter negotiations dominate trading. Exchanges in Brazil, Chile, and Mexico have instituted independent CCP entities that settle and clear trades in all markets (stocks, bonds, foreign exchange, and derivatives), as well as maintaining broker collateral against default. On the Colombian, Panamanian, Peruvian, and Uruguayan stock exchanges, stock and bond trades clear through the exchange itself. Bolsa de Colombia also operates a CCP for derivative and foreign exchange trades.

The global trend for stock exchanges to build strategic alliances through ownership stakes in each other is also occurring in Latin America. These alliances are entered into with the intention of facilitating cross-border transactions that will mobilize larger pools of savings to increase market size and trading activity and cut costs through scales of operation and back-office synergies. Many global

---

[2] Principles for Financial Market Infrastructure (PFMI) by the Committee on Payments and Market Infrastructure (CPMI) and the International Organization of Securities Commissions (IOSCO).

[3] Members of the board of the Bolsa Santiago voted to demutualize in April 2016.

banks and exchanges have stakes in Latin American stock exchanges, but regional cross-ownership is also on the rise. In early 2015, BM&F Bovespa purchased an 8 percent stake in the Santiago exchange and is working with it to set up an electronic derivatives market in Chile. In April 2016, BM&F also secured a 4.1 percent stake in the Mexican stock exchange BVM,[4] and it is said to be interested in acquiring stakes in the other Latin American Integrated Market (MILA) exchanges as well as the Bolsa de Buenos Aires. The acquisition in 2013 that gave the BVM an 8 percent stake in the Lima exchange was significant not only because it became the largest independent shareholder of the Peruvian Bolsa but also because it signaled BMV's commitment to join the MILA initiative. Regionalization is also expanding at the broker level. Several brokerages have obtained seats or licenses to be broker-dealers in other LA-7 markets. While their motivations could vary substantially, likely benefits would include reducing transaction costs for regional trades (compared with trades via correspondent brokers), broadening client bases, and increasing transaction volumes, which in turn could drive down average costs of back-office support. BTG Pactual has brokerages on the most dynamic regional exchanges, including Brazil, Chile, Colombia, Mexico, and Peru. Other investment banks and brokerages with intraregional operations include Itaú (Brazil), Sura (Colombia), Credicorp (Peru), GNB Sudameris (Colombia), and LarrainVial (Chile).

ANALYSIS

The concern regarding the withdrawal of global institutions from Latin America is much less pronounced for capital markets than it is for the banking sector. First, majority control of exchanges lies with domestic entities, while many of the foreign stakeholders are in fact other regional exchanges, not advanced economy entities looking to exit the region. At the brokerage level, while many brokers are subsidiaries of global banks from advanced countries, divestiture of operations has not occurred widely. Even when global banks leave a market (mainly retail banking), they often keep their brokerage operations open as, for example, HSBC has done in Colombia and Citibank in Chile. Retaining brokerage operations can help banks access fixed income and currency markets more efficiently. Brokerages may also signal sophistication of operations to large clients in advanced and emerging markets. Finally, the global regulatory agenda is not generating divestiture pressures for brokerages, given the substantial capital they must maintain with exchanges and the limited amount of lending they do to clients.

For regional capital markets, financial integration could facilitate financial deepening and development. Markets would especially like to see integration drive greater equity trading activity and liquidity conditions. Figure 6.3 shows that since 2013 liquidity measured as growth in value traded has declined for the

---

[4] http://ir.bmfbovespa.com.br/enu/2677/NM%20Investiment%20in%20Latin%20America_Bolsa%20Mexicana%20de%20Valores_2016.04.05.pd

Figure 6.3 Value Traded in Equities

(Three-month moving average of value traded in local currency terms, indexed to January 2007 = 100)

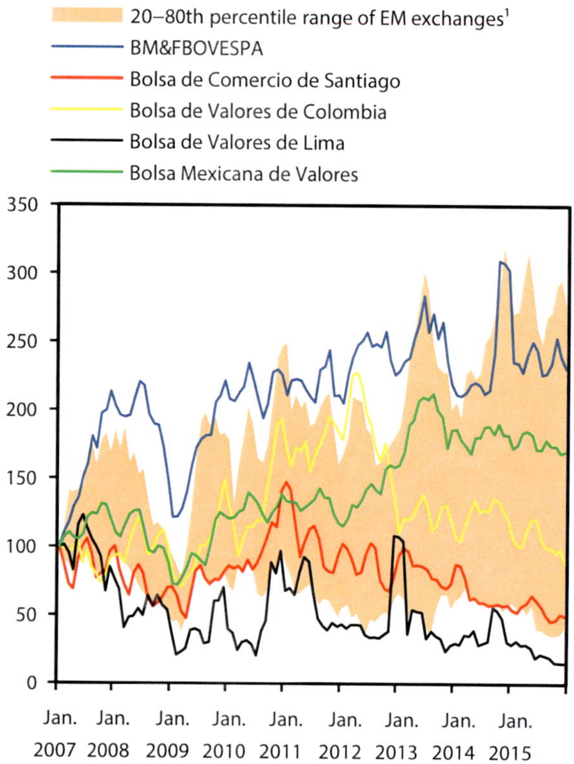

Source: World Federation of Exchanges.
[1]Selected emerging market (EM) exchanges in Argentina, Bermuda, Chile, China, Colombia, Cyprus, Egypt, Indonesia, India, Iran, Israel, Malaysia, Malta, Mauritius, Mexico, Panama, Peru, Philippines, Poland, Slovenia, Sri Lanka, South Africa, Taiwan, Thailand, and Turkey.

smaller equity markets (Chile, Colombia, and Peru) and remained largely flat for Brazil and Mexico. The drop in trading activity is likely tied to slowing macroeconomic prospects as the commodity super-cycle ended. This has raised concerns about a vicious circle in which lower trade volumes raise the cost of buying and selling large blocks, which further reduces market liquidity. Also, Latin American exchanges, noted for their high commission and settlement costs, need higher volumes of trades to push down per-trade transaction costs.

Experience with the MILA initiative has shown a demand for cross holdings of regional assets. However trading on the MILA exchange has not met expectations, with volumes averaging only about 260 trades per month at an average value of about $7 million since 2011. Several factors are cited as impediments to more robust trading on the MILA exchange in particular and among the LA-7 countries in general. These include the following:

- Higher costs to trade in regional markets compared with trading in advanced exchanges. Issues of high commission costs,[5] large bid/ask spreads in the region, and the fact that many shares trade only sporadically should be addressed to attract more regional participation.
- Operating in the cross-currency markets adds costs to transactions. If brokers, bankers, and institutional investors want to buy a foreign (regional) security and do not have internal access to foreign currency, they must first sell local currency for dollars (usually through New York), then buy the foreign currency (again through New York) before buying the asset. Both foreign exchange transactions incur charges and then they are charged again when they sell the position and repatriate the receipts. Capital controls in Brazil raise costs further for investors looking to enter the largest capital market in the region.
- Variance in tax rates/rules and administrative procedures. The opportunity exists to standardize and coordinate clearing and depository practices across the region.
- Poor sectoral diversity across some markets. The largest and most liquid debt and equity issuers in Chilean, Colombian, and Peruvian markets tend to be natural resource (mining) related firms which, over the past decade, have experienced highly correlated business cycles. Equity markets in Brazil and Mexico offer investors a variety of more diversified sectors from which to choose.

POLICY RECOMMENDATIONS

Broker-dealers should be permitted to operate across borders. They should be subject to supervision by both the home and host country regulatory agencies but should receive the same regulatory treatment as domestic firms.

Financial infrastructure should be harmonized across the region, including trading hours and interoperability of trading and settlement platforms. This would facilitate higher trading volumes, lower commission/settlement costs, and reduce reliance on more expensive correspondent brokerage services.

A special "bucket" should be introduced that would allow pension funds to hold regional securities that do not count against foreign securities asset class limits. As described in the recommendations for pension fund integration (Chapter 5), this bucket should have a small cap of 5 percent of assets and would apply only to countries that meet agreed-upon regulatory standards. This recommendation is motivated by the expectation that pension funds would be among the most active participants in regional capital markets if their holdings were not counted against the general foreign asset cap.

---

[5] Pagano (2009) finds median commission costs in South America to be more than two and half times those in the United States and higher than those in all other emerging market regions except the Middle East and Africa.

International Financial Reporting Standards should be used throughout the region. Countries that have not yet done so should adopt the multilateral memorandum of observance of principles and practices as set out by the Bank for International Settlements and IOSCO related to governance, monitoring, mitigating financial and operational risk, and exchanging information. Also, where they are not yet in effect, double taxation avoidance treaties should be signed and, over time, countries should seek convergence in their tax rates.

ANNEX 6.1. FOREIGN EXCHANGE TURNOVER OF LATIN AMERICAN CURRENCIES

Offshore trading continues to dominate turnover rates of Latin American currencies, with the majority of transactions taking place in the United States and the United Kingdom.[6] Foreign exchange turnover of emerging market currencies has been predominantly driven by the offshore component in many regions (Annex Figure 6.1.1), which testifies to the growing internationalization of currency, particularly as foreign exchange turnover expansion outpaces trade growth. Latin America continues to have the largest share of offshore currency trading among emerging markets, closely followed by central and eastern Europe (CEE), and well above emerging markets in Asia. The market patterns of offshore turnover of the currencies of Latin America, emerging Asia, and CEE appear to vary in response to geographic proximity as well as trade and financial linkages with offshore jurisdictions. Emerging Asian currencies, for example, have the lowest share of offshore trading, and nearly half of their offshore transactions occur in the regional financial centers: Hong Kong SAR and Singapore. Offshore trades of Latin American and CEE currencies, on the other hand, are largely concentrated in extraregional financial centers, given the absence of sufficiently large financial centers in the region. Although the majority of offshore turnover of CEE currencies occurs in the United Kingdom, financial centers in the United States constitute the largest markets for trading Latin American currencies, accounting for more than half of the offshore turnover.

Global turnover of Latin American currencies is dominated by the Mexican peso (about 65 percent of offshore turnover), followed by the Brazilian real. In 2013, the Mexican peso joined the ranks of the 10 most traded currencies, largely against the U.S. dollar and in the form of foreign exchange swaps and spot transactions (Annex Figure 6.1.2). In turnover ranking, the Mexican peso trails only the national currencies of the United States, the European Union, Japan, the United Kingdom, Australia, Switzerland, and Canada. The Mexican peso is fully convertible, free-floating, without any exchange controls, and widely accepted around the world. It experienced one of the biggest increases among the major emerging market currencies in market share up to 2013, when its turnover reached $135 billion, raising its market share in global foreign exchange trading to 2.5 percent (from 1.3 percent in 2010[7]) and significantly lifting Mexican peso turnover in the domestic market and in offshore jurisdictions. At 80 percent, the Mexican peso's share of offshore trading is among the highest among emerging markets, trailing only the Polish zloty and the Turkish lira.

Turnover in the Mexican peso increased largely as a result of increasing investor confidence and growing market liquidity. Unrestricted access (the Mexican

[6] Based on data and analysis from Bank for International Settlements, Triennial Central Bank Survey (April 2013).

[7] Because two currencies are involved in each outstanding contract, the sum of the percentage shares of individual currencies totals 200 percent.

Annex Figure 6.1.1 Offshore Trading of Emerging Market Currencies
(Percent of total onshore and offshore over-the-counter foreign exchange market turnover[1])

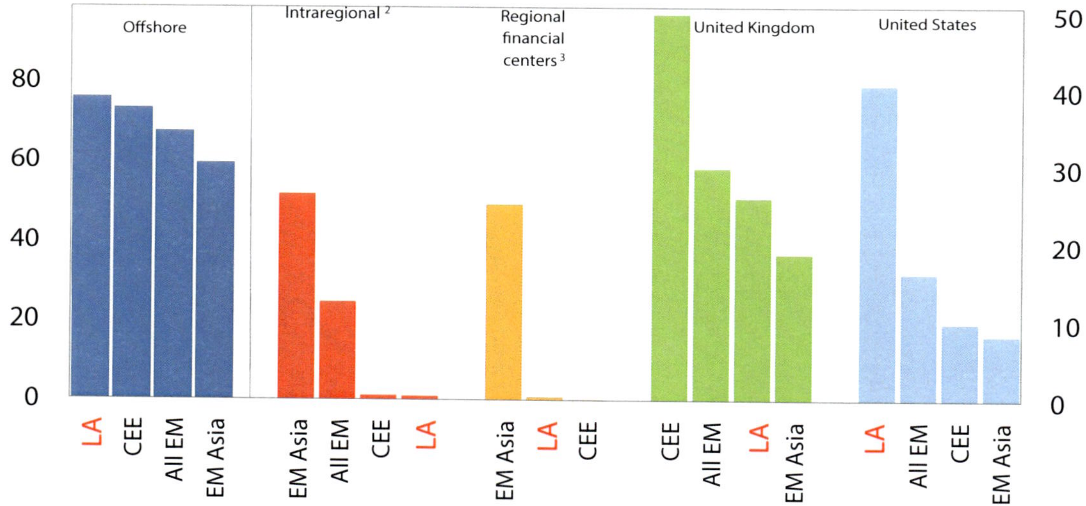

Sources: Bank for International Settlements (BIS), Triennial Central Bank Survey, and BIS staff calculations; and IMF staff calculations.
[1] Daily average in April 2013. Adjusted for local and cross-border inter-dealer double-counting (that is, net-net basis). Latin American currencies (LA) = Argentine peso, Brazilian real, Chilean peso, Colombian peso, Mexican peso, and Peruvian nuevo sol. Weighted averages based on foreign exchange turnover. Central and eastern European (CEE) currencies = Bulgarian lev, Czech koruna, Hungarian forint, Latvian lats, Lithuanian lats, Polish zloty, Romanian leu, Russian rouble, and Turkish lira. Emerging Asian (EM Asia) currencies = Chinese renminbi, Hong Kong dollar, Indian rupee, Indonesian rupiah, Korean won, Malaysian ringgit, New Taiwan dollar, Philippine peso, Singapore dollar, and Thai baht. All emerging market (All EM) currencies = Asia, Bahrain dinar, CEE, Israeli new shekel, LA, Saudi riyal, and South African rand.
[2] Intraregional is defined as all offshore trades within the respective EM region.
[3] Regional centers: Hong Kong SAR and Singapore for EM Asia; Brazil and Mexico for Latin America; and Turkey and Russia for CEE.

Annex Figure 6.1.2 Global Foreign Exchange Market Turnover by Currency

(Percent of global foreign exchange market, top 10 performers in 2013,[1] net-net basis[2])

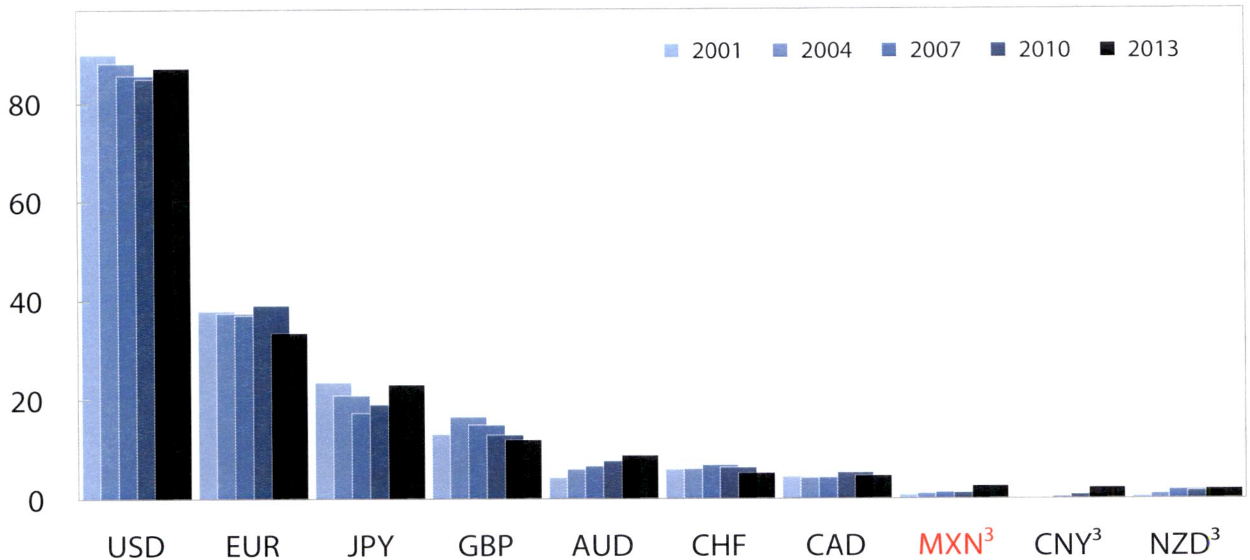

Sources: Bank for International Settlements (BIS), Triennial Central Bank Survey, 2013; BIS staff calculations; and IMF staff estimates and calculations.

[1] Percentage shares of average daily turnover in April.

[2] Because two currencies are involved in each transaction, the sum of the percentage shares of individual currencies totals 200 percent instead of 100 percent.

[3]Turnover for years prior to 2013 may be underestimated owing to incomplete reporting of offshore trading in previous surveys. AUD = Australian dollar; CAD = Canadian dollar; CHF = Swiss franc; CNY = renminbi; EUR = euro; GBP = pound sterling; JPY = yen; MXN = Mexican peso; NZD = New Zealand dollar; USD = U.S. dollar.

peso trades globally 24 hours a day) plays a fundamental role in its rising popularity. The high liquidity of Mexican assets also stimulates turnover of the domestic currency. Its popularity received a boost after the size of the Mexican bond market led Citigroup to add Mexican peso-denominated debt to its World Government Bond Index in late 2010, making Mexico the first Latin American country in the benchmark.

ANNEX 6.2. THE INTEREST RATE DERIVATIVES MARKET IN MEXICO

The bulk of the interest rate derivatives denominated in Mexican pesos are traded predominantly in the offshore markets, mainly in the United States. Mexico's vibrant interest rate derivatives market is composed primarily of TIIE (Tasa de Interes Interbancaria de Equilibio, the equilibrium interbank interest rate) interest rate swaps, with an overwhelming share of trading taking place outside of platforms via the over-the-counter (OTC) market. OTC turnover of single currency interest rate derivatives denominated in the Mexican peso stood at US$12.3 billion in April 2013,[8] representing about 0.4 percent of the global OTC single currency interest rate derivatives market, trailing only the OTC interest rate market denominated in the Brazilian real (Annex Figure 6.2.1).[9] However, less than a fifth (US$2.4 billion) of the Mexican peso turnover is cleared in Mexico, while the remaining 82 percent clears through offshore markets, mainly in the United States (Annex Figure 6.2.2).

A number of factors have accounted for the burgeoning offshore OTC market, including Mexico's close ties with the United States, delay in establishing a well-functioning trading platform, and lower costs of OTC transactions. Although it was established in the late 1990s, the Mexican derivatives platform MexDer (Mercado Mexicano de derivados) did not become an important financial player until a few years ago. Thus, until recently, in the absence of a well-functioning platform, interest rate hedging needs were predominantly met through the OTC market. Higher fees, associated largely with the technological and technical costs of the trading platform, continue to contribute to the general preference for the OTC market.

Recent regulatory adjustments in the European Union and the United States call for the trading of standardized OTC derivative contracts on exchanges or electronic platforms, and for their clearance through a recognized central counterparty (CCP), while non-centrally-cleared contracts would be subject to higher capital requirements. In the spirit of alignment with global standards, the Mexican authorities have introduced a new regulation, scheduled for gradual implementation, that will require OTC derivative trades to take place on exchanges or through interdealer brokers and that provides for a mandatory clearing of standardized derivatives through a CCP—Mexican (if established in Mexico and authorized by the Secretariat of Finance and Public Credit) or foreign (if recognized by Banco de Mexico). Since April 2016 compliance with the new regulation is required for transactions between Mexican entities; November 2016 marked the start date for transactions involving foreign financial institutions.

In addition to making derivatives markets safer, the new Mexican regulation is expected to improve competition between domestic and foreign clearinghouses.

[8] Based on the Bank for International Settlements, Triennial Central Bank Survey.

[9] Database covers the following Latin American countries: Argentina, Brazil, Chile, Colombia, Mexico, and Peru.

Annex Figure 6.2.1 Over-the-Counter Interest Rate Derivative Turnover Composition

(Billions of U.S. dollars, single currency, by instrument and currency, April 2013)

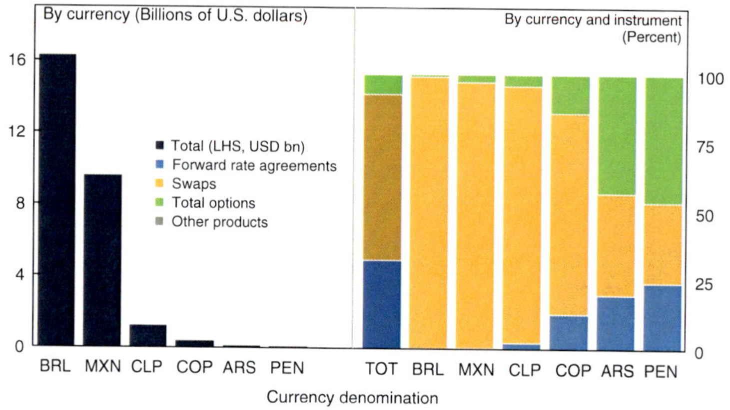

Sources: Bank for International Settlements (BIS), Triennial Survey 2013; and IMF staff estimates and calculations.
Note: ARS = Argentine peso; BRL = Brazilian real; CLP = Chilean peso; COP = Colombian peso; MXN = Mexican peso; PEN = Peruvian nuevo sol; TOT = all currencies.

Annex Figure 6.2.2 Over-the-Counter Interest Rate Derivative Turnover Country and Currency

(Percent, single currency, April 2013[1])

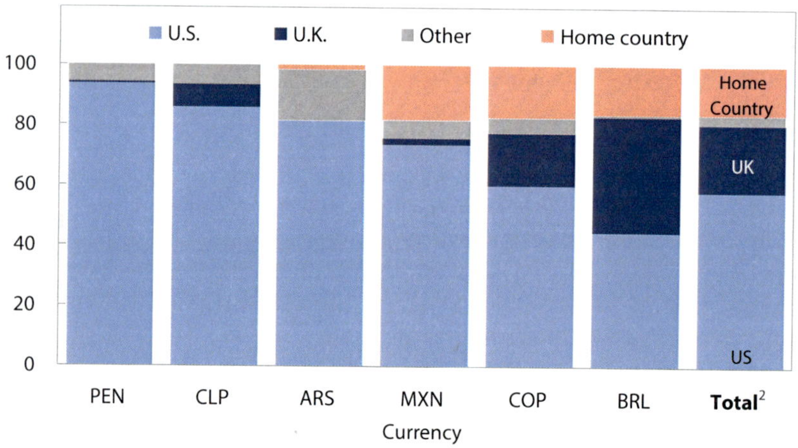

Sources: Bank for International Settlements, Triennial Survey 2013; and IMF staff estimates and calculations.
[1] ARS = Argentine peso; BRL = Brazilian real; CLP = Chilean peso; COP = Colombian peso; MXN = Mexican peso; PEN = Peruvian new sol. Forward rate agreements, swaps, options and other products. Adjusted for local inter-dealer double-counting (that is, "net-gross" basis).
[2] All Latin American currencies in the sample.

Over the medium term, the regulation is expected to increase the volume of contracts traded through MexDer and cleared through Asigna, the Mexican central clearinghouse for derivatives. However, given the large presence of foreign institutions, Asigna is likely to continue facing strong competition from offshore CCPs—such as Chicago Mercantile Exchange and LHC. Clearnet Ltd. (a European clearinghouse)—as foreign institutions are expected to continue clearing their derivatives offshore. By clearing through a CCP in the parent country, multinational entities can consolidate their operations by netting their derivative positions vis-à-vis the positions of the parent and other subsidiaries, thereby decreasing capital requirements. The operations of MexDer and Asigna are likely to continue expanding largely through the derivative trading businesses of Mexican institutional investors, such as pension funds. While the new regulatory changes constitute a welcome step toward market transparency and lower risk, additional technical and technological improvements are needed to boost Asigna's and MexDer's competitiveness.

REFERENCES

Ananchotikul, S., and B. Eichengreen. 2008. "Plumbing for Latin American Capital Markets." In *New Financing Trends in Latin America: A Bumpy Road towards Stability*, 110–39. Bank for International Settlements, Basel.

Pagano, M. 2009. "Which Factors Influence Trading Costs in Global Equity Markets?" *Journal of Trading*, 4 (1): 7–15.

Zervos, S. 2004. "The Transactions Costs of Primary Market Issuance: The Case of Brazil, Chile, and Mexico." Policy Research Working Paper 3424, World Bank, Washington.

CHAPTER 7

Legal Barriers to Regional Financial Integration in Latin America

LAURA LORENZO AND WOUTER BOSSU

Legal frameworks shape the context in which economic transactions take place, both within a given economy and between economies. Laws and regulations allow private economic agents to establish and (re)organize themselves, to seek finance, to enter markets by selling products and services, to enforce payment claims when customers are entering into default on obligations, and to exit a market in an orderly way when so desired or required. It is widely accepted that well-designed legal frameworks for market entry, operation, and exit can promote economic growth and, from a cross-border perspective, integration of economies and financial systems.

This chapter analyzes legal frameworks in the context of the cross-border integration of financial systems in Latin America. Specifically, the authors try to determine which legal barriers hinder the cross-border establishment of financial firms, the provision of financial services, and the flow of financial investments. The authors explore how carefully designed law reform could remove some of those barriers with a view to improving market access.

The specific perspective of this chapter is that, in designing legal frameworks for market entry and operation, the objective of openness must be balanced with the objective of financial stability. The goal is not to advocate the removal of *all* barriers. Many legal provisions that hinder financial activity (by imposing a cost on it) have been established for good reasons and should be retained. For example, this is the case for the minimum capital, governance, and "fit and proper" requirements placed on financial firms. However, in many jurisdictions, including in Latin America, potential market entrants face legal barriers that are not intended to ensure financial stability but rather to pursue other public policy objectives (for example, protecting the local market) or private economic interests (rents). Removal of such barriers can contribute to enhanced financial integration, which means more competition, more choice, and lower prices for consumers. In addition, some LA-7 countries[1] maintain certain legal instruments aimed

[1] LA-7 refers to Brazil, Chile, Colombia, Mexico, Panama, Peru, and Uruguay.

Figure 7.1 Financial Stability–Openness Frontier

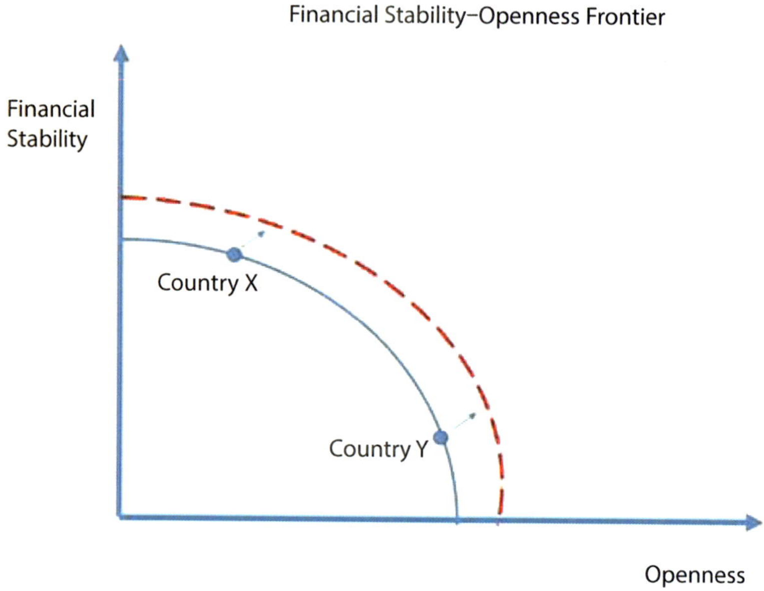

at pursuing financial stability that are actually not effective in that pursuit. In this regard, the authors recommend strengthening the legal framework so countries are better equipped to deal with the financial stability risk stemming from foreign entrants; in other words, to create a better equilibrium between openness and financial stability. Using a parallel with the economic concept of the "production-possibility frontier," we believe it is better, through the general improvement of the financial regulatory toolkit, to push the range of possible equilibria between financial stability and openness outward, as illustrated in Figure 7.1, instead of moving on the existing curve. This implies that, for most if not all countries, it is possible to seek both more financial stability and more openness.

The chapter provides a brief overview of the methodology designed by the authors to assess the existence of legal barriers, identifies such barriers in the LA-7 countries, and suggests mechanisms to remove the barriers and strengthen the legal underpinnings of financial stability.

METHODOLOGY

Analyzing all legal rules that have or may have an impact on all types of cross-border flows is potentially a huge endeavor. To make the exercise workable, it is therefore imperative to clearly define parameters for the analysis. The methodology developed for this purpose is limited and therefore imperfect, but it may serve as a template for similar analysis in other regions, or in the same region at a later time.

What Is Meant by "Regional Financial Integration" in a Legal Sense?

First, it is necessary to define the types of financial activities and transactions that are considered in this chapter and hence from a legal perspective as manifestations of regional financial integration. In line with the general practice of trade law analysis, the authors distinguish between (1) the right of cross-border establishment and (2) the right to provide cross-border services. They also analyze certain cross-border financial flows of financial firms.

- With regard to the *right of cross-border establishment*, the authors focus specifically on the legal framework for the cross-border opening of establishments by banks and insurance firms; investment firms (such as broker-dealers or asset managers) are not part of the exercise. They focus on the right of foreign firms to open establishments (in this chapter, subsidiaries and branches) in the host country and briefly address the right of firms under their home country rules to expand abroad. The difference between branches and subsidiaries is that subsidiaries have a separate legal personality under the law of the host country, whereas branches do not—they are legally one with the parent bank/insurance firm in the home country. Once licensed, both subsidiaries and branches are authorized to offer banking (taking deposits and making loans) and insurance services, albeit possibly under certain limitations, especially for branches. The third form of establishment, representative offices, is not allowed to offer banking or insurance services in the host country and is less relevant for this exercise.
- With regard to the *right to provide cross-border services*, the chapter concentrates mainly on two specific but interesting questions, and views them more from the perspective of the *acquisition* of services than the *provision* of services: (1) the right to acquire insurance coverage abroad and (2) the right of local pension funds to outsource part of their asset management tasks to foreign asset managers.
- With regard to *cross-border financial flows*, the chapter analyzes the extent to which pension funds and insurance firms are allowed to invest a part of their portfolios in foreign financial assets.

In many countries, the rules governing the cross-border right of establishment, provision of services, and financial flows do not distinguish between regional and other possible foreign entrants. In some countries, where the right of access is provided by treaty, such a distinction can be made. The authors consider that general openness constitutes regional openness and that, conversely, generally applicable barriers constitute barriers to regional integration.

Which Legal Rules Are Analyzed?

Many types of legal provisions and rules are capable of obstructing or hindering regional financial integration. To remain within the boundaries of the practically feasible, the chapter's analysis focuses on legal issues that directly hinder cross-border financial integration as defined in the previous paragraphs; namely, the opening of cross-border establishments by banks and insurance firms, the cross-border acquisition of certain financial services, and the cross-border flows of pension funds and insurance firms.

The analysis focuses on rules enshrined in primary legislation but, where relevant, also includes secondary regulation. In most countries, including most of the LA-7 countries, primary legislation provides the basic and most stable framework for financial market entry and operation. Many countries also include important rules regarding market access in secondary regulation, such as decrees issued by the government or regulations adopted by financial regulators. These rules tend to be more detailed and less stable (that is, they are modified more easily and more often).

Thus, the analysis of this chapter focuses on domestic law as established in internal constitutions, laws, decrees, regulations, and other local legal instruments. The authors do not analyze in detail the obligations of the LA-7 countries under public international law stemming from treaties and similar international instruments. However, the authors recognize that several of the domestic rules analyzed have been adopted pursuant to or shaped by international legal obligations. In one instance (Mexico), domestic rules make an explicit and direct reference to access rights acquired under public international law. Box 7.1 gives a brief overview of the role of public international treaties in regional financial integration.

Which Legal Rules Are Not Analyzed?

This chapter does not analyze certain legal frameworks even though they have a direct impact on cross-border financial integration; one such framework is the exchange controls rulebook. Several LA-7 countries still maintain exchange controls, and in some instances these controls may have a significant impact on the extent to which the local financial system is capable of integrating with those of other countries in the region. For example, some countries do not allow residents to maintain foreign currency deposits in local banks. The tax laws are also not analyzed in this chapter, although they obviously have a significant impact on cross-border financial flows.[2] For instance, the tax treatment of interest (coupon) payments of bonds determines the degree to which local bonds are attractive to investors from other countries.[3]

The authors recognize that the absence of a detailed analysis of exchange controls and tax frameworks makes the current exercise imperfect. However, it is widely accepted that strict exchange controls and convoluted taxation rules

[2] With regard to Latin America specifically, see Tanzi, Barreix, and Villela (2008).

[3] For a European Union perspective on this issue, see De Wolf (2005).

Box 7.1 The Role of International Treaties in Regional Financial Integration

Public international law can play a big role in opening countries' legal frameworks for the cross-border establishment of financial firms and provision of services. Important legal instruments in this regard are multilateral, regional, and bilateral free trade agreements (FTAs), as well as bilateral investment treaties.

The countries that make up the LA-7 (Brazil, Chile, Colombia, Mexico, Panama, Peru, and Uruguay) have made use of international treaties to open up their financial sectors, mainly through the General Agreement on Trade in Services (GATS). All LA-7 countries are members of the World Trade Organization (WTO), and in that capacity they are automatically also signatories to GATS. All LA-7 countries have undertaken specific commitments under GATS with regard to their financial sectors, thus submitting them to GATS' "market access" and "national treatment" principles, which have a liberalizing effect.

In this context, however, the LA-7 countries have also maintained many of the barriers discussed in this chapter as limitations to their specific commitments under GATS. Examples of this are the requirement under Mexican law that banks and insurance companies enter the market as subsidiaries or the requirement of a Presidential Decree imposed upon foreign financial institutions to access the market in Brazil. Both measures are excluded from the countries' specific commitments on market access.

Intra–LA-7 (pluri-lateral or bilateral) FTAs have until now rarely been used to achieve a much higher degree of regional openness than was achieved globally through WTO membership. GATS includes the option to grant preferential treatment (as an exception to Most Favored Nation treatment) among trading partners within a customs union or a free trade area. This offers to LA-7 countries the possibility to achieve a higher degree of regional openness without automatically granting similar treatment to WTO members from outside the region, at least at this stage. The LA-7 countries have made little or no use of this possibility. Many of their intra–LA-7 FTAs do not apply to financial services. Of the FTAs that apply to financial services, many include the barriers discussed in this chapter among their nonconforming measures, and in some instances the FTAs' provisions are too general to provide a robust legal basis for access.

Going forward, the scope of application of the intra–LA-7 FTAs could in some cases be expanded to include financial services, and nonconforming measures without direct bearing on financial stability (or other appropriate public policy objectives, such as social security) could be eliminated.

hinder cross-border financial integration. It is fair to say that the LA-7 countries would be well advised to regularly review their exchange controls and taxation rules to ensure that these frameworks do not excessively hinder cross-border financial transactions and operations.

This chapter does not address legal problems that hinder financial sector development more broadly without operating as direct cross-border barriers, such as creditor rights and quality of the judiciary. Well-designed contractual and collateral enforcement frameworks and a high-quality judiciary generally support growth of the financial system, thus creating an incentive for foreign entrants. Problems in these areas may constitute indirect barriers in the sense that well-connected local incumbents are probably better placed than new foreign entrants to navigate the legal complexities that arise in this context.

LEGAL BARRIERS TO REGIONAL FINANCIAL INTEGRATION

This section provides a relatively detailed overview of the manner in which the legal frameworks of the LA-7 countries authorize the forms of regional financial integration described above. The authors discuss direct barriers to entry and expansion as well as rules and mechanisms that hinder or could hinder the opening of certain forms of establishments.

Cross-Border Establishments of Financial Institutions

Outward Openness

All LA-7 countries generally authorize the opening abroad of establishments of their local financial firms, albeit sometimes under idiosyncratic conditions. All countries require prior approval of the home supervisor or—occasionally, for some operations—the ministry of finance.[4] Some countries impose the standard condition that the establishment abroad must allow for effective consolidated supervision of the bank.[5] Other countries, however, impose more onerous conditions. For instance, Brazil requires that expanding Brazilian banks, in addition to standard requirements, have been in business for at least six years and hold a capital surcharge of 300 percent.[6] In Chile, the capital of a branch established abroad must be no less than 3 percent of the bank's total assets.[7]

Inward Openness

The LA-7 countries differ considerably in the extent to which they authorize the opening of establishments in their own jurisdictions by foreign financial firms. Several countries (for example Colombia, Panama, and Peru) have open regimes as a matter of law: their financial legislation explicitly allows foreign banks and insurance firms to open both subsidiaries and branches. In most instances, such openings are subject to appropriate legal conditions in line with international good practices. For instance, in Colombia, foreign financial firms can establish subsidiaries, but the supervisor may condition such establishment on the existence of consolidated supervision of the foreign parent and the consent of the home supervisor.[8]

Several LA-7 countries maintain in their legislation formal legal barriers to the opening of certain types of establishments of foreign financial firms in their territory. Some of these barriers are fundamental in that they reflect a strong policy

---

[4] See, e.g., Article 87 of the Mexican Banking Law.

[5] In Brazil, see Article 2 of Resolution 2723/2000.

[6] Article 2 of Resolution 2723/2000.

[7] Article 81 No. 2, Chapter 11-7, III, 3(a) of the Instructions of SBIF "Recopilación Actualizada de Normas."

[8] Article 53.3.f. of Organic Statute of the Financial System.

preference of local authorities regarding whether or how foreign financial firms should enter their market, while others are more idiosyncratic.

- In Brazil, the key provisions of the framework governing the access of non-residents to the Brazilian financial market are included in the Constitution, which requires Congress to specifically enact legislation regarding the participation of foreign capital in the financial sector.[9] Until such legislation is enacted (and none has been enacted to date), nonresidents are not allowed to hold shares in domestic financial institutions (mainly banks but not insurance firms).[10] Shareholdings that existed when the Constitution entered into force on October 5, 1988, are grandfathered, but the constitutional prohibition extends to increases in equity stakes in domestic banks. The president of the republic can grant a waiver for this constitutional prohibition on the basis of (1) international agreements, (2) reciprocity, or (3) the interest of the government.[11] To obtain a presidential waiver, the central bank reviews and submits for the president's decision, the application for licensing of a bank in which a nonresident intends to hold a direct or indirect participation, or for acquisition of or increase in direct or indirect participation in an existing bank by a nonresident.[12]
- Mexico explicitly prohibits branches of foreign banks and insurance firms, and authorizes subsidiaries only under specific conditions. Only a foreign financial institution established in a country with which Mexico has entered into a treaty or agreement allowing for the establishment of subsidiaries may establish a subsidiary in Mexican territory.[13] Mexico also requires that a majority of the members of the board of directors and all members of the executive board of banks reside in Mexico.[14]
- In Uruguay, foreign banks are allowed to set up subsidiaries and branches in the country provided their by-laws or policies do not bar Uruguayan citizens from serving as directors, managers, or employees in their operations in Uruguay.[15]

Overly Broad Provisions

Even where legislative frameworks allow for entry, legislation in some LA-7 countries contains very broad provisions whose implementation may inhibit access to the local market for some types of financial firms.

[9] Article 192 of the Constitution.
[10] Article 52 of the Constitution, Transitional Provisions.
[11] The acquisition of nonvoting shares in a publicly traded financial institution is presumed to be in the government's interest, and the waiver is automatically granted (Presidential Decree of December 9, 1996).
[12] Article 1 of BCB Circular 3317/2006.
[13] Article 45-A of the Banking Law.
[14] Article 45-K and L of the Banking Law.
[15] Article 8 of Decree-Law 15322/1982.

- One example of such broad provisions is statutory conditions that make the licensing of the establishment of firms subject to a very broadly drafted "best interests of the economy" test. For instance, in Panama, the banking license can be refused if "the bank does not contribute to Panama's economy."[16]
- Some countries' supervisory legislation also features broad discretionary powers for supervisors in issuing normative instruments or individual decisions. For instance, in Panama, banking law authorizes the supervisor to make the license subject to "any criterion it deems pertinent."[17]

None of these provisions are restrictive per se or have been found in practice to have led to discriminatory treatment of foreign firms. Nonetheless, their very broad wording could, in principle, be used to restrict market access. Potential foreign entrants will naturally read those provisions in light of the supervisory practices and attitudes displayed by the supervisor and possibly also the government. Where those practices and attitudes are entrant friendly, the provisions are unlikely to cause much concern; however, where doubt exists, overly broad provisions contribute to uncertainty about the climate within which the request for licensing will be received, and this may discourage entry.

Restrictive or Discriminatory Conditions

Among the LA-7 countries where the legal right to entry of foreign financial firms exists, some subject branches of foreign banks to rules that effectively diminish the advantages of that business model. Compared to subsidiaries, branches are a low-cost form of entry (for example, the management structure is lighter, as there is no need to have a separate board of directors) and therefore often preferred by banks as an initial method of greenfield entry. However, where branches of foreign banks are regulated in exactly the same manner as locally incorporated banks, notwithstanding differences in circumstances,[18] this advantage vanishes, and foreign entrants basically have to carry a cost almost equal to the cost of establishing a subsidiary.

Specifically, several LA-7 countries impose identical capital adequacy requirements (CARs) on branches of foreign banks and locally incorporated banks. This ignores the fact that the branch's head office remains legally liable for the obligations of the branch, and imposes a high cost on the branch. Panama is one country that does not follow this approach: the CAR is not applied separately to the branch, although the parent must annually certify compliance of the parent's consolidated CAR with the home country's requirements.[19]

Several LA-7 countries apply discriminatory ring-fencing rules against foreign-owned branches. These rules provide that if a branch of a foreign bank enters into

---

[16] Article 48.3 of the Banking Law.

[17] Article 48.5 of the Banking Law.

[18] See, for example, Article 45A of the Colombian Banking Law and Article 39, 4th paragraph of the Peruvian Banking Law.

[19] Article 18 of Regulation No. 001-2015.

liquidation, the assets of the local branch will be distributed by priority to creditors of the local branch. (In other words, the assets of the branch will not be handed over to the home country liquidator of the parent bank, with the understanding that the host country creditors will file their claim on the estate of the failed bank according to home country rules.) Well-designed ring-fencing rules are nondiscriminatory and treat all creditors of the branch in a similar manner. Panama is a good example of a country with nondiscriminatory rules.[20] In contrast, under Chilean, Colombian, and Peruvian law, creditors who reside in the country are preferred over nonresident creditors of the local branch.[21] Such treatment discourages nonresident parties from maintaining deposits in or providing loans to foreign-owned branches: because the claims of such creditors would be subordinated to the claims of local creditors if the branch were liquidated, they are more likely to establish business relationships with locally incorporated institutions where such discriminatory treatment will not apply upon insolvency.

Cross-Border Acquisition of Financial Services

Several countries prohibit residents from acquiring certain types of financial services abroad. This chapter is not concerned with typical restrictions under an exchange control framework designed to support a country's exchange rate policy, such as rules that prohibit residents from holding foreign currency abroad or acquiring certain foreign financial instruments (such as bonds or shares). Rather, the chapter focuses on financial services provided by foreign providers that should have little impact on a country's balance of payments. For instance,

- In Panama and Mexico, local residents are precluded from acquiring certain types of insurance contracts abroad.[22]
- Most LA-7 countries impose restrictions on the ability of local pension funds to outsource part of their asset management tasks to foreign asset managers (this is allowed only in Chile).
- In Brazil, both retail and professional investors may invest abroad only through a locally registered investment fund.

Cross-Border Financial Flows

All the LA-7 countries allow insurance firms to invest in financial assets abroad; however, domestic legislations impose limits on these investments, typically in percentage of capital and technical reserves. Most legal frameworks establish a minimum percentage that must be invested in "safe" securities; namely, those

[20] See Article 221 of the Banking Law.

[21] See Article 34 of the Chilean Banking Law, Article 45B.2 of the Colombian Banking Law, and Article 39 in fine of the Peruvian Banking Law. Reservations to obligations under free trade agreements may include such ring-fencing; see for example Peru.

[22] See Article 153 of the Panama Insurance Law and Article 21 of the Mexican Insurance Law.

issued or backed by the (domestic) state or the central bank.[23] For the remaining percentage, laws or regulations set a general maximum limit on investments in foreign financial assets and, within that limit, some individual limits depending on the type of instrument.[24] Moreover, most legal frameworks grant the supervisory authority significant discretion to set additional limits, for example, for each issuance[25] or even more generally.[26]

A similar approach applies to investments by pension funds in the LA-7. Several of these countries have established different general limits for different classes of funds: the higher the yield of the fund, the higher the limit on foreign investments; the more conservative the fund, the lower the limit on foreign investments. In addition to such general limits and for purposes of risk mitigation, legal frameworks also set specific limits by issuer and for each issuance.

The imposition of such limits on foreign investments is not a barrier per se, as such limits are needed for the purpose of risk mitigation.[27] There are, however, two instances in which such rules could inappropriately hinder cross-border financial flows. First, the general or specific limits could be very low compared with stated public policy objectives. From a policy perspective it is possible to argue about the appropriate limit, but limits under 20 percent are considered very low.[28] Second, some supervisory authorities might be granted a very high degree of discretion to impose additional limits. In both instances, the concern arises that these limits could be used to artificially promote investment only in national instruments, thus creating a captive market to the detriment of sound risk diversification.

REMOVAL OF LEGAL BARRIERS

To the extent that barriers hinder regional financial integration without yielding significant financial stability benefits, countries should consider replacing them with legal provisions that yield a better equilibrium between the two public policy

---

[23] For example, in Colombia at least 40 percent of the technical reserves must be backed by investments in securities issued or backed by the Colombian state or the central bank, or by other highly liquid, secure, and profitable securities.

[24] In Chile, the legal framework establishes a general limit of 20 percent for foreign instruments. Within that limit, the law sets a 5 percent limit for debt securities, deposits, bonds, promissory notes, and other debt securities issued by foreign financial institutions with a rating under BBB or N-3, and a 10 percent limit for shares of foreign companies or corporations, shares in foreign mutual or investment funds, and shares in Chilean mutual or investment funds with investments abroad.

[25] That is the case in Chile: see Decreto con fuerza de ley 251, "Compañías de Seguros, Sociedades Anónimas y Bolsas de Comercio," Article 24.

[26] See Article 200, paragraph 8, of the Peruvian Banking and Insurance Law.

[27] The Organisation for Economic Co-operation and Development (OECD) "Guidelines on Pension Fund Asset Management" allow the inclusion of maximum levels of investment by category (ceilings) to the extent that they are consistent with and promote the prudential principles of security, profitability, and liquidity pursuant to which assets should be invested (OECD 2006). However, the OECD does not provide guidelines on appropriate quantitative limits.

[28] See, for instance, Chile's 20 percent limit on insurance firms and Uruguay's 15 percent limit for pension funds.

objectives. In some instances this will require enhancing the legal framework to effectively address the specific financial stability risks posed by increased foreign activity in a country's jurisdiction. The removal of barriers can take place at several levels.

First and foremost, regional financial integration would be supported if all countries across the region were to have in place objective and comprehensive entry regimes for foreign financial firms in primary legislation. Ideally, these regimes provide for entry in the form of both subsidiaries and branches of foreign firms. The use of primary legislation offers a more transparent and stable legal regime than secondary rules and regulations.[29] This approach also guides individual decision making by prudential supervisory authorities and shields them from excessive discretionary powers that can lead to the perception of arbitrary decision making. Overly broad best interest tests and discretionary licensing criteria are best avoided. If they cannot be avoided, safeguards can be provided in the form of transparent administrative guidance on how the tests and licensing criteria will be applied; for example, in the form of circulars from the supervisory authority.

Beyond the rules on access to the market, certain conditions imposed on establishments of foreign firms do not contribute to financial stability. Several Latin American countries maintain measures that, while increasing the cost of cross-border operations, are fully appropriate in light of the imperative to maintain financial stability; for example, limits on intragroup exposures for subsidiaries, local asset maintenance requirements for branches, and the power to ring-fence a local branch of a foreign bank in a nondiscriminatory manner. However, when those measures include excessive or discriminatory characteristics that hinder cross-border integration without yielding meaningful financial stability benefits, they could be modified to better balance financial stability with openness. Removing the discriminatory aspect of ring-fencing mechanisms for foreign branches (already done by Panama) would be particularly useful in this regard. Reconsidering residence requirements for directors and senior managers[30] (already done by most LA-7 countries) is also appropriate.

Rules prohibiting local residents from acquiring certain foreign financial services should also be reviewed. Chile, Colombia, and Peru present good examples of how barriers can be removed by explicitly authorizing in primary legislation residents to acquire foreign insurance coverage abroad.[31]

THE NEED TO STRENGTHEN SOME ASPECTS OF THE LEGAL FRAMEWORK

In search of a better equilibrium between openness and financial stability, some legal requirements for establishments of foreign firms are currently too weak or

[29] On this issue, see Bossu and Chew (2015).

[30] As provided for in NAFTA Article 1408.

[31] See Article 4 Decree-Law 251 in Chile, Article 38.2 of the Colombian Banking Law, and Article 10 of the Peruvian Banking Law.

poorly designed to achieve the objective of financial stability. This is particularly the case for some LA-7 countries with local asset maintenance requirements (LAMR) for branches of foreign banks. Conceptually, LAMR should require such branches to maintain in the country a certain amount of assets to satisfy liabilities of the branch in case of its insolvency (including insolvency of the parent firm), through the application of ring-fencing mechanisms. In the absence of LAMR, the branch may hold assets abroad under control of the head office, including in the form of deposits with or loans to the head office. In case of insolvency, this will result in branch assets being controlled by the liquidator of the head office or branch assets consisting of circular worthless claims.

To effectively operate as a safeguard for creditors of the branch, LAMR should be applied on a significant percentage of local liabilities, especially deposits. Colombia and Peru apply their LAMR only to the endowment capital of the branch,[32] which is just a small part of total liabilities and far too low to effectively protect depositors, thus inhibiting the effectiveness of the ring-fencing mechanisms the LAMR is supposed to buttress.

Combined with removing the discriminatory feature of the ring-fencing rule, these legal requirements should be significantly strengthened, specifically to require a higher amount of branch assets to be held locally. This should be achieved by requiring the local holding of assets equivalent to a high percentage of local (deposit) liabilities. Thus well-designed LAMR should give the assurance to host countries' supervisory authorities that they can manage adequately the specific risk stemming from branches of foreign banks. This may in turn lead to a more supportive attitude among local policymakers and supervisory authorities toward this form of cross-border establishments.

CONCLUSION

All in all, the LA-7 countries have made great progress in removing most of the legal barriers to cross-border financial operations. Several countries have open access regimes for establishments of foreign banks and insurance firms in their countries; however, some countries maintain certain formal barriers that hinder integration. These barriers reflect a reluctance on the part of policymakers and supervisory authorities, especially toward branches. Even in LA-7 countries that allow branches, the combination of, on the one hand, absence of a differentiated regulatory treatment of branches in spite of their specific legal nature, and, on the other hand, discriminatory ring-fencing rules combined with inadequate LAMR, points to an approach that diminishes the advantages of branches as well as the available legal instruments that allow a country to manage the risks while enjoying the benefits of opening to branches of foreign financial firms. It is hoped that the information in this chapter is helpful to authorities who seek to create a better equilibrium between financial openness and financial stability.

---

[32] See Article 2.36.12.2.2 of Colombian Decree 2555/2010 and Article 42 of the Peruvian Banking Law.

REFERENCES

Bossu, Wouter, and Dawn Chew. 2015. "But We Are Different! 12 Common Weaknesses in Banking Law, and What to Do about Them." IMF Working Paper 15/200, International Monetary Fund, Washington.

De Wolf, Joseph. 2005. "Tax Barriers on the Way towards an Integrated European Capital Market: The EU Savings Directive as a Challenge for Clearing and Settlement Systems." In *Legal Aspects of the European System of Central Banks*, p. 339. Frankfurt: European Central Bank.

Organisation for Economic Co-operation and Development (OECD). 2006. "Guidelines on Pension Fund Asset Management." Paris: OECD.

Tanzi, Vito, Alberto Barreix, and Luiz Villela. 2008. *Taxation and Latin American Integration*. Cambridge, Massachusetts and Washington: Harvard University Press and Inter-American Development Bank.

CHAPTER 8

Regional Initiatives to Achieve Financial Integration

CHARLES ENOCH AND IULIA RUXANDRA TEODORU

This chapter takes stock of existing efforts at regional financial integration. Integration initiatives have a long history in Latin America; however, many have lost momentum after initial enthusiasm. This chapter looks in particular at two ongoing regional initiatives that—among other objectives—are aiming at financial integration. It finds that prospects are good for both of them, and that they may be the most suitable vehicles for taking the integration process forward at this time.

MERCOSUR

Mercosur was established in 1991 through the signing of the Treaty of Asuncion by the presidents of Argentina, Brazil, Paraguay, and Uruguay. Venezuela joined in 2012 and Bolivia in 2015. Mercosur's founders were inspired by the example in Europe and aimed to go further. They intended the alliance to also be a tool to strengthen democracy as its members recovered from the dictatorships of the 1980s and hoped it would drive political integration. Progressive preferential trade liberalization among member countries took place from 1991 to 1994, and by the time the common external tariff was established in 1995, tariffs among members had been reduced for the most part. As a result, trade among Mercosur countries increased across the board throughout most of the 1990s (Figure 8.1). The establishment of a common external tariff was expected to lead to a customs union. However, the period from 1996 to 1999 saw a reversal in trade liberalization owing to external shocks such as the Brazilian financial crisis in 1999, as well as unilateral changes in the common external tariff by Brazil and Argentina. Both countries also introduced new nontariff barriers: import licensing requirements and antidumping measures. As a result, trade among Mercosur countries has declined since 2000.

In the Montevideo Protocol (1997), members made commitments to the liberalization of services, including financial services. The principles guiding the liberalization process were similar to those established in 1995 for multilateral liberalization in the General Agreement on Trade in Services (GATS) of the World Trade Organization (WTO). For example, modes of provision, rules of market access and national treatment, and complete liberalization were envisaged over a 10-year

Figure 8.1 Goods Trade within Mercosur
(Percent of national good trade)

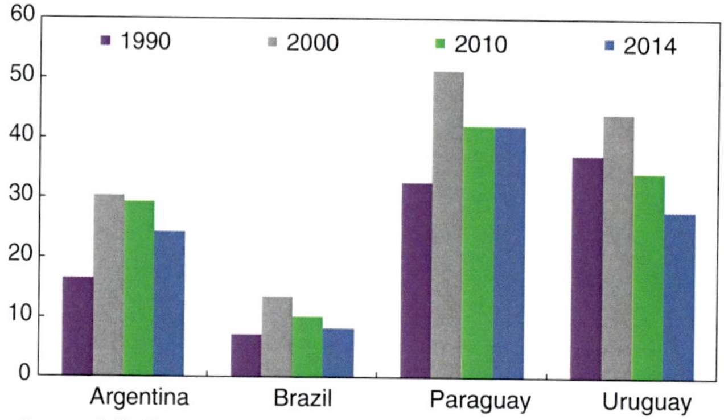

Source: IMF, Direction of Trade Statistics.

period. The list of initial commitments to liberalization under the Montevideo Protocol was marginally more extensive than the list negotiated in GATS. Argentina and Brazil maintained the liberalization levels they committed to in GATS, Paraguay committed less than the amount negotiated in GATS, and Uruguay increased its commitments, particularly regarding the presence of firms and of natural persons. Finally, Mercosur has a technical forum for financial issues—Financial Mercosur (SGT-4)—tasked with advancing the financial integration agenda.[1]

Financial services in Mercosur member countries were liberalized unilaterally in the 1990s, either simultaneously with or after the Mercosur agreement, which led to an increased presence of global foreign banks. The unilateral moves toward liberalization followed the Argentinean hyperinflation episode. Argentina instituted the "convertibility plan," which led to the deregulation of domestic markets, privatizations, trade liberalization, elimination of capital controls and a stable macroeconomic environment conducive to foreign investment. The Brazilian "*Real* plan"—introduced in 1994 to stabilize the economy after a bout of hyperinflation—led to the restructuring of banks, privatizations, and liberalization of the financial sector. To facilitate foreign bank entry, Brazil eliminated the restriction that the minimum capital for a foreign bank had to be twice as large as that required for a national bank.

Foreign claims of Brazilian banks[2] on Mercosur countries provide some evidence of increasing regional integration since 2008 (Figure 8.2). They rose from an average of 4 percent of total foreign claims over the period 2002–08 to a peak of 11 percent in 2011–12, after which they declined owing to a reduction in foreign claims on Argentina. Currently, foreign banks from Mercosur countries do not have important market shares in Brazil and Argentina, but they do hold 10 percent and 20 percent of assets in Uruguay and Paraguay, respectively (Figure 8.3). Seventeen percent of Brazilian Itaú's operations in Latin America are in

[1] The ultimate objective of SGT-4 is to create a single regional market for financial services while maintaining stability in the monetary and financial system.

[2] Brazil is the only Mercosur country that reports to the Bank for International Settlements (BIS).

Figure 8.2 Foreign Claims of Brazilian Banks on Mercosur
(Percent of total, immediate borrower basis)

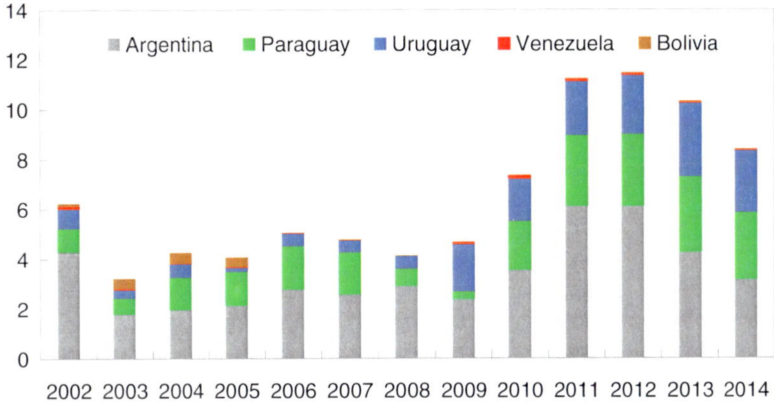

Source: Bank for International Settlements, Consolidated Banking Statistics.

Figure 8.3 Mercosur: Commercial Bank Ownership
(Mercosur bank assets in percent of total assets)

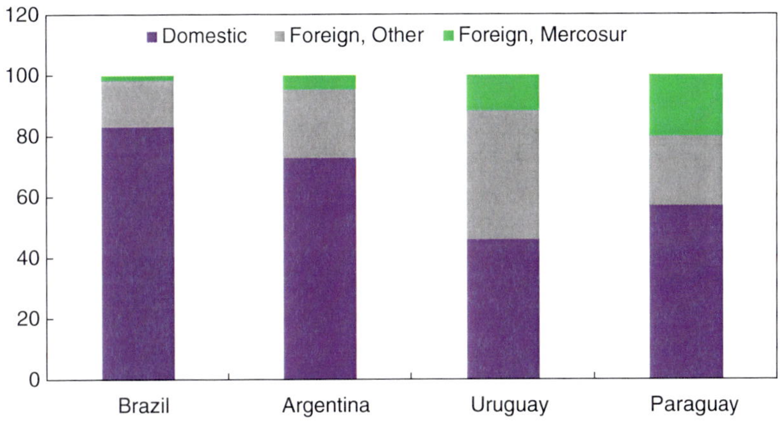

Sources: Bankscope; and Bureau van Dijk.

Mercosur countries; Itaú has market shares in the Paraguayan and Uruguayan banking systems of 18 percent and 11 percent, respectively.

Although the member countries committed to liberalizing financial services in the Montevideo Protocol, various indices suggest that certain restrictions to market access remain.[3] Argentina liberalized the most, but it maintained some level of protection in cross-border supply of financial services and presence of natural

---

[3] Hoekman (1995a; 1995b), Dee (2005), and Berlinski (2012) have constructed indices of restrictions for market access across the following modes of supply: cross-border supply, consumption abroad, commercial presence, and presence of natural persons, assigning values to liberalization commitments made by countries.

Figure 8.4 Portfolio and FDI Allocations to Mercosur by Other Mercosur Countries, 2003–13

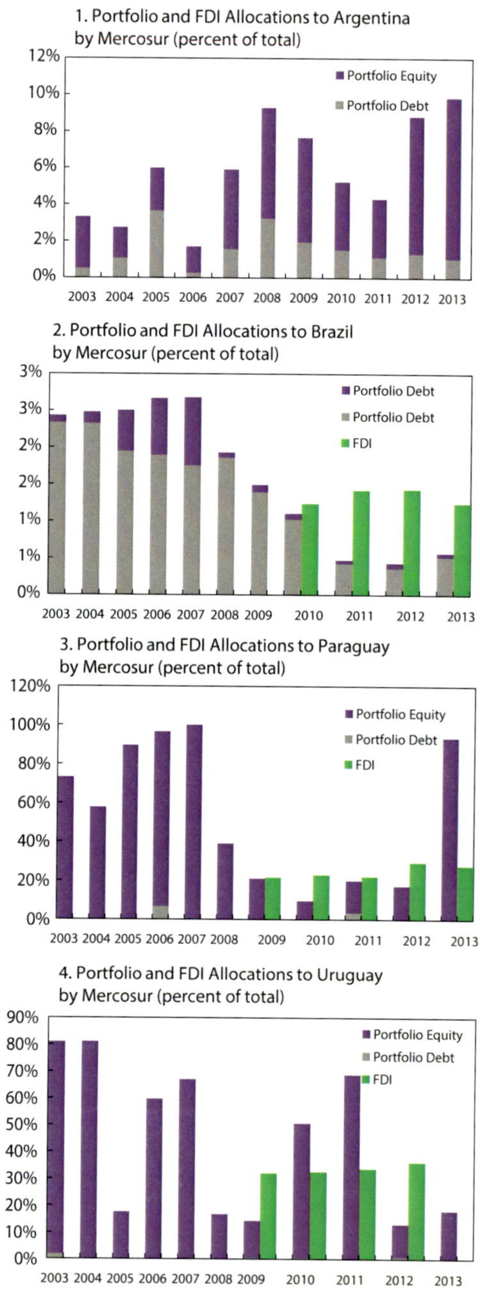

Sources: IMF, Coordinated Portfolio Investment Survey and Coordinated Direct Investment Survey.
Note: Mercosur includes Argentina, Brazil, Paraguay, and Uruguay. FDI = foreign direct investment.

persons. Brazil made no commitments to liberalize cross-border supply and consumption abroad, and kept some restrictions in commercial presence and presence of natural persons. Uruguay also had some restrictions across all modes of supply, while Paraguay had the most restrictions. Other indices of barriers to integration suggest some restrictions with respect to licensing for foreign banks (Brazil and Uruguay), foreign bank entry (Brazil), and movement of people (Argentina, Brazil, and Uruguay). Some indicators suggest an increase in restrictions to foreign bank entry and banking activities permitted in Argentina (Barth, Caprio, and Levine 2006, 2007), while restrictions on banking activities were lowered in Brazil from 2000 to 2006.

The Political Mercosur and the Commercial Mercosur are facing problems, but the Financial Mercosur is achieving some progress, especially on the convergence of the members toward best practices. Working Group No. 4 (SGT-4) comprises financial sector regulators (banking, securities markets, and insurance) from all Mercosur member countries to oversee the integration process. The ultimate goal is to create a regional common market in financial services.

Figure 8.4 shows the extent of cross-border portfolio and FDI allocations in four Mercosur countries.

This moment may be propitious for taking the process further. President Mauricio Macri of Argentina referred during his 2015 election campaign to the need to restore momentum to the Mercosur process. Regional integration may be a productive way for Argentina to begin to reintegrate into the global economy. In the coming years, Venezuela may face similar—albeit far more difficult—reintegration challenges. Meanwhile, members of Mercosur continue to integrate their economies. On December 2015, Paraguay and Uruguay signed an agreement to create a bilateral local currency payment system;[4] on April 20, 2016, Brazil and Paraguay signed a similar bilateral agreement. This followed an initial agreement between Argentina and Brazil in 2008; over the next five years, transactions using the Brazilian currency for invoicing trade and services between the two countries grew ninefold. These are voluntary agreements under which exporters may receive payment in the importer's home currency. The currency is remitted to the central bank, which nets the balances and pays the exporter in the home currency at the prevailing rate against the U.S. dollar. Over time such arrangements could perhaps become multilateral, allowing multilateral netting, perhaps based on the Brazilian currency. (The countries would have to take care not to violate their obligations under Article VIII of the Articles of Agreement of the IMF.[5])

---

[4] These agreements are known as SMLs, from their Spanish language acronym for the system of payments of local currency (Sistema de pago en Moneda Local).

[5] Article VIII covers restrictions on current payments, discriminatory currency arrangements, and multiple currency practices.

THE PACIFIC ALLIANCE

On April 28, 2011, then-President Alan Garcia of Peru—together with the presidents of Chile, Colombia, and Mexico—signed the Lima Agreement, which pledged the four countries to work together as the Pacific Alliance (PA) to foster "deep integration" in a wide range of areas. The signers agreed to the immediate abolition of tariffs on 92 percent of merchandise trade and made a commitment to abolish the remainder by 2020. Together the countries represent 36 percent of Latin American GDP, and they are the four largest exporters from the region.

The PA continues its high-level political commitment with biannual presidential summits. At a summit in Paracas, Peru, on July 2, 2015, the presidents reaffirmed their commitment to the PA and laid out new avenues for integration. On July 20, 2015, the framework agreement for the PA came into force. With the rotating presidency moving to Chile in 2016, the presidents met in Puerto Vargas on July 1, following a high-level business summit held in Santiago in June.

The Alliance has garnered wide international attention, and 34 countries are now observers at the PA meetings. Several smaller countries in the region are proceeding through the membership process or considering doing so. It has been suggested that the greatest achievement of the alliance is its ability to draw inward investment.[6] The PA explicitly sees itself as outward-focused and presenting an integrated economic face to the world. For example, the Association of Southeast Asian Nations (ASEAN) has been an observer at PA meetings, and the PA met with ASEAN in May 2015 and was an observer at the ASEAN summit in the Philippines in November 2015. In May 2016 ASEAN and PA officials met in Bangkok, along with academic and private sector participants. They agreed to define a general framework of cooperation between the two organizations' integration processes; this agreement was adopted during the subsequent third interregional ministerial meeting.

There is as yet no specific overall financial sector stream for integration among the PA countries, but it has taken over a private-led initiative for capital market integration. The stock exchanges of Chile, Colombia, and Peru agreed to merge under the Latin American Integrated Market (MILA) initiative (see Box 8.1). The initiative has received considerable publicity, and in 2014 Mexico joined, with an initial trade on December 2, 2014, of shares in Chilean retailer Falabella executed in the Mexican stock exchange. The Mexican stock exchange also bought 6.7 percent of the Lima stock exchange. The joint exchange is the second largest in Latin America, slightly smaller than Brazil's BM&F BOVESPA.

Actual results from the capital market initiative are minimal so far. Total trades in the five years since MILA was established are less than the volume traded in Mexico alone in a week. Two explanations have been put forward. The first is that MILA is redundant, as capital market needs can be serviced either domestically or outside the region, particularly in the United States. The second explanation is that the integration process so far has been insufficiently ambitious and that a

[6] *The Economist*, March 14, 2015.

Box 8.1 Integrated Securities Markets in the Latin American Integrated Market (MILA) Initiative

Background

Regional integration and cooperation in securities markets for LA-7 countries is crucial to address the increased intensity, growth, and importance of transnational and intraregional financial services. In particular, regional integration would intermediate the rapid growth and size of foreign direct investment (FDI) in financial institutions and cross-border transactions. Domestic securities markets in many LA-7 countries are restricted in size, in part owing to large fixed costs in setup and a lack of economies of scale. In addition, the limited nature of liquidity and risk diversification in such markets plays a significant role. MILA was announced in September 2009 and launched in May 2011 with the intention of bolstering trading volumes in three stock markets—Chile, Colombia, and Peru—and providing an alternative to the larger markets of Mexico and Brazil. Mexico joined MILA in December 2014. MILA exchanges are first in Latin America in the number of listed companies, second in market capitalization, and third in traded volumes.

Liquidity

Investors, issuers, and broker-dealers are less likely to participate in illiquid markets. Investors who hold securities in their portfolios require certainty of valuation and execution of sales of securities from such markets under appropriate pricing conditions should they decide to offset their positions. Liquid markets enable investors to meet these needs while benefiting from lower transaction costs. Large volumes and higher frequency of issuance of individual equity securities are necessary to create proper liquidity pools, attract investors, and generate a larger volume of transactions. This is a prerequisite for the development of efficient pricing in secondary markets. Moreover, liquid markets help investors diversify their risks.

Harmonization Challenges

MILA is a cross-border initiative to integrate equities markets without any real corporate merger of stock exchanges or depositories; it has enabled cross-listings and the use of technological tools to allow standardization of regulations on trading and custody across the separate MILA countries. Fuller integration would require deeper regulatory and supervisory harmonization, including delineated responsibilities for various securities supervisors, harmonization of regulatory standards, and supervisory approaches to best practice levels. The creation of a fully integrated regional equity market would require that all investors benefit from equivalent legal treatment and that a protection regime exists for all transactions made through MILA. Further tax and pension fund investment regime harmonization and unified resolution frameworks are important for more extensive integration of equity markets. There has been little or no progress in integrating fixed-income (bond), currency, derivatives, repos, and securities lending markets, partly because the rules for such securities are extremely challenging to integrate and, unlike equities, many of these securities are not fully traded electronically on exchanges, so the majority of trades are still over the counter (OTC). Foreign investors are not very actively involved in MILA, preferring to access local markets through well-established relationships with local custodians and broker-dealers; in this way they also benefit from tighter foreign exchange spreads when currency is converted and from delivery-versus-payment settlement (DvP).[1]

(*Continued*)

[1] DvP is a securities settlement mechanism that links a securities transfer and a funds transfer in such a way as to ensure that delivery occurs if and only if the corresponding payment occurs.

Box 8.1. (*Continued*)

Post-Trade Settlement and Counterparty Risk

MILA has so far been a trade-driven initiative with limited focus on essential back-office settlement issues to address settlement and counterparty risk. This operational factor is a major element restricting greater trading volume growth. Currently, counterparty risk is carried by local broker-dealers when they settle cross-border trades. This can result in contagion and systemic risk concerns if one of the broker-dealers cannot fulfill its payment or delivery obligations. Specifically, cross-border trades in MILA are conducted on a free-of-payment basis, in which the cash and securities do not move together on the settlement date. In fact, cash moves ahead of securities. For example, assume a Chilean broker-dealer buys Colombian equity for its Chilean investor through a Colombian broker. If the Colombian broker were to become insolvent and unable to deliver the securities, the Chilean broker would be liable to its Chilean investor. If the Chilean broker-dealer could not meet its obligations it could also fail and, if the failure was systemic, it could cause contagion and loss for other brokers and investors, and potentially cause wider systemic financial distress. Thus, a multilateral process is required for settling cross-border trades between brokers in MILA on a DvP basis. So far, options to facilitate that process through a regional clearinghouse or through the use of local custodians or central securities depositories have not materialized. One way forward would be to establish a mini regional bank under MILA auspices.

Conclusion

MILA represents an important staging post for further integration of securities markets in Latin America, increasing economic growth in the region through enhanced financial intermediation and financial resilience arising out of deeper and more liquid securities markets. Further integration of securities markets should involve harmonization toward best practices at an international level.

more comprehensive set of integration policies would enable the initiative to achieve "lift-off."

The number of actual integration measures to date has been limited. For instance, trades still have to be placed with a broker-dealer in the investor's country, who must then contact a broker-dealer in the investment's country. Also, the initiative covers only equities, although it is being expanded to cover government and corporate bonds. There has been no harmonization of operating hours and procedures, nor harmonization of tax systems to avoid double taxation. And—possibly most important—institutional investors in the participating countries, particularly pension and insurance funds, have limits on the shares of their portfolios they may invest across borders, including in fellow PA countries.

This would be an opportune time to use the political mileage achieved through the PA to implement a comprehensive set of interconnected measures to accelerate regional capital market integration, including through MILA. Such measures could include relaxing the share of portfolios that pension and insurance funds may invest cross-border or, preferably, allowing cross-border investments in other MILA countries to be counted as domestic. (For example, Chile restricts cross-border investment on the basis of country ratings; it might switch to using corporate ratings and foreign exchange position limits instead.) In addition, operational procedures—including all aspects of listing requirements—could be harmonized.

The PA agenda is carried forward largely by finance ministry officials in the country that holds the rotating presidency. This arrangement has a number of advantages—including keeping initiatives in line with national objectives—but it also has drawbacks. Primarily, the setup limits the administrative resources that can be put into the initiative and may limit it to moving forward through ad hoc measures. All the officials involved already have a full portfolio of other tasks, so PA work may at times be crowded out. And the periodic rotation of presidencies means an inevitable stop-start as the new team succeeds the old.

The authors therefore recommend that a small secretariat be established in one of the PA countries (see Box 8.2). The secretariat would not be an alternative to the rotating presidency but rather an instrument to make the presidency more

Box 8.2 The Pacific Alliance Secretariat

The Pacific Alliance Secretariat (PAS) would have overall responsibility for designing and providing advice on the operational requirements for the PA redefine financial sector work stream; it would translate the high-level pronouncements of the member country presidents (such as in the Paracas Declaration of 2015) into specific action. In establishing a secretariat, the PA would be following the practice of other regional bodies, such as the Association of Southeast Asian Nations (ASEAN), which established a secretariat in Jakarta in 1976 and has progressively assigned it additional functions.

The location of the secretariat would be determined by the member countries. It could be placed in the largest country, or the smallest, or the country with the best transport links. Some regional organizations have deliberately located the secretariat in a city that is not a capital city, to reduce the risk that one member will acquire disproportionate influence. However, choosing a city with good transport connections that is not a capital would narrow the range of choices. Sometimes the decision is the result of trade-offs; for example, one country might host the secretariat while another provides its first head. If other secretariats or agencies are being set up at the same time (for instance, there might also be a dispute resolution commission), such agencies could be distributed across the membership.

The proposed secretariat might start with no more than a dozen staff, drawn from across the PA membership. Staff might be secondees from central banks or ministries, selected by open competition across the member countries, or a combination. Diverse expertise would be required so that all facets of the integration agenda are covered.

The alliance would have to determine the role of the PAS vis-à-vis the member countries.[1] Because the PA operates through consensus, the secretariat would have to maintain very close contact with the member countries, probably with the same country officials who were previously responsible for PA work. Coordination could be facilitated by periodic meetings—say, twice a year—among the PAS, the country counterparts, and the informal group of country representatives, as part of the handover of the rolling presidency and the accompanying meetings of the PA presidents.

---

[1] Coordination among outside providers of assistance and expertise to the PA could also be useful. An important part of the forthcoming agenda for PA countries is likely to be the harmonization of accounting and prudential standards and of trading practices. Such harmonization should be based on international best practices, so coordinated advice from the multilateral agencies could make an important contribution. This might be facilitated by the establishment of an informal group of PA country representatives at the IMF, Inter-American Development Bank, and World Bank.

effective. Specifically, the secretariat should have overall responsibility for providing advice and executing the operational requirements for a PA financial sector integration stream. Work would include preparing and disseminating a comprehensive framework or action plan for integration, including timelines and sequencing, so as to maintain momentum for the process, ensure consistency, and gain the benefits of proceeding through reciprocity. The secretariat could also be the external face of the financial side of the PA, helping to secure foreign investment and other integration with the rest of the region and the wider world.

There has been some resistance to the establishment of a PA secretariat, primarily because of the number of bureaucracies already in existence in other regional institutions. It would be important therefore that the PA secretariat work closely with the political and economic leadership and that the present intensive series of political and economic meetings and programs be maintained or even intensified.

POLICY RECOMMENDATIONS

It is recommended that both the countries of Mercosur and those of the PA intensify efforts at financial integration, both at a country level and at the level of these regional arrangements.

Mercosur

This is a good time for Mercosur to revisit its plans for financial integration and consider how to take them forward. Prioritization and setting realistic timelines would be important. Many of Mercosur's members are in economic slowdown or recession; regional integration could be a component of a general rebalancing strategy.

Mercosur could demonstrate its revitalization by increasing its international profile; for instance, through joint roadshows to international financial centers and participation with other regional groups. It could seek to integrate its capital markets while providing assurances to the smaller countries that such integration would not bring about domination by the larger countries. Not all member countries may be ready to move forward right now. They could move forward on a bilateral basis insofar as this is compatible with Mercosur; for instance, as with the recent spurt in agreements on local currency payment systems.

The Pacific Alliance

The PA would benefit from establishing a small secretariat to support it in making decisions and implementing plans. The secretariat could work in the following areas:

- Permitting pension funds and insurance companies to count cross-border PA investment as domestic. Replacing remaining ratings-based country limitations on pension fund investments across MILA countries with specific foreign exchange and corporate limitations. Ensuring safeguards for foreign exchange and credit risks.

- Completing MILA expansion beyond equities (primary and secondary markets) to include sovereign and corporate bonds. Positioning MILA to focus on back-office issues, in particular postsettlement and counterparty risk.
- Harmonizing operational procedures, including all aspects of listing requirements, for capital markets.
- Ensuring that all countries have signed International Organization of Securities Commissions memorandums of understanding.
- "Passporting" the licensing of broker-dealers while keeping them subject to host as well as home regulation.
- Enhancing contacts among national regulators and supervisors, including through staff exchanges and secondments to the secretariat.
- Examining the potential for expanding the geographic scope of the PA.

REFERENCES

Barth, J., G. Caprio, and R. Levine. 2006. *Rethinking Bank Regulations (Till Angels Govern)*. Cambridge, U.K.: Cambridge University Press.

———. 2007. "Bank Regulations Are Changing: For Better or Worse?" Policy Research Working Paper 4646, World Bank, Washington.

Berlinski, J. 2012. "Banking Services Trade as Infrastructure in Mercosur: International Commitments, Domestic Regulations and Determinants of Argentina Banks' Performance." Montevideo: Mercosur Economic Research Network.

Dee, P. 2005. "A Compendium of Barriers to Services Trade." Canberra: Australian National University, unpublished. https://www.gtap.agecon.purdue.edu/resources/download/3492.pdf.

Hoekman, B. 1995a. "Tentative First Steps: An Assessment of the Uruguay Round Agreement on Services." CEPR Discussion Paper 1150, Centre for Economic Policy Research, London.

———. 1995b. "Assessing the General Agreement on Trade in Services." In *The Uruguay Round and the Developing Economies*, edited by Will Martin and L. Alan Winters. Washington: World Bank.

CHAPTER 9

Risks and Mitigation for Financial Integration

MOHAMED AFZAL NORAT AND CARLOS CACERES

Financial integration and the resulting interconnections among financial and nonfinancial institutions provide benefits and risks for countries. As articulated in earlier chapters in this book, financial integration can bring important benefits to both banks and clients, including lower funding costs, risk diversification, deeper liquid markets, increased competition, and efficiency in the financial system. At the same time, with conglomerates operating in multiple jurisdictions in the LA-7 countries (Brazil, Chile, Colombia, Mexico, Panama, Peru, and Uruguay) and across the Central American region, country-specific weaknesses in regulatory and supervisory frameworks or insufficient regional coordination may allow regulatory arbitrage. Moreover, financial integration can increase spillover risks and lead to contagion across the region in the event of a crisis.

The focus in this chapter is on the risks related to financial integration and the prudential tools required to mitigate them. The chapter uses market-based tools to assess current levels of systemic risk in LA-7 countries and the potential for contagion. It provides an overview of the importance of network analysis in mapping financial interconnections and how they add to systemic risk and the potential for contagion. The authors then undertake an overview of the importance of robust regulatory and supervisory frameworks and of consistency of prudential standards in the LA-7 to address the risks inherent in financial integration. Mapping the financial networks that have been created by conglomerates across the LA-7 countries illustrates the challenges faced by regulatory and supervisory frameworks and the importance of consolidated and conglomerate supervision. The authors suggest prudential tools (both micro and macro) that can be used to address the risks of interconnectedness and the possibility of contagion that are part of financial integration. The last section includes recommendations for pursuing financial integration within a robust framework that address its risks.

CURRENT STATE OF AFFAIRS

Systemic (or spillover) risk arises when the failure or weakness of one or more financial institutions or infrastructures disrupts financial services and imposes costs on the economy as a whole. The failure or weakness of multiple financial institutions

TABLE 9.1

Examples of Direct and Indirect Financial Interconnectedness

Examples of Direct Financial Interconnectedness			
Credit Exposures between Banks	**Financial Market Infrastructure Relationships**	**Vendors and Other Third-Party Relationships**	**Other Financial Service Dependencies**
Lending and borrowing	Payment	Service relationships	Hedging services
Buying and selling securities	Clearing	IT security protocols	Underwriting services
Derivatives trading	Settlement		Custodial services
Securities financing			Guarantee services
Interbank activity			
Examples of Indirect Financial Interconnectedness			
Exposure to Common Assets	**Mark-to-Market Losses**	**Margin Calls and Haircuts**	**Shadow Banking**
Market shocks	Fire sales	Holdings of securities	Money market funds
Market volatility	Collateral losses	Internal and external ratings	Mutual funds
Demand and supply dislocations	Liquidity pressures	Collateral framework	Pension funds
Pricing shocks	Funding pressures		Hedge funds
			Activities outside the banking system
Information Spillovers			
Crisis of confidence			
Negative signals about entities			

Source: Depository Trust and Clearing Corporation (2015).

may arise through a variety of direct and indirect mechanisms (Table 9.1).[1] Direct bilateral exposures across institutions are the most direct transmission mechanisms of shocks within a financial network. However, indirect linkages may arise from exposure to common risk factors, such as the adoption of similar business models, common accounting practices across financial institutions, the market perception of financial institutions' coincidence of fortunes, fire sales, and informational contagion. These risk factors can be as important as direct exposures.[2]

Contagion spillover risks in the LA-7 countries are currently at a low level. Although growing cross-border activity and financial integration increase the potential for contagion spillovers in a crisis, some quantitative analysis suggests that spillover risks among Latin American financial systems are currently contained (see the next section). The conglomerates operating in LA-7 jurisdictions and Latin

[1] According to Nier and others (2007), the failure or weakness of multiple financial institutions at the same time arises through four main mechanisms: (1) direct bilateral exposures between institutions, (2) correlated exposures of financial institutions to a common source of risk, (3) feedback effects from endogenous fire sale of assets by distressed institutions, and (4) informational contagion.

[2] Scott (2012) and the Committee on Capital Markets Regulation argue that asset and liability interconnectedness were not the main drivers of the systemic risk concerns during the recent financial crisis in the United States but that contagion was front and center.

America in general can act as pathways for increased regional banking and financial sector connectivity through their network of subsidiaries and intergroup and other counterparty exposures. Country authorities have begun to focus on these potential risks, in some cases limiting cross-border activities by imposing formal or informal restrictions. The current low levels of spillover risk leave room for further financial integration while regional supervisory and regulatory oversight is strengthened and any country-specific weaknesses in supervisory frameworks are addressed to avoid regulatory arbitrage. Contagion risks will naturally rise with greater integration or under adverse conditions. This potential requires that cross-border activity and exposures be monitored in a regionally coordinated manner.

QUANTIFYING MARKET-IMPLIED SPILLOVER RISKS

Market-based spillover analysis suggests that contagion risks among large financial institutions in Latin America are contained. This quantitative analysis looks at the market-based interlinkages of large financial institutions in six Latin American countries. In particular, the analysis quantifies potential spillovers across institutions through financial markets using data on traded securities. Overall, the relatively limited market-implied spillovers are in line with the current relatively low levels of cross-border balance sheet exposures within the region.

Financial linkages among financial or banking institutions can be broadly split into two categories: direct and indirect. Direct financial linkages denote explicit balance sheet positions from one financial institution onto another; essentially, assets or liabilities of financial institutions vis-à-vis each other. Indirect linkages arise when there are no explicit direct linkages among financial institutions, but their market indicators (for instance, stock prices or credit default swap spreads) tend to exhibit some degree of comovement or synchronicity. These indirect linkages could be the consequence of having similar business models or common exposures to related economic sectors, or simply of being perceived by the markets as being vulnerable to the same type of shocks (for example, a change in legislation affecting most banks in one country).

The aim of the market-implied interlinkage analysis is to quantify both direct and indirect linkages among financial institutions in Latin America. The sample includes the largest listed banks from Argentina, Brazil, Chile, Colombia, Mexico, and Peru; it covers the period 2005–16 and relies on publicly available daily time series of financial variables (Table 9.2).

The methodology relies on the computation of empirical distributions characterizing the joint and conditional probabilities of distress among financial institutions. This is largely based on Segoviano's (2006) Consistent Information Multivariate Density Optimizing Methodology.[3] In particular, two synthetic measures are used:

[3] Extensions of the methodology are described in Segoviano and Goodhart (2009), and a description of the main quantitative indicators used in this analysis can be found in Caceres, Guzzo, and Segoviano (2010).

TABLE 9.2

Latin American Banks Included in the Spillover Analysis

Bank Acronym	Bank Name	Country
BGALI	Banco de Galicia	Argentina
BVAAR	BBVA-Argentina	Argentina
BMACR	Banco Marco	Argentina
BDOBR	Banco do Brasil (BB)	Brazil
ITAUB	Itaú	Brazil
SANBR	Santander-Brazil	Brazil
SANCL	Santander-Chile	Chile
BDCHL	Banco de Chile	Chile
CORPB	Corpbanca	Chile
BCOLO	Bancolombia	Colombia
BDBOG	Banco de Bogota	Colombia
BANOR	Banorte	Mexico
INBUR	Inbursa, grupo financiero	Mexico
SCOPE	Scotiabank-Peru	Peru
BCREP	Banco de Credito del Peru	Peru

Source: IMF staff compilation.

1. The vulnerability index (VI), which measures the susceptibility of a particular institution to fall in distress given distress in other financial institutions (loosely speaking, it measures an institution's vulnerability to contagion from other financial institutions). Algebraically, the VI of a given financial institution "i" is given by:

$$VI(A_i) = \sum_{j \neq i}^{N} \alpha_j \, P(A_i \mid A_j)$$

where the weight $\alpha_j = \frac{1}{N} P(A_j)$, N denotes the number of financial institutions in the sample, and $P(A_j)$ is the probability that institution j falls in distress.[4]

2. The contribution to systemic risk, which measures the contribution of a given institution to changes in the vulnerability to contagion of other institutions (that is, its role as a source of contagion). In other words, it is the percent share that a given financial institution represents in the changes in the vulnerability index of all other institutions in the sample.

To analyze the dynamics of these two market-based measures, both are computed for a sample of 15 banks from six Latin American countries.[5] Figure 9.1

[4] Marginal probabilities of distress for the different individual financial institutions in the sample are obtained from Moody's KMV Expected Default Frequencies™ database.

[5] The country coverage and the sample are determined by data availability and are not the same as in the rest of this study. In general, any financial institution included in the sample must be listed and actively traded on the stock market. This is also a requirement for individual domestic subsidiaries of foreign banks.

Figure 9.1 Market-Based Interlinkages in Selected Latin American Banks

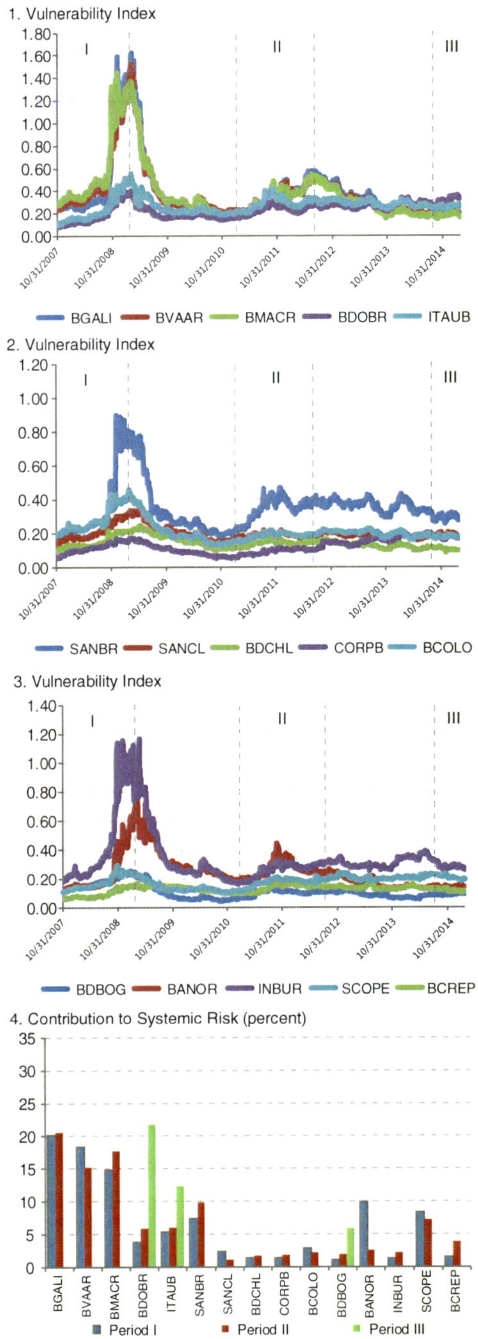

Sources: Moody's KMV; Thompson Reuters Datastream; and IMF staff calculations.
Note: See Table 9.2 for bank abbreviations used in this figure.

shows the evolution of the vulnerability index for the 15 banks (panels 1, 2, and 3). The figure also shows the percentage contribution of each of these banks to the rest of the system's change in vulnerability during three selected periods (panel 4). Argentinean banks and, to a lesser extent, Banorte (Mexico) appear to have been the most vulnerable to contagion during the global financial crisis (Period I). However, the relatively high market-implied interlinkages during that period appear to be important mainly among themselves (Table 9.3).

In the most recent period (Period III), Brazilian banks appear to be important drivers of the market-implied contagion (Figure 9.1, panel 4). However, in terms of absolute magnitude, the actual spillovers and VI outside of Brazil appear to be rather small compared with the VI levels observed during the global financial crisis. In other words, large domestic public banks in Brazil might be very important for the domestic market in Brazil, but they are not so important for the rest of the region. These market-based measures seem to be in line with the limited actual cross-border balance sheet exposures of the banking sectors in Latin America.

NETWORK ANALYSIS AND CONGLOMERATE CONNECTIVITY

Financial integration brings the prospect of increased financial network connectivity that is already established across the LA-7 and the Central America region through the growth of financial and mixed conglomerates. Banks, particularly from Brazil and Colombia, are becoming regional institutions, with the whole area as their home base. Some of this expansion was linked to the exit of some global banks from the region. Cross-border participation in stock exchanges is also apparent, with the Brazilian stock exchange purchasing 8 percent of the Chilean exchange. Nonfinancial corporations—particularly retail institutions from Chile and conglomerates from Brazil and Mexico—are expanding across the region. Since 2011, the presidents of Chile, Colombia, Mexico, and Peru have been meeting regularly to advance the Pacific Alliance (PA; see Chapter 8). Mercosur has brought six Latin American economies together with the objective of integration; although the Mercosur process has recently lost momentum, conditions may be favorable for a revitalization of the financial integration process. Regional financial integration moves have helped many systemic banks—as part of even more systemic conglomerates—create increased networks through headquarters–subsidiary linkages as well as regional bank linkages to U.S. global banks.

NETWORK STRUCTURES: INTERCONNECTEDNESS AND CONTAGION RISKS

Analysis of financial networks in Latin America can be a useful tool to capture interconnectedness and contagion (spillover) risks from financial integration. The expansion of systemic banks and financial and mixed conglomerates across Latin and

TABLE 9.3

Contribution to Systemic Risk during the Global Financial Crisis

	BGALI	BVAAR	BMACR	BDOBR	ITAUB	SANBR	SANCL	BDCHL	CORPB	BCOLO	BDBOG	BANOR	INBUR	SCOPE	BCREP
BGALI		3.9	3.3	0.4	0.7	1.2	0.4	0.2	0.1	0.5	0.2	1.9	0.2	1.5	0.2
BVAAR	4.2		3.3	0.4	0.7	1.1	0.4	0.2	0.1	0.6	0.2	1.9	0.2	1.5	0.2
BMACR	4.3	4.0		0.3	0.5	0.9	0.3	0.2	0.1	0.5	0.2	1.8	0.1	1.5	0.1
BDOBR	2.0	1.6	1.1		2.6	1.9	0.4	0.1	0.8	0.5	0.3	1.0	0.5	1.0	1.1
ITAUB	2.3	2.0	1.3	1.9		2.1	0.5	0.2	0.5	0.3	0.2	1.5	0.5	1.1	0.7
SANBR	3.0	2.5	1.8	1.0	1.5		0.4	0.2	0.3	0.4	0.1	1.5	0.3	1.4	0.3
SANCL	2.6	2.4	1.7	0.7	1.0	1.3		0.4	0.4	0.5	0.0	1.9	0.2	1.7	0.2
BDCHL	2.9	2.7	2.3	0.3	0.6	0.9	0.7		0.1	0.3	0.0	2.6	0.3	1.2	0.0
CORPB	1.8	1.4	0.9	2.1	1.8	1.7	0.7	0.1		0.5	0.2	0.6	0.5	1.5	1.2
BCOLO	3.2	3.0	2.3	0.6	0.6	1.0	0.4	0.2	0.3		0.1	1.3	0.1	1.8	0.1
BDBOG	3.7	3.3	1.9	1.2	0.9	0.9	0.0	−0.1	0.2	0.4		1.4	0.0	1.2	−0.1
BANOR	3.6	3.2	2.6	0.4	0.8	1.2	0.5	0.4	0.1	0.4	0.2		0.3	1.2	0.1
INBUR	2.4	1.9	1.1	1.6	2.0	1.6	0.3	0.3	0.5	0.1	0.0	2.0		0.9	0.4
SCOPE	3.3	3.0	2.6	0.5	0.7	1.3	0.5	0.2	0.3	0.7	0.2	1.4	0.1		0.2
BCREP	2.0	1.7	0.9	2.8	2.3	1.6	0.3	0.0	1.1	0.2	−0.1	0.8	0.3	1.1	
STD	**20.2**	**18.4**	**14.8**	**3.8**	**5.4**	**7.4**	**2.4**	**1.4**	**1.4**	**2.9**	**1.0**	**9.9**	**1.3**	**8.3**	**1.5**

Sources: Moody's KMV; Thompson Reuters Datastream; and IMF staff calculations.

Note: Data are for the period October 31, 2007, to March 2, 2009. See Table 9.2 for bank abbreviations used in this table.

Central America has led to increased direct and indirect financial interconnectedness, which could add to the propagation of shocks through interconnections in the LA-7 financial network. Risks within the LA-7 financial network also reflect the complex organizational structures and the risks inherent in the business models of the financial and mixed conglomerates in the network. A detailed mapping, monitoring, and analysis of the LA-7 financial network would allow supervisors and risk managers to determine: (1) at what point these financial networks become fragile; (2) how that fragility propagates through the network—through specific connections and through systemic conglomerates and other connected entities; (3) what type of financial network structures (topologies) are more fragile than others; and (4) how systemic risks in the network vary over time as a result of interconnectedness and contagion risks from greater regional integration in the LA-7. Network analysis using mathematical graph theoretical frameworks on data from various direct and indirect mechanisms of interconnections (see Table 9.1) can be an extremely useful complement to the analysis of systemic risks from market-based distress dependence models discussed earlier. Specifically, mapping, monitoring, and analysis of the LA-7 financial network provides a more detailed view of systemic risks from interconnectedness and contagion than the view from market-based models on their own.[6]

Financial and mixed conglomerate networks across the LA-7 countries are multilayered and complex, both domestically and across borders. Conglomerate financial networks in the LA-7 countries involve interconnections between systemic and nonsystemic financial and nonfinancial entities. Some of these interconnections are intraconglomerate—between parents (holding companies), subsidiaries, or branches—across multiple types of financial and nonfinancial institutions (multilayered). These networks not only extend across types of institutions but can also extend geographically on a cross-border basis, linked together through a multitude of direct and indirect connections (see Table 9.1). Using simple constructed examples, the authors show that network complexity can extend across multiple dimensions, moving from simpler domestic financial and mixed conglomerate networks to more complex multilayered cross-border networks (Figures 9.2 and 9.3). Domestic conglomerate networks (represented by the gray circle in Figure 9.2) are complex and challenging to supervise, but networks become much more complex and difficult to supervise when interconnections occur across borders (colored circles). This implies that systemic risk would be better estimated by mapping complex financial and mixed conglomerate networks across the LA-7 than by mapping simpler networks. As depicted in Figure 9.3, complex conglomerate networks have cross-border and multilayered dimensions that evolve dynamically over time. Thus, mapping, monitoring, and analysis of real-world complex financial and mixed conglomerate networks across LA-7 countries raises important supervisory, data, and coordination challenges for authorities, central banks, and supervisory agencies in the region.

---

[6] Markose and Giansante (2013) have argued that price-based models underestimate and are poorer at early warning of systemic risks compared to network balance sheet models, especially those based on granular balance-sheet and off-balance-sheet bilateral exposures.

Figure 9.2 Simplified Examples of Domestic and Cross-Border Conglomerate Networks

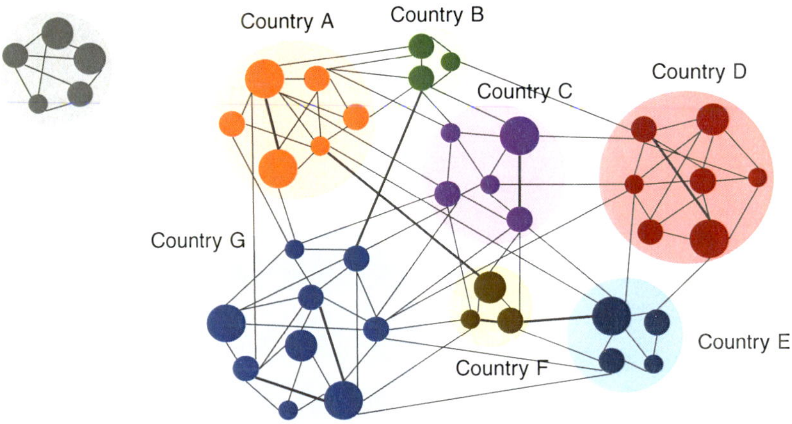

Source: IMF staff.

Figure 9.3 Complex, Multilayered Cross-Border Networks

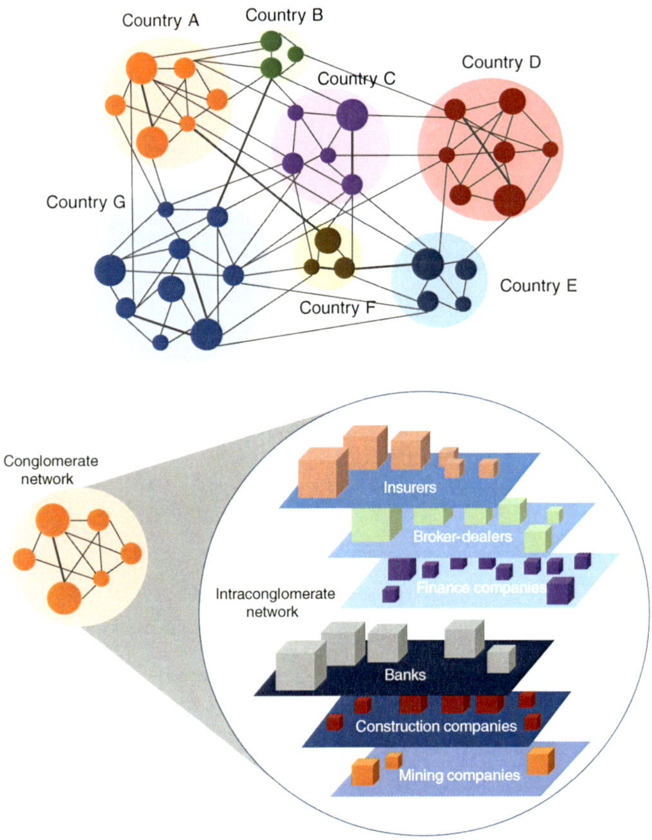

Source: IMF staff.

SOME RECENT NETWORK APPROACHES FOR LATIN AMERICA

Systemic risk in the Mexican banking system between 2007 and 2013 is underestimated by 90 percent when the focus is on a single exposure network rather than multilayered exposure networks. Recent work by Poledna and others (2015) for the Mexican banking system has shown that analyzing systemic risk contributions from four exposure layers of the interbank network (derivatives, securities cross-holdings, foreign exchange, and interbank deposits and loans) underestimates systemic risk by 90 percent if only a single interbank deposits and loans network is considered. Looking at financial market measures and market-based models using the VIX (the Chicago Board Options Exchange Volatility Index), credit default swap (CDS) spreads, or other market prices might also underestimate systemic risk ex ante.

Colombian multilayered financial institutions and financial market infrastructure networks (FMIs) are better able to capture systemic risks and insulate against them. Work by León, Berndsen, and Renneboog (2014) showed that Colombian transactions and exposures among financial institutions that are registered, settled, cleared, and safeguarded by FMIs can be expressed as multilayered networks. The analysis makes it clear that systemic risks would be much higher than those of each network in isolation. This result is due to consideration of cross-system risks. The study also suggests that integrating Colombian financial institutions' networks of transactions and exposures with FMI networks adds resilience to the multilayered network, as FMIs are able to isolate feedback and cascades. However, this result holds only as long as the FMI itself is functioning well and does not fail. The evidence presented makes clear the advantages of mapping, monitoring, and analyzing the real-world multilayered financial networks.

Network analysis has been applied to other regions of the Western Hemisphere outside of LA7 countries. For instance, network analysis of the Caribbean region, in the context of Caribbean Regional Financial Project (CRFP), showed that the financial system of the Caribbean is highly interconnected. However, the system was found to be resilient to a range of moderate to severe propagating shocks (Annex 9.1).

REGULATORY OVERSIGHT

A key precondition for substantial cross-border financial integration is having a robust and forward-looking best practice regulatory and supervisory framework in place. The global financial crisis highlighted the crucial need to enhance both domestic and international regulatory standards and to strengthen prudential requirements and develop macroprudential tools to reduce risks in the financial system, including cross-border risks. In Latin America, financial activity risks can be mitigated by having a suitable entry, operating, and resolution framework for cross-border institutions;[7] sound prudential standards and national regulatory frameworks that reflect appropriate timelines and banking system complexity (Basel III); a complete picture of the financial institution (needed for cross-border consolidated and conglomerate supervision); and macroprudential policies that protect the national and regional financial systems from systemic macro-financial stability risks.

CROSS-BORDER ESTABLISHMENTS

Legal and regulatory frameworks for subsidiaries and branches of foreign firms have been enhanced but could be further strengthened. The legal frameworks of the surveyed countries generally require that branches and subsidiaries follow all regulations and practices of the host countries. All countries require endowment capital for branches, and most authorities have the power to restrict subsidiaries' issuance of dividends and capital, including cross-border. In addition, the pricing of centralized functions such as IT and treasury is subject to oversight, thereby avoiding circumvention of the restrictions on dividend and capital transfers. However, there is room for improvement. Local asset maintenance requirements for branches and limits on intragroup exposures for subsidiaries could usefully be reviewed. In the context of a broader update of bank resolution frameworks, powers to deal with cross-border coordination should be strengthened, including by removing the automaticity and discriminatory features of ring-fencing mechanisms.

BASEL III: CAPITAL, LIQUIDITY, AND LEVERAGE REQUIREMENTS

The LA-7 countries have made progress in adopting the Basel standards (Figures 9.4, 9.5, and 9.6). The Basel Committee's Eighth Progress Report on the adoption of the Basel regulatory agenda shows rapid recent progress in many emerging markets. Brazil and Mexico are fully compliant with the Basel III capital standard, the liquidity standard, and the leverage ratio. They also are compliant with regard to Basel II and Basel 2.5. Other LA-7 countries are implementing at a pace they consider in line with the complexity and development of their banking systems. With financial integration, many large banking groups and conglomerates face the prospect of varying regulatory capital regimes across the LA-7 countries in which they operate. This creates the potential for adverse incentives to grow in LA-7 countries where capital standards are weaker. A move to the Basel III capital definition across the LA-7 would remove the potential for regulatory arbitrage and—by coalescing on a consistent, high-quality capital measure—would

[7] The assessment of emerging markets in Latin America on the basis of the key attributes of effective resolution regimes for financial institutions (IMF 2016) is limited and will require further work. In late 2015 Colombia underwent a pilot assessment that will provide useful inputs to the Financial Stability Board from the emerging market perspective.

Figure 9.4 Progress in Implementing Basel II

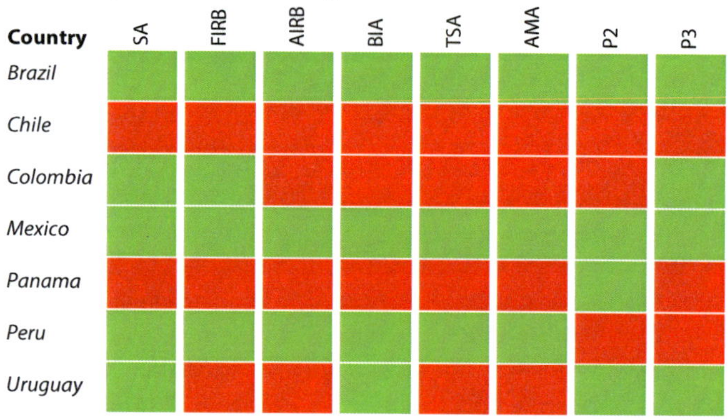

Sources: Data for Brazil and Mexico are from the Basel Committee on Banking Supervision (2016); for other countries, from the Bank for International Settlements (2015).
Note: AIRB = advanced internal ratings-based approach; AMA = advanced measurement approaches; BIA = basic indicator approach; FIRB = foundation internal ratings-based approach; P2 = Pillar 2; P3 = Pillar 3; SA = standardized approach; TSA = alternative standardized approach.

Figure 9.5 Progress in Implementing Basel 2.5

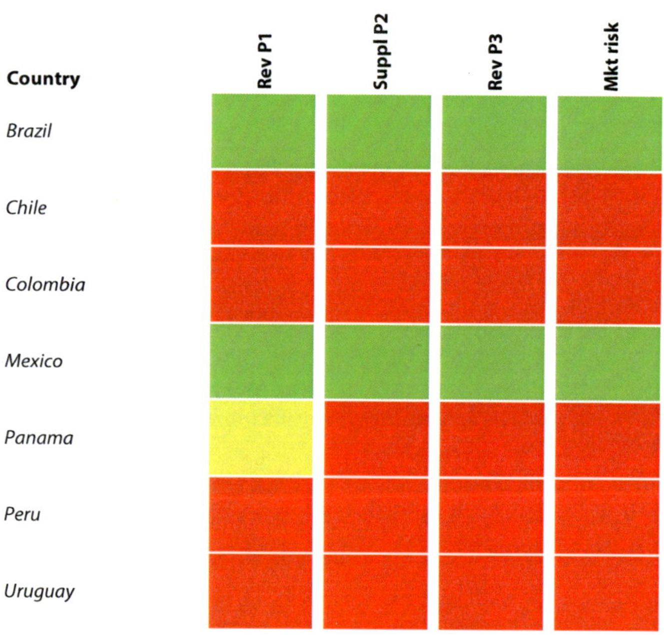

Sources: Data for Brazil and Mexico are from the Basel Committee on Banking Supervision (2016); for other countries, from the Bank for International Settlements (2015).
Note: Mkt risk = revisions to the Basel II market risk framework; Rev P1 = revisions to Pillar 1; Rev P3 = revisions to Pillar 3; Suppl P2 = supplemental Pillar 2 guidance.

Figure 9.6 Progress in Implementing Basel III

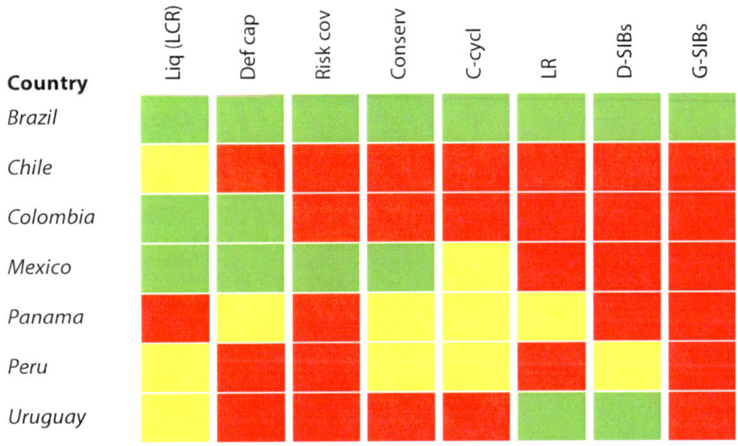

Sources: Data for Brazil and Mexico are from the Basel Committee on Banking Supervision (2016); for other countries, from the Bank for International Settlements (2015).
Note: C-Cycl = countercyclical buffer; Conserv = conservation buffer; Def cap = definition of capital; D-SIBs = domestic systemically important banks; G-SIBs = global systemically important banks; LCR = liquidity coverage ratio; Liq = liquidity; LR = leverage ratio; Risk cov = risk coverage.

enhance macro-financial stability by increasing loss absorbency against potential spillover risks (see Annex 9.2).

IMPORTANCE AND BENEFITS OF CONSOLIDATED AND CONGLOMERATE SUPERVISION

Forward-looking domestic and cross-border consolidated and conglomerate risk-based supervision is a key supervisory approach to address the complexity and potential underestimation of systemic risks inherent in conglomerate networks in the Latin and Central American region. Many supervisory agencies in the LA-7 countries have moved to a forward-looking risk-based regulatory and supervisory framework that uses supervisory tools such as macroeconomic, multiyear credit, market, and liquidity stress tests to flag solvency (capital) and liquidity vulnerabilities of financial institutions. However, this approach does not fully account for systemic risks, and even the use of price-based models would underestimate systemic risks arising from financial and nonfinancial institutions' interconnectedness and potential contagion risks. Adopting a domestic and cross-border consolidated and conglomerate supervisory approach would help prioritize the mapping, monitoring, and analysis of financial and mixed conglomerate networks, including through network stress tests as well as onsite and offsite work. This approach would help: (1) fully capture systemic risks, (2) identify vulnerable financial and nonfinancial institutions, (3) identify fragile transactions and exposures, and (4) flag key pathways for contagion. Knowledge of institution and system fragility would enable countries to tailor prudential and macroprudential tools to mitigate risks and ensure macro-financial stability.

The evidence from recent financial stability assessments conducted by the IMF and World Bank under the Financial Sector Assessment Program (FSAP) is that the countries in the region have a ways to go in improving their supervisory frameworks in terms of consolidated and conglomerate supervision. Legal restrictions in some countries prevent full achievement of best practices, in particular in the handling of the nonfinancial components of conglomerates. Although subsidiarization, and regulatory and resolution ring-fencing, can dampen cross-border spillovers, cross-border safety requires that the institution be supervised on a consolidated basis. International best practices for consolidated supervision call for establishing robust supervisory regimes, cross-border supervisory processes, joint monitoring programs, and coordinated corrective/supervisory actions among all parts of a cross-border financial institution or conglomerate.

The structure of Latin American financial institutions makes consolidated supervision particularly important because many are parts of conglomerates. In a number of cases the nonfinancial parts of these conglomerates have already expanded cross-border to a much greater extent than the banks. Even where there are no direct financial flows between the bank and nonbank parts of a conglomerate, problems in the nonbank part can have major knock-on effects on the bank. For example, problems in the retail arm of the group with the first Chilean bank to move cross-border led to financial pressures and ultimate sale to another regional bank, although the Chilean bank itself had faced no difficulties and was making substantial profits.

There is increasing awareness of the importance of consolidated supervision. Uruguayan regulators declined to license a regional bank that was seeking to acquire a bank being sold in Uruguay on the grounds that the regional bank's supervisor was not conducting consolidated supervision.

Conglomerate supervision complements supervision of individual sectors by adding a layer to the solo and consolidated sectoral supervision. Individual supervision faces limitations in dealing with double gearing of capital, conflicts of interest, risks of contagion, concentration, and other specific group risks that may hamper financial stability. Conglomerate supervision should detect and monitor these risks while avoiding unnecessary duplication with sectoral prudential standards.

Internationally agreed upon documents provide national authorities with a set of principles that support consistent and effective supervision of financial conglomerates. The main references are the Basel Committee on Banking Supervision's "Core Principles for Effective Banking Supervision" and the Joint Forum's "Principles for Supervision of Financial Conglomerates."[8] Focusing on both the cross-border and cross-sector dimensions of the process, these principles set expectations for supervisory powers and responsibilities, corporate governance, prudential requirements, and risk management. They focus on closing regulatory gaps, eliminating supervisory blind spots, and ensuring effective supervision of risks

[8] The Principles were released in 2012 by the Joint Forum's parent committees: the Basel Committee on Banking Supervision, the International Organization of Securities Commissions, and the International Association of Insurance Supervisions.

arising from unregulated financial activities and entities. Colombia is currently seeking parliamentary approval for a bill to provide supervisors with powers over the holding companies of financial conglomerates. However, the law would provide only limited reach into mixed conglomerates; much of their activity would remain outside the scope of the financial supervisory and regulatory perimeter.

The Principles are flexible and take a nonprescriptive approach to the supervision of financial conglomerates in order to cover a wide range of structures. They emphasize the importance of recognizing structural complexity and the potential risks it poses. This includes risks arising from all entities—unregulated or regulated—that affect the financial conglomerate's overall risk profile. The flexibility of this framework is intended to enable policymakers and supervisors to appropriately regulate and supervise financial conglomerates while limiting the scope for regulatory arbitrage.

Beyond consolidated supervision, there is also a need for increased cooperation and data sharing among supervisors to tackle conglomerate and cross-border risks more broadly. Supervisory colleges have been established for major banks in the region. Colombia has gone further with regard to Central America, where its banks have established significant positions in most countries. These countries have established a multilateral memorandum of understanding, a regional council of finance ministers, a regional monetary council, and a joint council of supervisors. The analytical work on cross-border multilevel financial networks highlights the need for more granular direct and indirect data for both on- and off-balance-sheet items (see Table 9.1). However, important data confidentiality concerns must be overcome on a cross-border basis, new analytical tools are needed to handle very large data sets, and investment is required in staff who can work with financial risk modeling tools.

PRUDENTIAL AND MACROPRUDENTIAL MEASURES

Prudential tools allied with forward-looking, risk-based supervision can address systemic risk arising from financial and mixed conglomerate networks across Latin America. The tools described here are designed to address interconnectedness and contagion (spillover) risks.[9]

- *Microprudential exposure limits.* Microprudential exposure limits are normally designed as non-risk-sensitive backstops to limit concentration from a microprudential perspective, but they are also relevant from a macroprudential point of view.
- *Capital charges, particularly for systemically important financial institutions (SIFIs).* Capital requirements in Basel I and II did not directly account for interconnectedness (concentration) and contagion risks, but Basel III minimum capital rules were formulated with explicit consideration for concentration and systemic risk.

---

[9] See Arregui and others (2013) for more details.

- *Liquidity regulation and limits on liquidity mismatches.* The lack of liquidity requirements encouraged reliance on central bank and wholesale funding in the global financial crisis, increasing interconnectedness and contagion risks among financial institutions. Basel III liquidity requirements (the Liquidity Coverage Ratio and Net Stable Funding Ratio) can mitigate systemic risks by limiting liquidity contagion and reducing funding and counterparty interconnectedness.
- *Clearing of over-the-counter derivatives on a central counterparty (CCP).* CCPs increase transparency regarding the amount and distribution of risk exposure, helping clarify interconnectedness risks. They also help mitigate contagion by mutualizing losses among all clearing members.
- *Structural limits on activities.* Direct restrictions on the scope of business of global SIFIs, conglomerates, or large and internationally active banks can help reduce the complexity of business models, which directly reduces interconnectedness and contagion risks.
- *Resolution frameworks and insurance.* Effective cross-border resolution frameworks can help insulate institutions from each other with regard to failure, which reduces the impact from interconnectedness and contagion risks.

Arregui and others (2013) note that prudential measures can interact bilaterally, either complementing each other in reducing systemic risks or conflicting with one another. Depending on the degree of complementarity or conflict, we can make a qualitative assessment of how each prudential tool is likely to address interconnectedness (concentration) and contagion risks and how difficult it can be to implement from a regulatory or bank perspective (Table 9.4). Prudential tools may be less effective for mixed conglomerates than for financial conglomerates, because they may apply only to supervised and regulated entities within the mixed conglomerate structure.

Since the global financial crisis there has been considerable global progress in designing and implementing a macroprudential toolkit. If they consider that cyclical conditions warrant, macroprudential authorities have the power to impose additional capital charges beyond those imposed institution by institution. Specific instruments—such as limits on loan-to-value and debt-to-income, and sectoral risk weights or floors—can be helpful.

Such instruments are likely to be designed and implemented at the national level, given the different risk exposures of each country. However, where cross-border financial activity exists, especially in the case of financial and mixed conglomerates, there is a clear need for coordination and reciprocity to avoid arbitrage and macroprudential leakage across countries. In addition to the complementarity and conflicts among prudential tools, there are complementarities and conflicts when prudential and macroprudential tools operate together to address systemic risks. Policymakers need to address this tension when they design policy frameworks and institutional mechanisms, to ensure effective coordination between these tools.

TABLE 9.4

Interaction of Prudential Tools

Tools[1,2]		Microprudential Exposure Limits	Capital Buffers (SIFIs)	Limits on Liquidity Mismatches (LCR, NFSR)	Limits on Activities[3]	Resolution Frameworks	CCP Clearing Requirements
Microprudential exposure limits							
Capital buffers (SIFIs)							
Limits on liquidity mismatches							
Limits on activities (structural)							
Resolution frameworks							
CCP clearing requirements							
Overall Complementarity							
Impact on concentration		↓↓	↓	↓↑	↓↓	↓	↑
Impact on contagion		↓↓	↓	↓	↓↓	↓	↓
Overall reduction in interconnectedness		HIGH	LOW	MEDIUM	HIGH	MEDIUM	LOW
Complexity of implementation	Regulators	LOW	MEDIUM	HIGH	HIGH	HIGH	MEDIUM
	Banks	MEDIUM	LOW	HIGH	HIGH	HIGH	LOW

Source: IMF staff compilation.

Note: CCP = central counterparty; LCR = liquidity coverage ratio; NFSR = net funding stable ratio; SIFIs = systemically important financial institutions.

[1] Fully complementary: tool mutually reinforces the intended objective of another tool (dark blue); partially complementary: tool may have a partially offsetting impact on the intended effects of another tool (light blue); partially conflicting: tool has a conflicting but not major impact on the intent of another tool (light red); not related or not contradictory (white).

[2] Arrows indicate an increase (↑) or decrease (↓) in resulting impact.

[3] Refers to the Volker, Vickers, and Liikanen structural measures—see Pazarbasioglu and others (2013).

POLICY RECOMMENDATIONS

Latin American countries can benefit from taking a regional approach to implementing the remaining elements of the global regulatory agenda and developing their emerging prudential and macroprudential toolkits to address systemic risks. They should do the following:

- Align timelines while reflecting international commitments and local circumstances as national authorities move forward with implementing the regulatory agenda.[10]
- Invest in staff and resources to fully capture systemic risks through the use of new data analysis tools and mapping, monitoring, and analyzing financial and mixed conglomerate networks that can be integrated with solvency and liquidity stress tests. Coordination across the LA-7 in sharing such information (legally enshrined, if possible) would help the region tackle appropriate systemic risk analysis and address data confidentiality concerns as well.
- Introduce or strengthen consolidated supervision—with technical assistance from the IMF or other sources—in line with recommendations from the IMF FSAPs and the Joint Forum's Principles.
- Introduce or enhance conglomerate supervision, including establishing regulatory limits for intragroup exposures within banking groups and between bank and nonbank segments of conglomerates.
- Continue the development of macroprudential tools through regional conferences and possibly a more formal regional arrangement, so that tools can be designed and implemented on a regional basis to avoid cross-country regulatory arbitrage and coordinate dealing with spillovers.

[10] As members of the Basel Committee and the Financial Stability Board, Brazil and Mexico are required to abide by the international timeline for implementation.

ANNEX 9.1. THE CARIBBEAN REGIONAL FINANCIAL PROJECT[11]

The Caribbean Regional Financial Project sought to map the structure of interconnectedness within the Caribbean financial system and, given that structure, to assess potential transmission of shocks through financial channels. The project entailed collecting a unique dataset on interconnectedness covering the banking systems of Barbados, Belize, the Eastern Caribbean Currency Union (ECCU), Guyana, Jamaica, Suriname, The Bahamas, and Trinidad and Tobago, as well as the insurance sectors of Barbados, Belize, Guyana, Jamaica, Suriname, and Trinidad and Tobago.[12] After mapping the financial system, the analysis consisted of using the network structure to simulate how financial and economic shocks might propagate through the system. The aim was to assess the adequacy of Caribbean financial systems' capital buffers to withstand such shocks and to understand which were the key regional financial sectors and clusters within the region.

The unique dataset collected suggests that the Caribbean financial sector is highly interconnected, both within the Caribbean and with the global financial system.[13] Caribbean banks in particular, have important cross-border claims on sovereigns, banks, and insurers, representing, on average, 15 percent of GDP and 12 percent of total assets. In contrast to banks, Caribbean insurers' cross-border claims are relatively small compared to the size of the economy, representing, on average, 5 percent of GDP, but are considerably larger as a share of their total assets than banks' cross-border claims, suggesting a larger degree of interconnectedness in the insurance segment of the financial sector. Other key findings from the mapping exercise included the following:

- The Caribbean financial sector's exposure to cross-border sovereign risk appears to be concentrated primarily in the insurance sector, and within that sector, primarily to sovereigns from within the region. By contrast, banks' cross-border claims on sovereigns represent a relatively small share of their total assets, and these claims are relatively diversified across the Caribbean and globally.
- Caribbean banks are interconnected with other banks, particularly global banks, likely related to the significant presence of three Canadian banking groups in the Caribbean. Claims are primarily in the form of relatively low-risk deposits. Caribbean bank claims on banks domiciled in other Caribbean countries are relatively minor.
- Insurers generally have limited interconnections with banks, with the exception of a few jurisdictions that are home to the largest regional insurers.

[11] Prepared by Elie Canetti and Kimberly Beaton.

[12] The data were provided to IMF staff at the aggregate banking and insurance system level rather than at the level of individual institutions for confidentiality reasons.

[13] The data were collected in 2015, but in order to use audited accounts, were based on accounts as of June 30, 2013.

- Caribbean banks' exposures to cross-border risks from the insurance sector appear to be negligible, but Caribbean insurers appear to have important exposures to global insurers.
- Network maps show that the most interconnected banking sectors in the Caribbean region are those in Barbados, The Bahamas, the ECCU, Guyana, Jamaica, and Trinidad and Tobago, while the key insurance sectors are in Barbados and Trinidad and Tobago (Annex Figure 9.1.1). The financial systems of Belize, Haiti, and Suriname appear to be on the periphery of the system.

The analysis of how financial and economic shocks could propagate through the Caribbean financial system suggested the system was resilient to a range of moderate to severe shocks. The simulations gauged Caribbean financial systems' systemic importance and susceptibility to spillovers stemming from potential depletion of bank capital (solvency channel) and funding pressures (liquidity channel).[14] Most banking systems were in a position to withstand substantial losses on total loans and on sectoral loans without falling below conventional capital adequacy ratio (CAR) thresholds. In general, propagation risks appear limited. Only one simulation, involving a simultaneous solvency and liquidity shock, was able to trigger a second-round (that is, indirect) spillover effect.[15]

The network was also exposed to simulations of both single-sector shocks (tourism, construction, real estate, households, energy sector, and the sovereign) and multisector shocks:

- Several financial systems were exposed to sovereign risk. Simulations of simultaneous and uniform haircuts on Caribbean sovereigns pushed a number of jurisdictions' banking systems below the Basel I/II minimum capital threshold. However, although the size of the simulated haircuts was based on historical experience with debt restructurings in the region, it should be noted that simultaneous haircuts on all sovereigns in the region would constitute a very extreme shock. All but one insurance sector were able to stay above the same Basel I/II minimum CAR threshold in such cases.[16]
- Among the single-shock scenarios, shocks to real estate and household loans had the largest impact on banking systems' capital adequacy. Substantial

[14] With aggregate data, it would be unrealistic to assume that spillovers occur only when the capital of the financial system is depleted. Aggregate capital would typically remain positive even during severe crises, but this would not preclude failures of individual institutions. Therefore, we modeled a systemic crisis as a capital shortfall (a capital adequacy ratio below 8 percent) rather than as an insolvency.

[15] It is important to realize that these simulations can test shock propagation only through fundamental financial linkages. However, crises and spillovers can lead to purely panic-driven contagion across countries, even in the absence of fundamental linkages.

[16] Although Basel I/II applies to banks, the same threshold was used for insurers for consistency. That said, the threshold treats insurers, in effect, somewhat more conservatively than banks because it measures capital adequacy in terms of total assets instead of risk-weighted assets.

Annex Figure 9.1.1 Caribbean Financial Interconnectedness

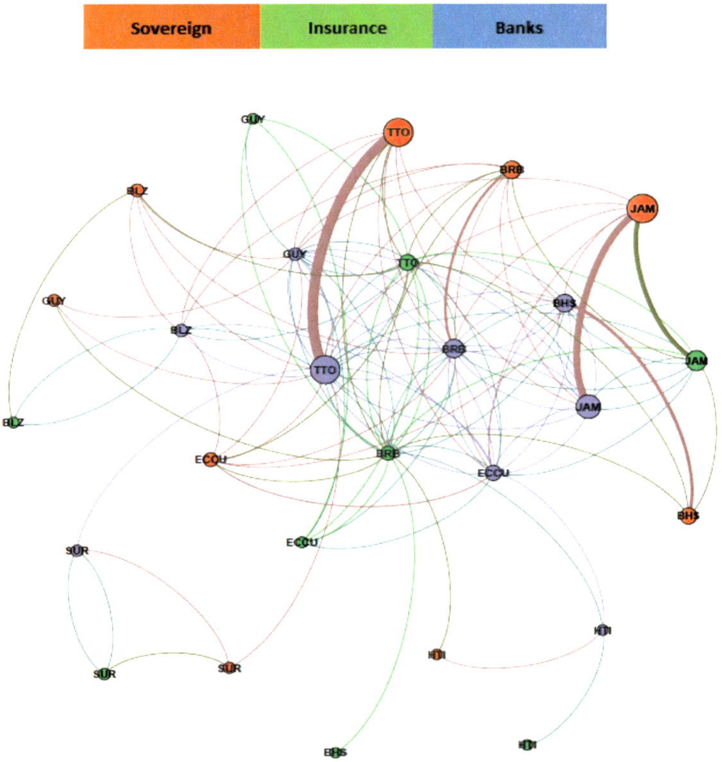

Source: Country authorities; and IMF staff calculations.
Note: Based on data as of June 30, 2013. BHS = The Bahamas; BLZ = Belize; BRB = Barbados; ECCU = Eastern Caribbean Currency Union; GUY = Guyana; HTI = Haiti; JAM = Jamaica; SUR = Suriname; TTO = Trinidad and Tobago.

losses on real estate loans would have materially affected the capital adequacy of a few banking systems. However, these tests did not take into account collateralization of real estate lending, and partial recovery of such collateral would in fact mitigate the risks to bank capital.

- Losses arising from single shocks to tourism, construction, and energy loans were relatively small as these sectors tend to be at least partially financed by foreign direct investment or by foreign banks.
- Combinations of severe shocks to tourism, construction, and the sovereign would have significantly weakened the capital buffers of a number of national banking sectors. A moderate across-the-board haircut to sovereign debt, if combined with simultaneous losses on tourism and construction loans, did not push any banking sectors below the Basel I/II minimum capital adequacy threshold, although one banking sector came close.

- Cross-border spillover risks among the Caribbean insurance sectors appeared largely contained owing to robust capital buffers.
- Spillovers through solvency channels are more predominant than spillovers through liquidity channels. This appears to reflect that banks are primarily funded by deposits rather than interbank borrowing, reducing funding vulnerabilities.

ANNEX 9.2. CAPITAL DEFINITIONS AND CAPITAL RATIOS ACROSS LATIN AMERICA

Background

A robust bank capital framework helps ensure financial stability and sustain bank lending during economic downturns. Bank provisions and profits are an important buffer; provisions in particular can absorb expected losses. However, in the event that losses exceed earnings, capital provides banks with a cushion to absorb unexpected losses to reduce the risk of bank failure and prevent interruption of banking services and financing to the real economy. Unfortunately, loss absorbency elements such as provisions, capital definitions, and actual regulatory capital levels are not easily comparable across Latin America, even using harmonized market-based measures.

Capital Definition and Adequacy

Capital definitions differ across Latin American countries, and comparisons must be made with utmost caution. Some cross-country differences in the computation of capital include treatment of the revaluation of fixed assets, accounting of profits from current or past accounting periods, treatment of investments in capital instruments or requirements on donated capital, treatment of some deductions from capital (goodwill, intangibles, and deferred tax assets), and grandfathering of some capital (debt) components. Capital also differs depending on the degree of consolidation undertaken, whether at the individual (solo) bank level, the banking group level, or even the financial conglomerate level. In different jurisdictions, the regulatory risk weights applied to the same asset classes can be quite different. Differences in the national definition of capital, the Basel framework in use, and accounting standards across Latin America suggest that any direct comparison of total regulatory capitalization should be interpreted with caution.

Market-Based Estimates of Capital

Some systemic Colombian banks have lower levels of capital in excess of the regulatory minimum than their regional peers. Regulatory capital requirements differ across Latin American countries (Annex Figure 9.2.1), with some higher than Colombia's 9 percent (Brazil, 11 percent; Guatemala, Peru, and Uruguay, 10 percent) and some lower (Argentina and Chile, 8 percent; Mexico, 10.5 percent). The decision to choose a given level of national minimum regulatory capital reflects multiple factors, including supervisory judgment and discretion. The four largest banks in Colombia have lower levels of capital than the large banks in some other Latin American countries.

Total capital ratios in excess of the regulatory minimum requirement stood at 2.9 percent, the lower end of regional peer comparisons. Rating agencies have tried to obtain a more consistent, harmonized measure of capital across Latin

Annex Figure 9.2.1 Regulatory Capital Requirement and Total Capital Above Requirement
(*Percent*)

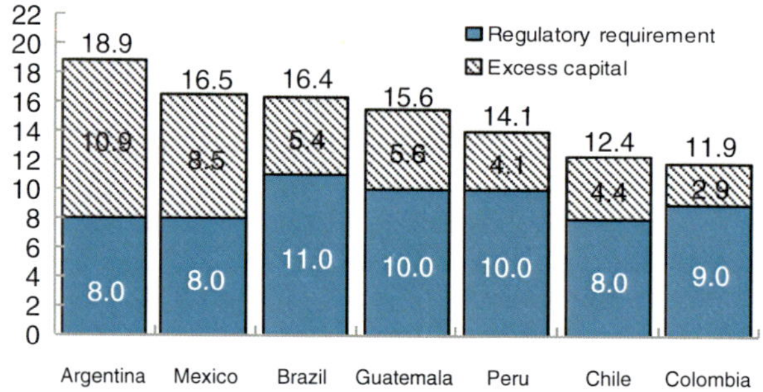

Sources: Bankscope; company filings; IMF, Article IV Consultation staff reports, and Financial Sector Stability Assessments.

America, but comparisons on quantity and quality of capital vary depending on the measures used. For example, Colombian banks have lower levels of capital according to Standard and Poor's risk-adjusted capital measure, which deducts all goodwill on the balance sheet from banks' total adjusted capital (Annex Figure 9.2.2). This measure is important, as Colombia experienced a large number of mergers and acquisitions following the financial crisis of the late 1990s that, together with the geographic expansion of the largest banks over the past few years, created large amounts of goodwill assets. Using the Fitch Core Capital (FCC) measure, Brazil, Chile, and Colombia have much lower capital levels, owing to higher leverage of the system, sizable investments in insurance

Annex Figure 9.2.2 Risk-Adjusted Capital Ratios for the Largest Rated Latin American Banks
(*Percent*)

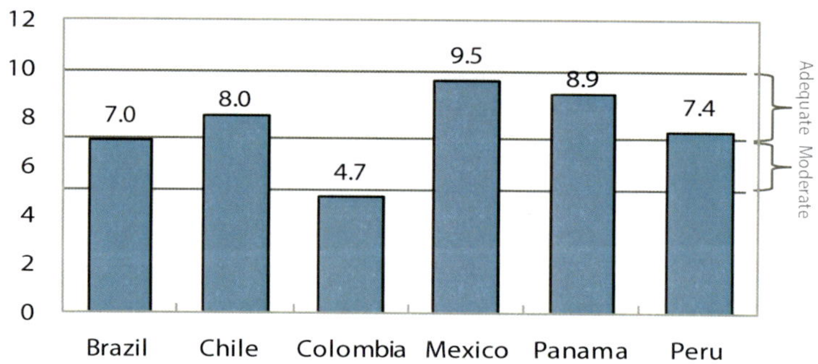

Source: Standard & Poor's.

Annex Figure 9.2.3 Fitch Core Capital
(Percent)

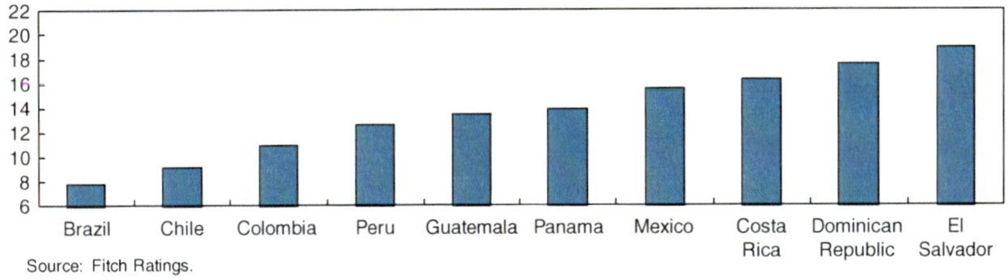

Source: Fitch Ratings.
Note: Data for 2013. Figure shows generally adequate capital ratios in Latin America.

companies, and high levels of goodwill and deferred tax assets, all of which are deducted from equity to reach FCC levels (Annex Figure 9.2.3).

Additional Loss Absorbency and Basel III

Although capital ratios on market-based measures may seem low for some Latin American countries, these countries have additional loss absorbency in their banking systems. Many banks hold high levels of provisions (Brazil and Colombia), lower levels of nonperforming loans (Colombia), or more conservative risk weights (Chile and Colombia). Many Latin American countries are adopting Basel III standards, albeit at different paces. This should help address inconsistency of capital definitions, with recent work by the Basel Committee ensuring harmonization of risk weights. Notwithstanding the move to Basel III, actual implementation may still result in differentiation of capital stemming from differences in the adoption of above-minimum levels (Pillar 2 and conservation, countercyclical, and domestic systemically important bank buffers). These differences may reflect the need to address supervisory failings and the desire to tailor capital to bank risks, which may be above Basel III voluntary minimums in some Latin American countries.

Conclusion

The addition of more consistency to the already robust capital framework across Latin America will help ensure financial stability and sustain bank lending during economic downturns. Challenges from moderating economic growth, a low yield environment, volatility around U.S. monetary policy normalization, cross-border risks, and conglomerate expansion require that Latin American banks adopt a more conservative long-term capital planning approach. Moving to Basel III should help, and this is attainable for most Latin American banking systems, as current capital is sufficient to support transition and additional loss absorbency exists beyond capital.

REFERENCES

Arregui, N., M. Norat, A. Pancorbo, and J. Scarlata. 2013. "Addressing Interconnectedness: Concepts and Prudential Tools." Working Paper 13/199, International Monetary Fund, Washington.

Bank for International Settlements. 2015. "Financial Stability Institute Survey: Basel II, 2.5 and III Implementation." Bank for International Settlements, Basel, July.

Basel Committee on Banking Supervision (BCBS). 2016. "Tenth Progress Report on Adoption of the Basel Regulatory Framework." BCBS, Basel, April.

Caceres, C., V. Guzzo, and A. Segoviano. 2010. "Sovereign Spreads: Global Risk Aversion, Contagion or Fundamentals?" Working Paper 10/120, International Monetary Fund, Washington.

Depository Trust and Clearing Corporation (DTCC). 2015. "Understanding Interconnectedness Risks to Build a More Resilient Financial System." White Paper, DTCC, October.

International Monetary Fund (IMF). 2016. "Technical Assistance Report: Detailed Assessment of Observance of Key Attributes of Effective Resolution Regimes for Financial Institutions—Pilot of the Draft Assessment Methodology." Washington, April.

León, C., R. Berndsen, and L. Renneboog. 2014. "Financial Stability and Interacting Networks of Financial Institutions and Market Infrastructures." Discussion Paper 2014-011, Tilburg, European Banking Center.

Markose, Sheri M., and Simone Giansante. 2013. "Pigou Tax of Systemically Important Financial Intermediaries." In *Financial Networks: An Empirical Application of Systemic Risk Monitoring and Governance*. Workshop: Twenty Years after Cadbury, Ten Years after Sarbanes-Oxley. Challenges of Corporate Governance June 24–25, Bath Management School, University of Bath, Bath, United Kingdom.

Nier, E., J. Yang, T. Yorulmazer, and A. Alentorn. 2007. "Network Models and Financial Stability." *Journal of Economic Dynamics and Control* 31: 2033–60.

Pazarbasioglu, C., J. Surti, A. Narain, M. Erbenova, and J. Chow. 2013. "Creating a Safer Financial System: Will the Volcker, Vicker, and Liikanen Structural Measures Help?" Staff Discussion Note 13/4, International Monetary Fund, Washington.

Poledna, S., J. L. Molina-Borboa, S. Martínez-Jaramillo, M. van der Leij, and S. Thurner. 2015. "The Multilayered Network Nature of Systemic Risk and Its Implications for the Costs of Financial Crises." *Journal of Financial Stability* 20: 70–81.

Scott, H. 2012. "Interconnectedness and Contagion." Discussion Paper, Committee on Capital Markets Regulation, Cambridge, Massachusetts, November.

Segoviano, A., and C. Goodhart. 2009. "Banking Stability Measures." Working Paper 09/4, International Monetary Fund, Washington.

Segoviano, M. 2006. "Consistent Information Multivariate Density Optimizing Methodology." Discussion Paper 557, Financial Markets Group, London School of Economics, London, United Kingdom.

Appendix 1. Brazil[1]

Brazil's financial system is by far the largest in Latin America. Commensurate with the size of its overall economy, Brazil's total financial sector assets dwarf those of other regional peers. Brazil's nominal GDP amounted to about $2.4 trillion in 2014 (Appendix Figure 1.1), comparable to that of the next five largest economies in Latin America combined. Accordingly, Brazil's banking system is the largest in absolute terms. Furthermore, at total assets close to $2.4 trillion, the banking sector is also one of the largest in percent of GDP, representing close to 117 percent.

The banking system in Brazil remains dominated by large public banks. Publicly owned banks represent about half of the entire banking system. Furthermore, the banking sector remains highly concentrated, with the eight largest banks accounting for about 85 percent of the banking sector (Appendix Figure 1.2). Moreover, the financial system is characterized by a high degree of conglomeration. Interest margins are high, which are partly reflected in high profitability, particularly for the large banks. However, the system appears to be still stuck in a "high interest rate and short duration" equilibrium, which limits capital market development and thus potential growth.

In terms of nonbanks, the insurance sector appears to be performing well. Profitability in the insurance sector has been relatively high over the past few years, likely benefiting from high interest rates, which has translated into solid solvency ratios. Mutual funds and banks appear to be highly interconnected through repo operations and the holding of deposit and bank-issued bonds by the funds. Pension funds are sizable in Brazil, with assets under management close to $280 billion. Nevertheless, essentially all these assets are invested domestically.

Itaú is the only universal Brazilian bank with a significant presence in the region. Most Brazilian banks tend to be inward looking. This reflects in large part the significant share of publicly owned banks, as well as a large domestic market to service. Itaú, which is the largest privately owned bank in Brazil, has nevertheless sizable stakes in the region, representing almost 10 percent of the banks' total assets. The bank is present in Argentina, Chile, Colombia, Mexico, Paraguay, and Uruguay. In terms of more specialized Brazilian banks, BTG Pactual is trying to position itself as a regional investment bank. These banks have the advantage of operating with smaller balance sheets, hence the potential ability to be profitable without the need for large scale. This is also reflected in terms of their capital costs, with capital requirements (that is, risk-weighted assets) mainly driven by market risk considerations rather than credit risk.

However, foreign claims of banks in Brazil remain concentrated in a few advanced economies. Claims of Brazilian banks on countries such as the United Kingdom or the United States completely dwarf claims on other Latin American countries (Appendix Figure 1.3). The only exception is Chile, where Itaú has a significant presence. Interestingly, the Cayman Islands appears to have a

[1] Prepared by Carlos Caceres.

Appendix Figure 1.1 Brazil's GDP and Banking Sector Assets Compared with Regional Peers

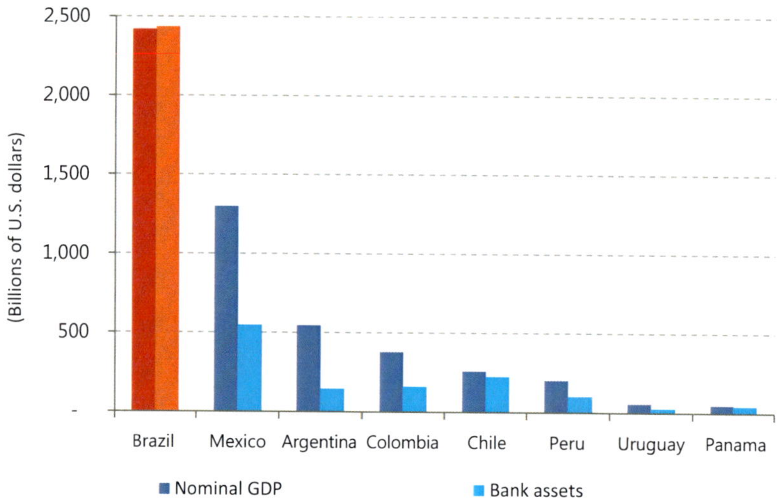

Sources: Bankscope; Haver Analytics; national statistics; and IMF staff calculations.

Appendix Figure 1.2 Ownership in the Brazilian Banking System

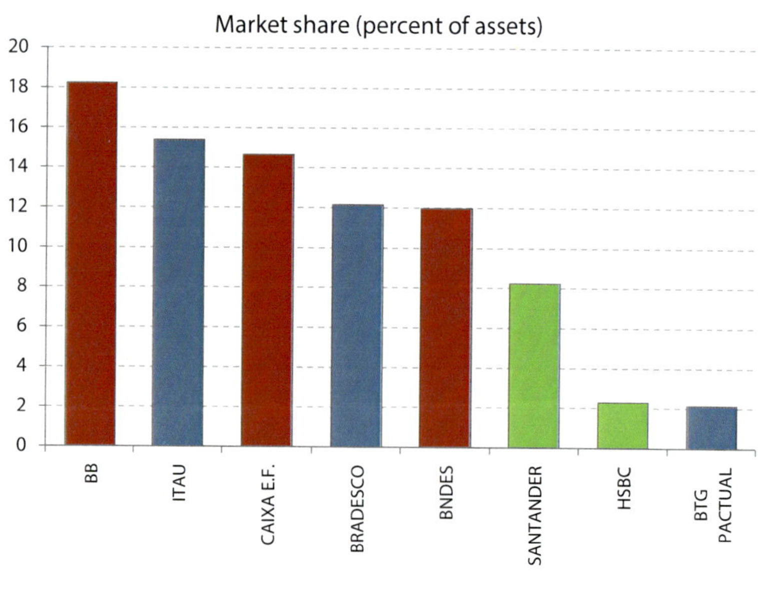

Sources: Bankscope; national statistics; and IMF staff calculations.

Appendix Figure 1.3 Claims of Brazilian Banks on Banks in Other Countries

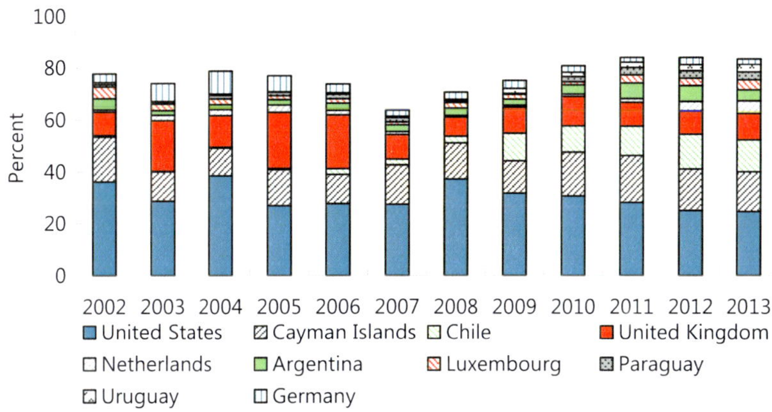

Sources: Bank for International Settlements (BIS); and IMF staff calculations.
Note: Figure shows consolidated foreign claims of BIS-reporting banks in Brazil on the top 10 individual countries, sorted by 2013.

noticeable share of Brazilian foreign claims. However, most Brazilian banks establish operations there so they can offer their Brazilian clients investments denominated in foreign currencies.

Foreign financial claims on Brazil have been growing rapidly for most of the 21st century. Indeed, foreign claims have more than quadrupled since 2005, and stand at about $442 billion (roughly 18 percent of GDP). Spain has the highest foreign claims, representing close to 7.5 percent of GDP, reflecting the significant presence of Spanish banks in the country, most notably Santander. In recent years, however, the total amount of foreign claims seems to have stabilized. This would be consistent with the slowdown in growth observed in the domestic economy over this recent period. Furthermore, Brazilian financial institutions present a relatively low ratio of foreign liabilities to credit to the economy (about 10 percent). This suggests a relatively low reliance on foreign funds as a source of funding, limiting the effects of any potential global liquidity squeeze.

Banking sector flows appear to be present in places where real activity linkages exist. There are likely a large number of drivers behind Brazilian cross-border financial flows. However, most banks report the desire to establish operations in those locations where Brazilian clients are present or have any significant interest. Indeed, there is some evidence that cross-border banking sector flows in Brazil tend to be associated with trade linkages as well as foreign direct investment. Furthermore, there has been a noticeable increase in bank as well as nonbank issuance abroad by Brazilian corporations.

Brazil's regulatory framework is broadly adequate. The last IMF Financial Sector Assessment Program (which took place in 2012) characterized financial sector oversight as strong, but there is room for improvement in some areas to stay ahead of a rapidly evolving system. Compliance of banking supervision vis-à-vis the Basel Core Principles is one of the highest in the region (100 percent of principles were found to be "Compliant" or "Largely Compliant").

Significant regulatory barriers exist, potentially hindering Brazil's further integration into the region and elsewhere. For instance, foreign banks need special presidential approval to operate in the country, even under the subsidiary model. This is not the case for domestic banks. Furthermore, Brazilian banks are not allowed any significant position in their balance sheet (loans or deposits) denominated in foreign currencies. Although this clearly minimizes potential foreign exchange–associated risks (both market and credit risks), most countries tend to allow some small open foreign exchange position on banks' balance sheets. In addition, natural barriers such as Brazil's large relative size and the degree of market concentration represent further hurdles for regional players to enter the domestic market.

Appendix 2. Chile[1]

Chile has a deep financial system with a large presence of institutional investors. Assets of the banking system amount to about 125 percent of GDP. Pension funds account for about 75 percent of GDP, while mutual funds and insurance companies are significantly smaller (20–25 percent of GDP). All institutions combined, the financial sector is close to 250 percent of GDP.

Chile is a very open economy with large cross-border financial linkages. Chile's net international investment position has hovered around –15 percent of GDP since 2008, and is stronger than other countries in the region. Chile has a net negative foreign direct investment (FDI) position, reflecting large inflows in the mining sector, and a net positive equity position, with the financial sector (pension funds, mutual funds, and insurance companies) being the main holders of foreign assets. FDI inflows are an important source of investment in Chile, in particular for the mining, financial, and utilities sectors. FDI inflows have increased from an annual average of 6 percent of GDP in the early 2000s to 8½ percent in recent years. The Netherlands, Spain, and the United States represent the main source markets. Portfolio investment amounted to 30 percent of GDP in 2014 (based on international investment positions stock data). U.S. residents hold nearly half of total portfolio investment assets (both equity and debt) vis-à-vis Chile, followed by Luxembourg and the United Kingdom (each 10 percent). Nonresidents hold about 5 percent of Chile's sovereign bonds.

The Ministry of Finance (MoF), the Central Bank of Chile (BCCh), and the three supervisory agencies are responsible for financial regulation and supervision. In addition to their responsibilities for the issuance of norms, particularly concerning corporate governance, credit classification, and provisioning, the three supervisory agencies are responsible for the supervision of financial entities: the Superintendencia de Bancos e Instituciones Financieras supervises banks, the Superintendencia de Valores y Seguros supervises insurance companies and security companies, and the Superintendencia de Pensiones supervises pension funds. The MoF is responsible for the preparation of financial sector laws. In addition to having an advisory role regarding the preparation of laws, the BCCh is directly responsible for the determination of liquidity requirements, regulation and supervision of derivative operations, and the payments system. The BCCh conducts twice-a-year top-down stress tests that focus on both credit and market risk for the banking sector, and shares these results with the supervisory agencies. Coordination among all these entities has been improved through the creation of a Financial Stability Council in 2011.

THE BANKING SECTOR

There is a large foreign presence in the banking sector in Chile. Foreign banks account for 35 percent of total banking sector assets, including Chile's largest

[1] Prepared by Luc Eyraud and Diva Singh.

bank, Banco Santander-Chile, which is a subsidiary of the Spanish banking group. BBVA, Itaú, and Scotiabank are also subsidiaries of foreign banks. Banco de Chile is a domestic bank but it is jointly owned by U.S.-based Citigroup and a Chilean conglomerate. The share of foreign banks, however, is not unusually high and is close to the average of LA-5 countries. Itaú-Corpbanca (whose merger is expected to be finalized in 2016) has become a regional bank with a presence in Brazil, Colombia, and Chile.

Conversely, Chilean banks do not have a large presence abroad. Corpbanca was an exception, with its acquisition of two Colombian banks a few years ago. One explanation is the small size of the financial sector relative to Chile's neighbors. Chilean banks are too small to compete with Brazilian banks, for instance, particularly because Chilean banks are not allowed to invest more than 40 percent of common equity in a single market (in shares of a foreign bank).[2] In any case, there are few potential candidates (only four large domestic banks, of which one is public). In addition, if subsidiaries of foreign banks are willing to expand outside Chile, they will proceed from their headquarters, not from Chile.

The banking sector appears generally healthy. Bank capitalization is adequate. Banks' profitability remained strong in 2014, although it declined in 2015 mainly because of a smaller positive impact of inflation. Banks' nonperforming loans have decreased slightly from already low levels, and capital ratios are above regulatory thresholds. Domestic deposits are the main funding source; the banks' reliance on external funding sources is relatively moderate (at 12¼ percent of their total funding needs, up from about 9½ in August 2012).

The authorities are in the process of adapting Basel III standards to the Chilean banking system. Currently, banks operate under an amended Basel I framework with additional capital requirements for market risk. A leverage ratio is already imposed, but there is no capital charge for operational risk. A new banking law was submitted in March 2016. The new law will adapt Basel III capital standards to Chilean banks on a transitional basis and introduce a capital surcharge for domestic systemically important banks. Basel III capital guidelines should be published in 2016 to ensure compliance by the 2019 deadline. In addition, a new liquidity regulation became effective from August 2015. It improves the quality and frequency of information provided to regulators and specifies the minimum requirements for monitoring the liquidity coverage ratio and net-funding stable ratio.

PENSION FUNDS

Pension funds, with total assets above 70 percent of GDP, are key players in Chile's financial system. Chile has a three-pillar defined contribution system.

---

[2] The 40 percent limit applies to each country, meaning that a bank could invest up to 80 percent of its regulatory capital in two countries, for instance.

Under the mandatory contribution pillar, employees are required to contribute 10 percent of their wage or salary to an individual account and choose one of the six private pension funds (Administradoras de Fondos de Pensiones or AFPs) to manage their account. Employees also choose between five portfolios (A to E) depending on their desired level of risk. Two pension funds were bought by U.S. groups in 2013. Today, four AFPs are foreign owned and two are Chilean. AFP assets are managed by international and domestic fund managers, who invest mainly in mutual and exchange traded funds, with a strong focus on emerging markets. The authorities plan to establish a new public pension fund to increase competition and coverage.

In recent years, pension funds pressured by the low-yield environment have been restructuring their portfolios toward riskier, foreign, and/or less liquid assets. Expansion abroad has mainly been in response to the lack of investment opportunities in the domestic market. Most foreign investment is in mutual funds and equities, mainly in the United States and emerging Asia assets.

AFPs are subject to a number of limits on their allocations of risky assets. These limits are intended to encourage diversification and protect pensions from contagion and spillover problems. In the past AFPs could invest in only fixed-income securities, but limits have been relaxed over time, and gradually the scope was extended to riskier and more diversified instruments.

For each type of portfolio (A to E), there are limits on how much the AFP can invest in "restricted instruments" (non-investment-grade fixed income and stocks that exchange in a market with a rating lower than AA). For instance, for the riskiest portfolio (type A), the limit is 20 percent of assets under management. The assessed risk of direct equity holdings is assigned to the sovereign risk rating of the country where the firm is domiciled; however, this can be somewhat circumvented by purchasing mutual funds or exchange traded funds through investment-grade financial centers such as New York or Luxembourg. AFPs are not allowed to invest directly in alternative assets (such as private equity or real estate) but are required to invest through a mutual fund.

In addition, AFPs are subject to two types of limits on their foreign investment. The first limit is specific to each portfolio (for instance, 90 percent of portfolio B can be invested in foreign assets). The second limit concerns the aggregate portfolio: AFPs are allowed to allocate up to 80 percent of their total assets under management abroad; currently, the actual share is 45 percent on average, up from 35 percent at end-2011.

INSURANCE AND MUTUAL FUNDS

The insurance sector is the largest sector after banks and pension funds. This competitive market (60 companies) is dominated by life insurance companies, which represent 90 percent of assets. Its growth has been spurred by the pension system.[3] In life insurance about a third of the market share is held by foreign companies. International companies need to be based in Chile to operate in the domestic market, and their risk rating needs to be equal to or above BBB. Most insurance companies are part of conglomerates.

Pressured by the low-yield environment, like pension funds, insurance companies have increased their asset allocations in real estate, as well as lower-rated domestic and foreign corporate bonds. Insurance companies cannot invest more than 20 percent of their assets abroad (and 5 percent for foreign high-yield bonds), which makes the limit significantly more binding than that applied to pension funds. The 20 percent limit has recently become binding for several life insurers and is an active constraint on portfolio management. A new regulation introduced in 2015 requires insurance companies to define their risk appetite and introduces "own risk and solvency assessment" (an internal procedure for risk assessment). The draft law that introduces risk-based supervision for insurance companies (and risk-based capital requirements) is still in Congress.

The mutual fund sector has grown very rapidly in recent years. Its share of GDP has tripled since the early 2000s. Mutual funds are often affiliates of banks, such as Banco de Chile, Santander, or BCI. Investment abroad is relatively low: about 10 percent of assets under management are foreign (mostly in the United States). Mutual funds invest mostly in money market funds, although the share of bonds in their asset portfolios is increasing. Mutual funds do not have to comply with standardized liquidity requirement but they are subject to restrictions on foreign investment abroad (depending on the quality of the foreign market's supervision and regulation).

THE STOCK MARKET

Market capitalization is quite large, at about 90 percent of GDP.[4] This is partly because of the role and importance of pension funds in Chile. Since the mid-1990s, the stock market has gone through several rounds of modernization via the adoption of "MK laws." The last round in 2010 (MK III) included numerous provisions to foster the openness of capital markets to international investors. It exempted capital gains obtained by foreign institutional investors on the sale or transfer of some securities (which was previously seen as a factor behind the low participation of foreign investors in the fixed-income market in Chile). The law authorized representative offices of foreign banks to advertise in Chile the products or credit services offered by the parent company. The law also promoted the local trading of registered foreign securities by allowing their denomination in Chilean pesos (such peso-denominated foreign securities are now payable in an authorized foreign currency or in Chilean pesos).

[3] At retirement, a retiree has the choice between either buying an annuity from an assurance company or leaving the money in the pension fund and drawing it on a monthly basis. In most cases, retirees chose the first option and pension funds are converted into annuities.

[4] As measured by the World Federation of Exchanges.

The liquidity of the Chilean stock market has declined over the past few years and is relatively low compared to other economies. Compared to other emerging markets, since the global financial crisis Chile's stock market has gone from being one of the most liquid to being one of the least liquid. This is reducing the attractiveness of the Chilean market for foreign investors. Several reasons have been provided. Pension funds, which are large market players in Chile, are to a large extent buy-and-hold investors. Large conglomerates also reduce the amount of float (because of the large intro-group debt). The tax system may have encouraged companies to issue debt rather than equity. Another factor is poor corporate governance: informational asymmetries (corporate insiders using private information to extract rents from other market participants) may discourage trading activities.

FINANCIAL CONGLOMERATES

Both financial and mixed conglomerates have a strong presence in the financial sector. According to the Chilean authorities, conglomerates comprise 16 systemically important domestic institutions, with assets totaling 125 percent of GDP as of the end of December 2011 (the last time the authorities measured these assets on a consolidated basis). Conglomerates held more than one-third of the assets of local pension funds and life insurers, which totaled some 60 percent of GDP at the end of December 2011, as sign of the concentrated holdings among these conglomerates.

Most conglomerates operate in the financial sector. Out of the 16 conglomerates, as measured by their asset holdings with respect to total assets, five conglomerates focus on banking activities, four concentrate in the insurance and pension sectors, and four focus on both the banking and insurance sectors. Many banks operate within conglomerates, perhaps because of the required separation of financial activities.

Conglomerates are well integrated into international financial markets. Out of the 16 conglomerates, two are led by major international banks and four by major international insurance companies. In addition, four local mixed conglomerates have significant operations in both the financial and nonfinancial sectors of neighboring countries, underlining the importance of establishing coordination with other regulators in the region.

Improving the supervision of conglomerates is on the agenda of the Chilean authorities. Currently, the supervision of conglomerates relies on a sector or silo approach, with each type of financial institution (banks, pension funds, insurance companies) being supervised by a separate superintendency. Nonetheless, the Financial Stability Council law has strengthened consolidated supervision of financial conglomerates. The law removed all barriers to information sharing among supervisors, expanded their power to request information from the final owners of financial institutions within the conglomerate, and established solvency requirements for the controlling shareholders of banks and insurance companies. However, supervisors still lack the powers and authority to conduct comprehensive group-wide supervision (including setting risk-based minimum prudential standards and monitoring conglomerates' compliance with limits on risk exposure). The 2011 Financial Sector Assessment conducted by the IMF recommended stronger coordination among supervisors and the identification of a group-level supervisor with enhanced powers, including that of establishing risk-based minimum prudential standards for financial conglomerates.

Appendix 3. Colombia[1]

Robust growth of financial assets has led to an increased importance of the financial sector in Colombia resulting in greater macro-financial linkages. Financial assets were equivalent to about 150 percent of GDP at end-2015 (Appendix Figure 3.1). Assets of the banking system are about $175 billion, or 65 percent of GDP. Nonbank financial intermediaries (largely private pension funds, trust companies, and insurance companies) account for another 90 percent of GDP. The financial system has continued to grow and deepen macrofinancial linkages recently despite lower oil prices and large depreciation shocks.

Colombia has a concentrated financial system, dominated by complex financial conglomerates. Large domestic complex conglomerates dominate the financial landscape, with 10 holding about 80 percent of total financial sector assets. Many bank and nonbank entities are part of the same conglomerate. In the banking sector, the top three banks (Bancolombia, Banco de Bogota, and Davivienda) hold about 50 percent of banking system assets. Loan portfolio concentration is high, given that banks extend 90 percent of their commercial loans to 7 percent of borrowers. Foreign banks hold only 24 percent of banking system assets (one of the smallest shares in the LA-7), of which regional banks hold 8 percent.

Financial intermediation is among the lowest in the LA-7, but financial deepening and inclusion has been improving, including last year. Credit to the private sector and bank deposits (49 and 39 percent of GDP, respectively), and ATMs are low compared to the region, reflecting in part the large informal sector. Most credit is commercial credit (about 30 percent of GDP), while another 20 percent of GDP is consumer and housing credit. In 2015, credit institutions' loans and macro-financial linkages to various real economic sectors continued to increase; only loan growth to the mining, quarrying, and oil sectors fell, reflecting lower commodity prices, large losses, and some defaults in the sector. In terms of financial access and inclusion, 75 percent of all adults in households having access to some type of financial products (especially banking products). Mobile banking and correspondent banking have been growing rapidly too.

Colombia's capital markets reflect mainly activity in government debt and equity markets, with capitalization reaching 45 percent of GDP at end-2014. Nongovernment fixed income remains undeveloped (4 percent of GDP). The investor base for government debt comprises mainly domestic investors—banks, pension funds, insurance companies, and mutual funds. Foreign investors' ownership of government debt rose to 14 percent of the total at end-2014, fueled by a reduction in the withholding tax charged on foreign investors' income and capital gains. The authorities intend to raise foreign investors' participation in the government debt market to 15–20 percent to diversify the investor base.

The main nonbank financial intermediaries are the private pension funds, which manage IRA-type pensions, while insurance companies are much

[1] Prepared by Iulia Ruxandra Teodoru and Mohamed Afzal Norat.

Appendix Figure 3.1 Financial Assets (in U.S. Dollars)

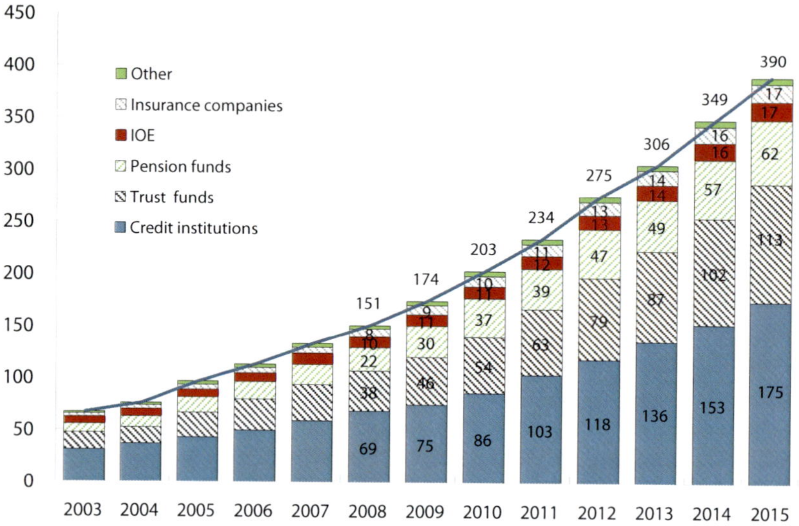

Source: Financial Superintendency of Colombia.
Note: IOE = Instituciones Oficiales Especiales.

smaller. Since 2008, assets under pension funds' management increased by about half through a combination of healthy returns and rising contributions. Industry concentration is high, as the two largest private pension funds in Colombia, Porvenir and Proteccion, manage more than 70 percent of industry assets. Pension funds remain under the sole stewardship of domestic asset managers, and foreign pension funds are nonexistent due to legal restrictions. In the insurance sector, premium growth, one of the highest in the LA-7, was 24 percent for the life segment, and 4 percent for the non-life segment in 2012–13. Premiums per capita (at $200) and insurance penetration are below other Latin American countries, but similar to Mexico's premiums per capita and insurance penetration. The insurance sector is relatively concentrated. The 10 largest companies account for almost 80 percent of the market. Foreign insurance companies are virtually nonexistent. Recently, the pension, insurance and trust funds sectors have grown less rapidly, partly reflecting poorer asset performance due to larger volatility in asset prices and limited availability of higher-yielding longer-term assets.

Colombia has important and growing financial linkages with the rest of the world, including recently with Chile. Foreign claims on Colombia have increased nine times since 2005 and twice since 2008, and are now $45 billion (11 percent of GDP). These foreign claims originate mostly from European banks ($21 billion)—of which $18 billion are from Spanish banks—U.S. banks ($10 billion), and Japanese banks. Most foreign claims are on the non-bank private sector.

High bank concentration made it hard for regional banks to break into the Colombian market when foreign banks withdrew. High bank concentration and tight linkages of conglomerates to the private sector hinder entry of big foreign players. A Colombian bank, GNB Sudameris, acquired HSBC's assets in 2014, which resulted in a consolidation of the market. However, efforts were made to open up, and Chilean Corpbanca acquired the business of Banco Santander, as well as Helm Bank in 2012–13. Currently Bank Itau is merging with Corpbanca, which will place it fifth in terms of market share.

Beyond banking, regional financial integration started through broker dealer acquisitions. Brokerage firms are less concentrated than banks or pension funds, allowing entrance of new players more easily. A Peruvian broker bought Correval, as the two countries integrate their securities markets, and a Chilean broker is planning to enter the market. However, concentration in terms of issuers and the investor base is high in each of the four MILA capital markets (two to three conglomerates are the main issuers, and they are the same buyers), which will be hard to break to allow more players on both sides. BTG Pactual, a Brazilian investment bank, acquired Bolsa y Renta, Colombia's biggest brokerage firm, attracted by a high return on equity and underdeveloped capital markets, including the need to for instruments to finance large projects in the energy and infrastructure sectors.

In terms of outward regional expansion, Colombian financial institutions have a significant presence in Central America and, to a lesser extent, South America (Appendix Table 3.1). The expansion was due to a combination of factors: withdrawal of foreign banks since 2008, increased economic integration with Central America, as well as similarities in culture and language that fit with Colombian banks' business plans to expand in geographically proximate regions. Colombian banks have attained a significant market position in Central America (on average: 22 percent). Banco de Bogota acquired Panama-based conglomerate BAC International and Guatemala-based Grupo Reformador, and focuses on

APPENDIX TABLE 3.1

Assets of Colombia Banks in the Region (*Percent of parent banks' assets*)	
Bancolombia	29.1%
in CA and other Caribbean	7.5%
in Panama	21.6%
Banco de Bogota	43.0%
in CA and other Caribbean	26.7%
in Panama	16.3%
Davivienda	21.6%
in CA and other Caribbean	17.1%
in Panama	4.5%
Occidente	9.3%
in CA and other Caribbean	1.9%
in Panama	7.4%
Sudameris	24.5%
in Peru	15.9%
in Paraguay	8.6%

Source: Financial Superintendency of Colombia.

consumer credit and mortgage lending in these markets. Bancolombia bought El Salvadorian-based Banco Agricola and HSBC's assets in Panama, as well as a minority stake in Guatemala-based Grupo Agromercantil, and its portfolio comprises corporate lending as well as consumer credit and mortgage lending. Banco Davivienda acquired most of HSBC's operations in the region, notably those in Costa Rica, El Salvador, and Honduras, and provides consumer lending. Banco GNB Sudameris bought HSBC's remaining operations in Latin America, specifically in Paraguay and Peru, and focuses on corporate lending. There has also been expansion by Grupo Sura, which is the largest shareholder of insurance company Suramericana and asset management company Sura Asset Management (76 percent of assets are in the rest of Latin America).

Going forward, Colombian banks are planning to consolidate their acquisitions in Central America, while seeing limited scope for going elsewhere, at least in the short run. They cite consolidation and size of the market, as well as language, as significant impediments to establishing in Brazil. While considering Peru and Chile as attractive markets, they see current prices of assets as prohibitive and markets as extremely concentrated.

Financial integration through foreign investment by pension funds is picking up. The share of foreign assets held by pension funds in their portfolios in Colombia is still less than half of that in Chile and Peru, but comparable to that in Mexico, and has been picking up in recent years. An easing of regulatory restrictions allowed, for instance a multifund system, which allows risk profile differentiation and thus larger shares of investments in variable rate instruments and higher limits on foreign securities investments. Investments abroad are about 30 percent of total assets, close to the 40 percent statutory limit for the Conservative Fund. In December 2015 investments in pesos in domestic public debt represented 50 percent of total investments, followed by investments in dollars, which were

Appendix Figure 3.2 Investments by Pension Funds

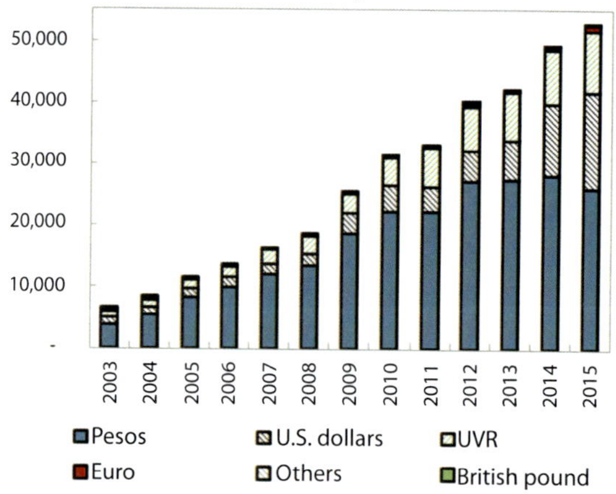

Source: Financial Superintendency of Colombia.
Note: UVR = Unidad de Valor Real.

30 percent (Appendix Figure 3.2). Recently, there has been a sizeable portfolio shift toward investments in dollars. Insurance companies largely choose to invest in debt securities, where about three fourths of investment portfolio allocations of life insurers are held in bonds, and not at all in foreign assets.

The Colombian authorities have finalized legislation that would help address cross-border risks. Laws granting independence and legal protection of the supervisor have come into effect in January 2016 and laws awarding regulatory powers over holding companies of financial conglomerates currently lie before Congress. The Financial Superintendency of Colombia continues to consolidate and make consistent its risk-based supervision to enable the supervisor to tailor prudential requirements of banks and nonbanks to the risks that their operations entail.

Appendix 4. Mexico: Financial System Overview[1]

FINANCIAL SYSTEM OVERVIEW

The Mexican financial system continues to remain relatively open and competitive, while growing at a significant rate. This helped turn Mexico into a top-tier destination for foreign investors seeking emerging market returns with advanced economy ease of entry and exit. The rebirth of Mexico as an open and modern financial market dates to the aftermath of the 1994 "tequila" crisis. Its response, which was cemented in both domestic reforms and international treaties like NAFTA, opened the financial system to foreign participation in order to attract needed investment and managerial expertise, as well as to develop the moderating virtues of markets that could reduce the extent and frequency of public sector interventions when economic volatility rises.

Today, while Mexico's financial system remains small relative to its size and the level of development, it continues to expand robustly. Over the period 2010–14, the Mexican financial system increased on average by 2.5 percentage points of GDP annually, with total assets accounting for about 83 percent of GDP in 2014.[2] Banks account for slightly less than half the assets of the financial system. With the relatively low lending-deposit spreads and a large number of banking institutions—which stood at 44 at end-2015—the market appears fairly competitive. The bulk of financial sector growth, however, has largely concentrated in the nonbank financial sector, where private pension funds and insurance funds in nominal terms together about tripled between 2005 and 2015. Private pension funds are rapidly developing in size and sophistication. Each pension manager maintains four funds comprising different risk tolerances that progressively and automatically reduce risk exposure based on the age of the contributor. Managers can invest in currencies, equities, Mexican private equity funds and real estate trusts, structured assets, and more recently swaptions and Real Estate Investment Trusts (REITS) (up to certain prudential limits), among others. The insurance market, however, remains a relatively small component of the financial sector. There are about 100 insurance companies that jointly capture premiums of about 2.7 percent of GDP[3] and hold nearly 6 percent of GDP in assets. With an expanding middle class, demand for insurance is growing fast, though penetration still remains well below the Organisation for Economic Co-operation and Development (OECD) countries' average, and among the lowest in Latin America. Mexican capital markets are the second largest, behind Brazil, in the LA-7. They are well regarded in Latin America for the ease with which investors can enter and exit the market, the robust liquidity conditions, and the wide array of securities that can

[1] Prepared by Alla Myrvoda and Bennett Sutton.

[2] Based on Banco de Mexico, Secretaría de Hacienda y Crédito Público (SHCP), Comisión Nacional del Sistema de Ahorro para el Retiro (CONSAR), and Comisión Nacional de Seguros y Fianzas (CNSF) data.

[3] March 2015 CNSF data.

be traded, including bonds, foreign and domestic equities, exchange traded funds (ETFs), mutual funds, REITS, and derivatives tied to stocks, indices, interest rates, bonds, and currencies.

REGIONAL INTEGRATION IN THE BANKING SECTOR

In efforts to recapitalize the banking system, after the 1994–95 crisis, Mexican regulators lifted important restrictions on foreign investment in domestic banks and developed a regulatory regime that strongly favors domestically supervised subsidiaries (to the exclusion of the branch model), which operate as autonomous financial institutions with significant operational independence and funding structures that rely almost entirely on local deposits and Mexican wholesale markets. Today about 70 percent of banking assets are controlled by subsidiaries of foreign institutions. Large international players include the Spanish banks BBVA Bancomer (22 percent of assets) and Santander (15 percent); Banamex (a subsidiary of Citibank at 15 percent); and HSBC (7 percent).[4]

With its high participation of foreign banks, the Mexican banking market can be described as highly integrated *globally*, but the activity of regional banks is quite limited. The regional banking sector players regard the inherent structure of the market as a significant barrier. In order to justify in terms of profitability a new market entrance, the institution needs to obtain on average a top 10 ranking. However, in an environment of larger banks holding a competitive advantage, obtaining the desired 7–10 percent market share proves challenging either via greenfield investment or through the acquisitions of smaller banks. At the same time, valuations of top five banks are often regarded as too expensive (justified by substantial market share and profitability) to lure regional competitors. Nevertheless, at a time when global banks may be divesting from some emerging markets (for reasons discussed in Chapter 3), going forward, Mexico may see some valuation growth deceleration given the dominance of foreign subsidiaries. In terms of Mexican investment abroad, the expansion of domestic banks into other countries so far has been limited, largely since banks recognize the growth potential domestically and also given the fact that few domestic banks in Mexico possess the necessary size to make substantial acquisitions abroad. At the end of 2015, only one Mexican bank, Banco Azteca, which held about 1.6 percent of the market share in Mexico, operates subsidiaries in other countries of the region (Panama, Guatemala, Peru, and Brazil).

REGIONAL FINANCIAL INTEGRATION IN THE PENSION FUND SECTOR

Mexican pension funds represent the second-largest segment of the financial system. Assets under management have well outpaced the growth of the capital

[4] As at end-2015; CNBV statistics.

Appendix Figure 4.1 Mexico: Pension Funds' Composition of Investments

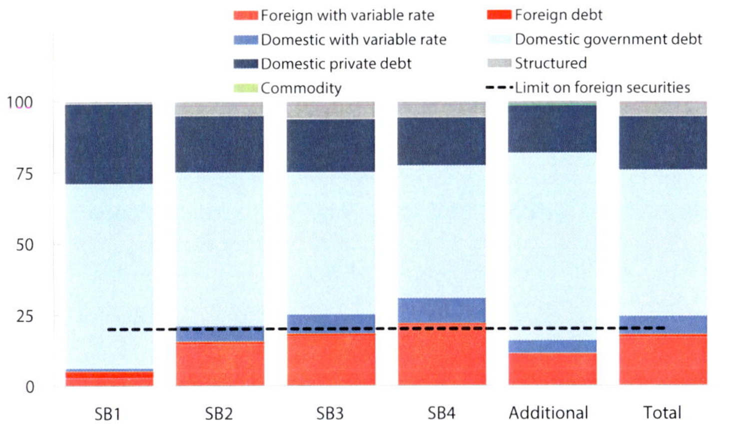

Sources: CONSAR; and IMF staff estimates and calculations.
Note: SB (siefore basica) refers to the type of fund, which varies by the degree of riskiness of the portfolio. Estimates as of June 2015.

markets, more than doubling in percent of GDP and growing by about 260 percent in USD terms between 2005 and 2015. This is largely the result of increasing numbers of participants since the establishment of the pension scheme in 1997 and reforms to the participation of public sector employees in 2007. By end-2015, assets under AFORES' (pension fund managers) management constituted about 14 percent of GDP. Rapid asset and management fee growth has partly spurred substantial mergers and acquisitions activity, including by foreign fund managers. The number of administrators peaked at 21 at end-2007, but stands at 11 as of end-2015. The acquisition of ING Afore in 2012 by a Colombian asset manager—Grupo Sura—was the first entrance of a regional player into the Mexican pension fund market. By mid-2015, Sura AFORE held 15 percent of the industry assets and was the third-largest pension fund in Mexico. The three afores managed by the U.S. entities constituted about 26 percent of the market share, while the remaining 60 percent of the assets fell under the management of domestic pension funds.

The degree to which the Mexican pension fund system can further regional integration through its asset allocations is limited by a ceiling (20 percent) of foreign assets (Appendix Figure 4.1). Originally instituted to stimulate domestic financial deepening (especially capital markets) and to protect contributors from excessive risk concentration, many funds have reached the cap as growth in assets under management has outpaced the supply and issuance of new instruments in the domestic capital market. Moreover, within the foreign securities segment, the composition of investments is dominated by instruments from the United States and Europe. Efforts to reduce high transaction costs including brokerage fees and currency conversion and to increase capital market liquidity in the LA-7 need to advance more quickly in order for Mexican pensions to broaden their regional holdings. Domestically, both pension fund regulators and pension fund managers agree on the urgency of increasing the foreign security holding limit, but the process is complicated by the required approval of Congress. Nevertheless, raising the foreign securities cap would facilitate optimal portfolio allocation and potentially increase regional cross holdings. Given the vibrant domestic debt market and the stalled Mexican equities market, AFORES report a greater need for diversification of equities, rather than debt instruments, through foreign holdings. The current shares of debt instrument holdings remain significantly larger than in other OECD countries, while domestic holdings of equity remain relatively low, given the small size of the equity market in Mexico. This is exacerbated by the growth of AFORES, whose demand for assets may have inflated bubbles in the domestic capital markets. Thus, any further increases in the foreign security holding limits are likely to be largely used for equity diversification. Currently, holdings of securities from other Latin American markets are reported to be limited. While investments in Brazil are stalled due to the perceived excess volatility in the market, investments in Chile, Colombia, and Peru are restrained by the relatively small size of these markets. Investments in individual markets, and particularly other LA countries, are reportedly discouraged by the need to employ specialists for stock picking due to insufficient familiarity with these markets, thus encouraging investment in mutual funds. The Mexican market, on the other hand, provides an attractive opportunity for the Chilean and Peruvian pension funds, among others, for diversification purposes, given the disparate business cycles between Mexico and Latin American commodity exporters.

REGIONAL FINANCIAL INTEGRATION IN THE INSURANCE SECTOR

Liberalization of the Mexican financial sector has resulted in an open insurance market with about 100 insurance companies providing life insurance policies (40 percent of the market), damages (19 percent), and auto insurance (19 percent). The unrealized potential of the domestic insurance market, along with a strong regulatory framework—Mexico implemented the Solvency II-type standard in 2015—constitute the main drivers of entry, including cross-border. Nevertheless, the structure of the distribution channels generates some implicit impediments, since the life insurance products are mainly distributed through agents (nearly half of the market), and developing a sound agent base can be expensive and lengthy and potentially serve as a deterrent for market entry.

Most insurance companies in Mexico have ties to foreign institutions, mostly in the United States and Europe. Thus, among the largest 10 institutions, which comprise about 70 percent of the market, 60 percent of premiums are captured by foreign-owned entities. The five largest institutions—MetLife Mexico (U.S.), Grupo Nacional Provincial (domestic), AXA Seguros (France), Seguros Banames (U.S.), and Seguros Banorte Generali (domestic)—control nearly half of direct premiums. The expansion of the Mexican insurance companies abroad, on the other hand, has been limited, arguably due to the sizable unrealized potential for growth of the domestic market. Expansion to other Latin American (LA) countries is also dampened by the elevated levels of market concentration of the insurance industry in LA-7 countries.

Financial integration through holdings of foreign assets is rather limited in the Mexican insurance sector. The investment strategy of the Mexican insurance companies is largely dictated by the structure of the offered insurance products and the associated liabilities they incur. At present, insurance companies invest a large share of assets in the domestic debt securities. Given the small size and the low turnover and liquidity of the domestic equity market, access to domestic equities remains limited. Maturity matching for long-term products like annuities and life insurance products demands long-term Mexican peso–denominated assets. Ideal instruments with long maturities of 20 or 30 year are rarely available in local markets. While longer-dated instruments are available in foreign markets, insurers generally abstain from them to avoid currency mismatches. Consequently, the share of foreign investments is often well below the regulatory limits and rarely comprises regional securities. However, adoption of Solvency II-type regulation is expected to slightly increase the foreign asset holding limit in order to accommodate the expected rise in non-life products denominated in foreign currency.

REGIONAL FINANCIAL INTEGRATION IN CAPITAL MARKETS

Development of the foreign exchange and debt markets has advanced with an increasing number of listings and liquidity in the past few years, while growth in the domestic equity market has stalled. The Bolsa Mexicana de Valores (BMV), on which stocks and bonds are traded, is a demutualized, publicly traded company and is the second-largest trading house by volume of trades and market capitalization in Latin America, trailing only Brazilian BM&F Bovespa. The number of listed firms has increased only marginally (135 to 143 between 2010 and 2015) while the overall domestic market capitalization remains relatively small at about 35 percent of GDP. The low level of new issuance is explained by a preference for debt financing among Mexican corporates with tightly controlled ownership structures. While the fairly small pool of retail investors limits broad market appreciation, the bond market plays a much more important role in sovereign and corporate financing. According to Bank for International Settlements (BIS) statistics, the value of domestically issued bonds outstanding in 2014 was 46.0 percent of GDP, making it smaller (relative to GDP) than in Brazil (81.6 percent), Chile (50.9 percent), and Uruguay (51.2), though liquidity measured by the number of trades is considerably higher than in any other LA-7 country. Banks and the general government are the primary beneficiaries of domestic bond financing, with only about 15 percent (each) of their bonds outstanding being placed abroad. Nonfinancial corporate, however, sought 72 percent of their bond financing from foreign markets. Derivatives trading is dominated by interest rate swaps, largely TIIE swaps (Tasa de Interes Interbancaria de Equilibrio, the equilibrium interbank interest rate), as the volume of forward rate agreements, options, and other products remains rather limited. The over-the-counter single currency interest rate derivatives turnover in Mexico stood at U.S.$2.4 billion as of April 2013, representing about 0.1 percent of the global interest rate derivatives market. This is the second-largest market in Latin America, trailing only Brazil. Most OTC single currency interest rate derivatives trading denominated in Mexican pesos, however, occurs in the U.S. markets, with only 18 percent executed domestically. This is not unusual in Latin America, as OTC derivatives of other LA-7 countries are largely traded on the U.S. and U.K. markets as well.

The Mexican peso has been among the 10 most traded currencies since 2013, largely against the U.S. dollar and in the form of foreign exchange swaps and spot transactions. The Mexican peso is convertible and free floating, with turnover reaching U.S.$135 billion in 2013, raising its market share in the global FX trading to 2.5 percent, from 1.3 percent in 2010. The U.S. dollar vis-à-vis Mexican peso currency pair trading comprises the majority of Mexican peso trading, and constitutes about 2.4 percent of the global foreign exchange (FX) market transactions. Since the vast majority of these transactions take place offshore, the Mexican domestic market only manages about 0.5 percent of global foreign exchange market turnover. Exchange-traded derivatives are traded on the Mercado Mexicano de Derivados (MexDer, the Mexican derivatives exchange platform) and are cleared through a central counterparty clearing house (CCP) ASIGNA, both of which are subsidiaries of the BMV. MexDer's turnover remains small, with a reported market share in the low single digits. The establishment of MexDer has not resulted in a significant shift of OTC transactions to the Mexican electronic platform, largely because trading OTC is more cost competitive than MexDer, which is in need of higher trade volumes to drive down the higher fees to cover its technical and technological costs. Activity on MexDer is also hindered by the high foreign presence in the Mexican markets, the close trade and financial ties of Mexican companies to the United States, and regulatory bias toward trading on recognized exchanges, which have also pushed the derivatives market outside of Mexico, mainly to the United States, United Kingdom, and Europe.

The global financial crisis prompted changes in the regulatory frameworks in many countries, including Mexico, aimed to provide transparency and reduce counterparty risk. Regulatory adjustments to the G20 frameworks, the Dodd-Frank law in the United States, and European Market Infrastructure Regulation (EMIR) in the European Union, in line with the Basel III standards, introduced largely comparable regulatory modifications aimed to eliminate counterparty risk, increase price and valuation transparency, and collect information. The new regulations call for all standardized OTC derivative contracts to be traded on exchanges or electronic trading platforms and cleared through CCPs, while non-centrally cleared contracts would be subject to higher capital requirements. In the spirit of improving transparency and strengthening the derivatives market, and largely in line with the global regulatory changes, the Mexican authorities introduced a new regulation, scheduled for gradual implementation. In April 2016, compliance with the new regulation will be required for transactions between Mexican entities, while November 2016 is the start date for transactions involving foreign financial institutions. The new Mexican regulation will require derivative trades to take place on exchanges or through interdealer brokers, and call for a mandatory clearance of standardized derivatives through a CCP—Mexican (established in Mexico and authorized by the SHCP) or foreign (if recognized by Banco de Mexico).

Higher CCP clearance volumes will also generate competition between ASIGNA and global CCPs, such as CME (Chicago Mercantile Exchange). While the volume on ASIGNA is expected to be driven largely by Mexican pension funds, clearance through CME is likely to remain significant given the large share of transactions involving multinational institutions headquartered in the United States. A large share of counterparties involved in derivatives trading are subsidiaries of foreign entities or have ties to other countries, as testified by the overwhelming majority of foreign subsidiaries among the "eight market makers"—the most active participants in the Mexican capital market. By clearing through a CCP in the parent country, foreign multinationals are able to consolidate operations through netting their derivative positions, thereby decreasing capital requirements. Thus, ASIGNA may maintain its domestic market share, and could become the primary vehicle for trading with regional participants, including through Latin American Integrated Market (MILA), while foreign CCPs, such as CME, would largely handle the business involving the global multinationals.

Appendix 5. Panama[1]

Panama is an important regional financial center, especially for Central America and part of South America. Banking assets are over US$100 billion, or about 240 percent of GDP at end-2015, with over 30 percent held by regional banks (and another 20 percent held by other foreign banks). Panama's banking center includes a sizeable offshore sector. Of the 76 banks licensed in Panama, 49 operate with a general license (onshore; includes two state owned), and 27 have an international license (offshore). Offshore banks' assets are 40 percent of GDP. The offshore sector is largely disconnected from the rest of the Panamanian financial system, and serves for such operations as foreign currency lending to Latin American or international corporates by banks outside their home jurisdiction. Domestic capital markets are the smallest in the LA-7 (bonds outstanding are 12 percent of GDP), compared to 33 percent of GDP for international bonds outstanding, and the domestic stock market capitalization is 33 percent of GDP. The range of activities undertaken by Panamanian financial institutions is relatively narrow: there is no significant activity on derivatives, structured products, or foreign exchange.

Both insurance companies and pension funds are small compared to the size of the banking sector, but are expanding rapidly. Insurance companies' assets account for roughly 5 percent of GDP, and foreign insurance companies own about half of the assets. Premium growth has been 12 percent for the life segment annually, and 8 percent for the non-life segment. Premiums per capita and insurance penetration figures are high relative to other LA countries (premiums per capita are US$320 and premiums amount to about 3 percent of GDP). The insurance sector is relatively concentrated. There are 33 companies, of which the three leading companies are of similar size and jointly account for 49 percent of total premiums. Insurance brokers monopolize the distribution of insurance products, and commissions are relatively high, making micro-insurance and other low cost products unattractive. The two local pension funds, one public and the other private, account for about 0.7 percent of GDP. Since 2008, assets under pension funds' management increased by about half.

Panama has important and growing financial linkages with the region and the rest of the world. According to the BIS, international banks have significant claims on Panamanian borrowers. Foreign claims (ultimate risk basis) on Panama have doubled since 2005 and were US$40 billion in 2014 (90% of GDP). Claims by the United Kingdom, which were among the highest until 2013, have dropped (likely due to the exit of HSBC), and foreign claims by Germany and Spain (likely due to the exit of BBVA) also fell that year.[2] Most foreign claims are on the nonbank private sector. Foreign claims of Panamanian banks on other countries have more than doubled since 2002 (US$21 billion in 2014), with lending to the

[1] Prepared by Iulia Ruxandra Teodoru.

[2] Colombian banks, significant holders of important claims on Panama, do not report their foreign claims to the BIS.

remaining LA-6 representing 30 percent of total claims on others (Appendix Figure 5.1).

The withdrawal of global banks starting in the 1990s first led to a consolidation of the market and, more recently, to mergers and acquisitions by Latin American banks. Foreign banks (that is, Bank of America, Societe General, seven Japanese banks, as well as some Swiss, Dutch, and Spanish banks), controlling 70 percent of assets in the 1970–80s, withdrew in the 1990s. Their assets were mostly acquired by domestic banks, which led to a consolidation of the market (for example Primer Banco del Istmo doubled its market share to 12 percent of total assets between 2000 and 2008). Since 2008, banks from Colombia acquired assets of withdrawing banks and institutions (that is, HSBC, BBVA, and GE). In 2010, Colombian Grupo Aval, through Banco de Bogota, bought GE's 75 percent share in BAC International. In turn, BAC International acquired BBVA in 2013. The same year, the largest Colombian bank—Bancolombia—acquired HSBC's assets. Colombian banks own 22 percent of assets in Panama.

Cross-border credit to the region is important. Credit to GDP is 90 percent (one of the highest in the LA-7), but credit growth has remained in line with nominal GDP growth in the past four years. Credit to nonresidents is 30 percent of total credit and 30 percent of GDP, and has recovered following a sharp deceleration associated with HSBC's departure. Costa Rica, Brazil, Mexico, and Colombia are among the largest borrowers, and receive 45 percent of foreign credit (Appendix Figure 5.2). Foreign investments, foreign loans, and deposits in foreign banks (as many banks hold sizable deposits at their parent banks or other banks abroad) are about 40 percent of total bank assets. Half of the securities bought are foreign (US$7.5 billion), and most investments are made in securities in the United States (30 percent of total foreign securities), Costa Rica, Mexico, Colombia, and Brazil.

Appendix Figure 5.1 Consolidated Foreign Claims of Reporting Banks in Panama on Top 10 Individual Countries

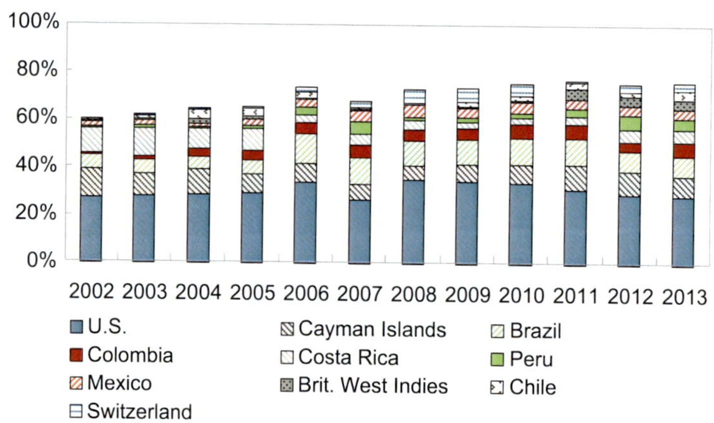

Source: BIS; and IMF staff calculations.

Appendix Figure 5.2 Foreign Credit by Country, 2014 (percent)

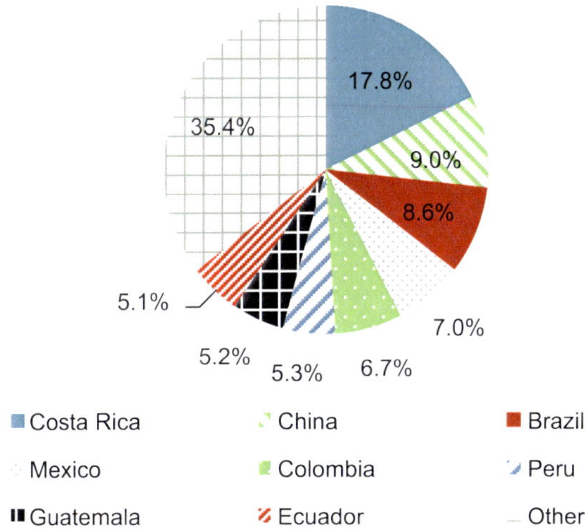

Acquisitions by regional insurance companies and pension funds remain limited. Only the Colombian insurance company Suramericana has expanded to Panama, and several other Central American countries, and has a strategy of expansion to LA. Foreign investments by insurance companies and pension funds are very small. Investments by pension funds are concentrated in local bank deposits (50 percent) and domestic fixed-income securities (less than 10 percent). Only 2 percent of total investments are invested abroad (most in Latin America). The rest is invested in equity and nonfinancial institutions. Investments by insurance companies are concentrated in equities (80 percent), while 20 percent is invested in bonds, and similarly only about 2 percent abroad.

CHALLENGES FOR FINANCIAL STABILITY IN THE CONTEXT OF INCREASED REGIONAL INTEGRATION

Complex conglomerates with cross-border operations raise important challenges for effective supervision and the assessment of macro-financial stability. The conglomerates operating in Central America have complex corporate structures, including overlapping layers of holding companies (one of which could be in Panama) and entities (bank, nonbank, and real sector) in several financial sectors (including in Panama), and thus fall under different supervisory authorities that may not cooperate sufficiently. In Panama, there appeared in the past to be incentives to attract financial business through laxer regulation and requirements. This model is obsolete, with outside supervisors increasingly imposing home country requirements across the whole financial institution, and with the threat of large fines on the institution in the event of lack of full compliance with the requirements of the home country authorities. Coordination among supervisory agencies in the region has been improved through the establishment of a Council of Supervisors (FCC) for all supervisors in Central America and Colombia, and efforts are under way to further enhance supervisory capacity.

Slow progress in implementing Basel III, including capital definitions, liquidity and leverage rules, and capital buffers, could lead to inadequate identification of cross-border and interconnected risks and insufficient capital held against such risks. The absence of a well-articulated framework and available capital buffers (Pillar 2, D-SIB buffers) could result in lower levels of loss absorbency and risk mitigation exposing complex conglomerate structures to own risks, but given their size and the complexity of their cross-border operations could lead to systemic risks as well.

Appendix 6. Peru[1]

The financial system in Peru is relatively small, but growing solidly. Between 2006 and 2014 the broad financial system including insurance and pension funds grew from US$52.3 billion (58.1 percent of GDP) to US$175.8 billion (90.8 percent of GDP). Most of the financial system (except for the stock exchange) is under the consolidated purview of the superintendent for banks, insurance, and pensions (SBS). The banking system is assessed to be largely Basel II-compliant, with SBS reporting that Basel III compliance expected in the next few years. Some of the larger, particularly foreign-owned, banks have already adopted many Basel III principles. All firms traded on the Bolsa de Lima must file IFRS-compliant annual reports to the securities regulator. Even with a high level of dollar deposits, the banking system maintains relatively low foreign asset exposure (2 percent of assets) though the share of foreign liabilities is on the rise, but still less than 15 percent of the system's balance sheet (Appendix Figure 6.1). The importance of insurance and pension funds deposits in the banking system has declined markedly, but they still account for 11 percent of total deposits.

There are no legal impediments to foreign financial institutions entering, operating in, or exiting Peru. The legal regime provides for equal treatment of foreign and domestic entities. Foreign institutions are free to operate as either branches or subsidiaries, though currently there are no branch operations of foreign banks. Within the four largest banks, accounting for about 85 percent of total assets and credit, two (Banco del Credito and Interbank) are controlled by domestic conglomerates and two are foreign-owned institutions. BBVA (Spain) purchased half the controlling interest in Continental bank in 1995 to become the second-largest bank by assets. Scotiabank (Canada) purchased the operations of two smaller banks in 2006 and is now the third-largest bank. The SBS supervisor reports strong interest from many foreign financial firms to obtain operating licenses. The insurance sector in particular has seen many new applications and entrants from abroad.

Highly concentrated market structures as well as tax and supervisory issues are the most commonly cited impediments to foreign investors. As in other countries of the region, the dominant market shares of the largest firms in the banking, brokerage, and pension management sectors mean potential targets for acquisition are either too small or too expensive. As noted in the financial system chapters, the difficulty of building market share organically leads most international banks to target only the largest three to four institutions in a country for acquisition. The top four banks are sufficiently large and profitable that buying into Peru is considered to have become cost prohibitive, while the small market share of remaining banks would require significant business development to achieve critical mass. Also, the SBS's exhaustive efforts to document ownership structures to ensure compliance with a prohibition against multiple licenses to subsidiaries of the same parent may draw out the licensing process, and dissuade some potential

[1] Prepared by Bennett Sutton.

Appendix Figure 6.1 Peru: Selected Indicators of the Financial System, 2015
(Percent of GDP)

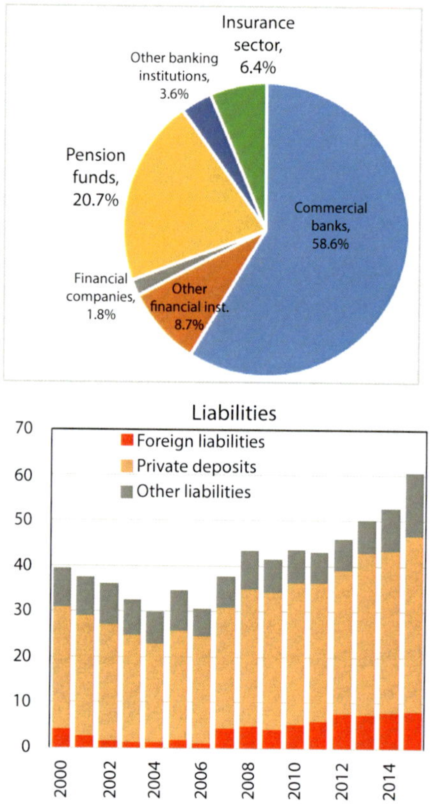

Sources: SBS financial supervisor; and IMF, International Financial Statistics.

buyers. Moreover, the 30 percent tax on dividend repatriation may weaken the incentive for foreign institutions to operate in the country.

Divestiture of regional operations by global banks, and the special skills developed by Peruvian banks, may present expansionary opportunities for some Peruvian banks. Banco del Credito del Peru, a subsidiary of the Creditcorp conglomerate, the largest bank by assets and deposits in Peru, already owns the fourth-largest private bank in Bolivia and an asset management/insurance company in Chile, and is likely seeking opportunities in other countries. Interbank, the fourth-largest bank, and its conglomerate parent, Intercorp, are focused on developing organic growth in Peru, though Interbank's strength in retail banking and reaching underserved segments could be leveraged in other countries with high informality.

Appendix Figure 6.2 Peru: Insurance Market Development, 1996–2015
(Percent of GDP)

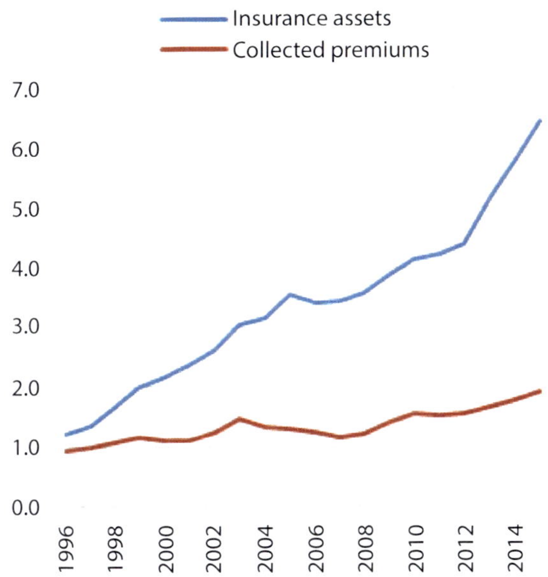

Sources: Superintendencia de Banca, Seguros y AFP (SBS); and IMF staff calculations.

Private pension funds have been successful at drawing out domestic savings and broadening the formal financial system. About 5 million adults (out of nearly 20 million ages 15–64) are enrolled in Peru's private pension fund system. The system caters to formal sector employees, who are required to contribute 10 percent of their salaries to funds administered by one of four fund managers (AFPs).[2] Under each administrator there are three age-determined, risk-tolerant funds. Funds for the youngest workers have the highest risk tolerance, while the risk profile for funds reserved for people closer to retirement is less aggressive. Younger participants may elect to save in the more conservative pool, but older subscribers are prohibited from moving into riskier funds. Unlike pension funds in other LA-7 countries, upon retirement, a lump sum is not paid to the individual. Rather, the AFP is charged with a fiduciary responsibility to provide a stream of income for the remaining years of life proportionate to the accumulated savings of the individual. Strong domestic growth has increased both the number formal employees and their salaries such that in 2015 participants paid in over US$230 million each month (US$115 million net of fees and paid benefits).

[2] However, it is estimated that only about half the 5 million contribute regularly as the others are independent or contract workers. Reforms are under consideration to facilitate contributions by independent, contract, and other workers in the informal sector.

The supervisors penalize funds that do not yield a minimum level of returns, and organize a competitive auction every two years to contain management fees. Minimum financial returns are determined as the average systemic return less 2 percent over the previous 36 months. Fund managers must "top up" returns from their own capital if they fail to meet minimum returns. As in other countries with minimum return requirements, AFPs tend to mimic each other's asset class holdings yielding very similar risk/return profiles. Consequently, it is considered that competition to attract competitors' clients is based more on marketing than net returns. All new subscribers are enrolled with the same AFP; however, every two years, the SBS solicits proposals for this designation in which the winner is the one with the lowest proposed management fee. If the lowest fee is lower than the current rate, the new lower rate is then applied to all of its subscribers. After the initial two years, subscribers are free to move their savings to a different AFP.

The rapid growth of assets under management now exceeds the capacity of domestic capital markets to provide a sufficient portfolio of securities. While about 180 shares and over 350 bonds are listed on the Lima exchange, the aggregate value of stocks and bonds traded in 2014 was about US$5.8 billion, or 3.7 times annual net contributions. The universe of investable domestic securities for pension funds shrinks further once small cap and infrequently traded listings are excluded. Deposits in the banking system have also become less attractive as easier external financing conditions and solid fiscal and macro-management have combined to push down treasury and deposit yields. With increasingly limited domestic investment options, the supervisor has had to increase the limit on foreign asset holdings several times; it now stands at 50 percent[3] and the limits are effectively binding on nearly all funds. Financial market participants and regulators are looking to raise the foreign asset limits, if implemented gradually, to avoid abrupt sales of nuevo soles in the onshore market.

As in other countries of the region, insurance markets in Peru are small, but developing steadily (Appendix Figure 6.2). In 2014, the industry collected about US$3.4 billion in premiums and held $11.1 billion in assets (1.8 percent and 5.8 percent of GDP, respectively). The sector is fairly concentrated, with six of 18 firms accounting for about 75 percent of premiums and 72 percent of assets. While several foreign firms are active through local subsidiaries (Mapfre and Sura being the two largest foreign subsidiaries), most insurers are domestically owned. Premiums between life insurance and property/casualty policies segments are evenly split at about US$1.7 billion. Insurance policy issuance is largely marketed to formal, high-wage earners, so deeper penetration is considered dependent on higher incomes generated by macroeconomic development and a larger share of the workforce joining the formal sector. Most policies are written in nuevo soles: thus, for currency matching reasons firms generally have fewer foreign holdings than the statutory limit of 40 percent of assets. Insurance companies reportedly

[3] Fifty percent is the statutory limit, though the regulator currently limits holdings to 42 percent as the effective cap is raised slowly to stem large capital outflows and volatility in the onshore FX market.

face difficulties finding sufficient long-term local currency assets in domestic capital markets in order to match the long-term liabilities in the life policy segment.

Peruvian equity markets are modest in size; domestic bond markets are significantly smaller than in LA-7 counterparts (except Panama and Uruguay), and both suffer from falling liquidity. At end-2015, equity markets had 212 domestically listed firms and a market capitalization of nearly 30 percent of GDP. Liquidity concerns are also apparent in the low frequency of IPO issuance, the muted volume of shares traded, and the large number of infrequently traded firms. In 2015, the authorities introduced exemptions on capital gains and other reforms related to short-selling, automated trading, and market makers to encourage higher trading volumes. Domestic bond markets are characterized not only by their small size and low trading volumes, but also by the limited number of long-term bonds. While trading in the money market is quite active, especially for corporate issuers, only a small number of securitized instruments are listed on the Bolsa de Valores de Lima (BVL), and derivative products are not traded domestically.

Appendix 7. Uruguay[1]

Uruguay's financial system assets amount to about 92 percent of GDP, making it larger, in GDP-weighted terms, than the financial systems of Colombia and Peru, but smaller than Brazil, Chile, and Panama. While the size of the system relative to the economy does not draw attention, there is much scope for financial deepening, as Uruguay's private credit intermediation ratio is one of the lowest in the region. Banks dominate the financial landscape, but pension funds have grown in recent years and are the main institutional investors. The state plays a predominant role in Uruguay's financial sector, with public institutions controlling 45 percent of banking system assets, 60 percent of pensions, and 80 percent of the insurance market.

Credit to the private sector in Uruguay, at just 25 percent of GDP, is among the lowest in the region. The high degree of financial dollarization in Uruguay (80 percent of deposits and 60 percent of loans are in U.S. dollars) is a key factor. Given the history of high inflation and currency devaluations, people have a preference for holding their savings in U.S. dollars, but the majority of lending to households is in pesos. Since the bulk of banks' liabilities are in dollars, they limit their peso lending to avoid currency mismatches on their balance sheets. Dollar credit is stifled by high reserve requirements for foreign currency deposits on the supply side, and high transaction costs coupled with easy access to direct lending, bond markets, and high levels of foreign direct investment on the demand side.

The crisis of 2002 left a legacy for Uruguay's financial system. The role played by foreign banks, FX deposit withdrawals (especially by nonresidents) and relatively lax regulations during the crisis have shaped the current policy mindset and supervisory framework. When the crisis erupted in 2002, key prudential regulations for FX-related risks (liquidity, reserves, capital requirements) were virtually nonexistent, even though almost 50 percent of total deposits were from nonresidents. By the end of that year, the banking system had lost 46 percent of total deposits, and the level of nonresident deposits had fallen by 65 percent; the bank run had led to the closing of one bank and the intervention/restructuring of three. The government provided US$2.4 billion in liquidity support. In December 2002, a new banking law was passed that strengthened regulations to limit liquidity and FX risks significantly. The system remains heavily regulated. At the same time, the 100 percent backing of U.S. dollar demand and savings deposits—but not time deposits—in 2002 likely still impacts the choices of Uruguayans when putting their money in banks (90 percent of total deposits today are in short-term demand or savings deposits). The legacy of 2002 has led to a preference for caution and liquidity—which to a certain extent may have worked against deepening.

The banking system in Uruguay comprises two public banks and nine private banks—all of which are foreign owned. Commercial banks account for almost three-quarters of total financial system assets. The banking system is

[1] Prepared by Diva Singh.

concentrated with the large public bank, Banco del Republica Oriental de Uruguay (BROU), holding 40 percent of total banking assets, and the top four banks holding three-quarters of assets. There is only one large regional bank: Banco Itaú of Brazil. The sector is marked by a high degree of segmentation between the public and private banks. Until recently, BROU enjoyed a monopoly on public employee accounts by law,[2] which has given the large public bank a majority share of the peso deposit market (largely at zero cost), and thereby facilitated its strong presence in the high-spread peso retail lending market. The foreign banks, on the other hand, have highly dollarized deposit bases, and cater to commercial, higher-income, and some retail segments, in a highly competitive environment.

High operating costs and relatively low profitability have led to a process of consolidation in Uruguay's banking sector. Banking fees and rates in Uruguay are high compared to the region because labor and operating costs are very high, while the high degree of competition among private banks operating in a dollarized environment has constrained their profitability. Consolidation of the sector, from 20 private banks in 2002 to just nine private banks today, has been driven at least in part by the search for efficiency gains through greater scale in this environment. Most of the consolidation has taken the form of mergers between foreign-owned banks' operations in Uruguay: in 2008, Santander and ABN Amro merged; in 2011, BBVA and Credit Agricole merged. Most recently, in December 2014, Scotiabank signed an agreement to buy Israel's Discount Bank Latin America, Uruguay's ninth-largest bank, that will make Scotiabank the fourth-largest bank by assets. Given the need for scale, it is likely that regional banks wanting to enter the Uruguayan market would have to do so through similar mergers rather than as greenfield entrants.

The absence of private domestic banks in Uruguay, and the lack of focus of the BROU on regional opportunities, has dampened the extent of cross-border and regional activity by Uruguayan banks. When Scotiabank entered Uruguay in 2011, it did so by acquiring Banco Comercial, the last private domestic bank operating in Uruguay. Following this acquisition, Uruguay was left with only foreign private banks. This has had a material impact on cross-border regional banking activity. While Banco Comercial (and other private domestic banks) had historically maintained significant cross-border business ties with Brazil and Argentina, as well as non-negligible investments in regional banks, the entrance of Scotiabank severed these ties. The foreign private banks must abide by parent country regulations and compliance standards that are becoming ever more stringent. Many of these global banks have subsidiaries in various countries in the region, which operate as independent entities and are not allowed to pool their capital for projects. As a result, foreign assets of the banking system have reduced considerably in the past decade, as have nonresident deposits (which have shrunk to just 15 percent of total deposits, from 50 percent during the 2002 crisis).

[2] The new financial inclusion law allows public employees to choose private banks for their payroll accounts.

Banks' financial soundness indicators are adequate but there is heterogeneity, and overall banking profitability is low compared to the region. Uruguayan banks have adequate capital levels and ample liquidity. Resilience indicators are generally strong, with NPL ratios at less than 2 percent of total loans, loan-loss provisions on average three times larger than NPLs, and net foreign exchange positions below 1 percent of capital.[3] Nevertheless, a few soundness indicators have weakened slightly in recent years—in particular, foreign currency lending to un-hedged borrowers has risen steadily, from 26 percent of total private sector loans in 2010 to 31 percent in 2014.[4] Bank profitability on the whole remains subdued given the high levels of deposit dollarization and dollar liquidity, low interest rates on U.S. dollar assets, and high operating costs. That said, there is significant heterogeneity between BROU and the private banks, with the former enjoying higher profitability aided by its predominant position in the peso market.

Pension funds are the main institutional investors in Uruguay. There are four pension fund managers, with collective assets under management amounting to US$11 billion (20 percent of GDP). The defined-contribution pension system is characterized by two funds (an accumulation fund and a retirement fund). The largest of the fund managers is the publicly-owned Republica AFAP, with almost two-thirds of pension assets (US$6.2 billion). The three private AFAPs are all regionally owned: AFAP SURA from Colombia (US$1.99 billion); Union Capital, owned by Itaú (US$1.82 billion); and AFAP Integracion, owned by the Venezuelan Banco Bandes (US$998 million). Given the small size of Uruguay's private capital markets, nearly 80 percent of the pension system's assets are invested in government bonds and held to maturity. The investment regulations governing the funds currently permit only 15 percent of assets under management to be invested abroad. Expanding this limit would not only diversify the investment portfolio of the pension funds from a risk management perspective, but also mitigate against the present crowding out of retail investors in the face of the limited investment opportunities in the domestic market. Enhancing regional integration and perhaps including a separate investment limit for regional investments could be a solution—particularly as the three private AFAPs are owned by regional pension fund managers and could capitalize on the expertise of each for regional investments.

The insurance market in Uruguay is small and dominated by the large state insurance company. Total assets of insurance companies in Uruguay amounted to US$3.2 billion at end-December 2014 (6 percent of total financial system assets, or 5 percent of GDP). There are 15 insurance companies operating, but the sector is dominated by the state-owned Banco de Seguros del Estado, which controls 82 percent of the insurance market.

The capital markets in Uruguay are small but there is purportedly a large informal market and much scope for deepening. While total risk capital managed by brokers in Uruguay is projected at about US$5 billion (10 percent of

[3] Staff Report for the 2014 Article IV Consultation, No. 15/81.

[4] Ibid.

GDP), only 5 percent of this goes through the formal Bolsa de Valores. There is a large informal market a significant volume of direct placements of securities between securities issuers and the pension funds. Given high brokerage fees, it is less costly for private companies to go directly to banks for private placements than to go through brokers. Formal capital market activity has also been dampened as the global banks have withdrawn their brokerage activities in Uruguay. Becoming an integrated member of a regional capital market initiative could be beneficial to Uruguay given the relatively small size of its market, need for scale, and room for deepening.

Index